Teaching and Learning in Context

This book is a product of the CODESRIA Textbook Programme.

Teaching and Learning in Context

Why Pedagogical Reforms Fail in Sub-Saharan Africa

Richard Tabulawa

CODESRIA

Council for the Development of Social Science Research in Africa
DAKAR

© CODESRIA 2013
Council for the Development of Social Science Research in Africa
Avenue Cheikh Anta Diop, Angle Canal IV
BP 3304 Dakar, CP 18524, Senegal
Website: www.codesria.org

ISBN: 978-2-86978-569-4

Typesetting: Alpha Ousmane Dia
Cover Design: Ibrahima Fofana

Distributed in Africa by CODESRIA
Distributed elsewhere by African Books Collective, Oxford, UK
Website: www.africanbookscollective.com

The Council for the Development of Social Science Research in Africa (CODESRIA) is an independent organisation whose principal objectives are to facilitate research, promote research-based publishing and create multiple forums geared towards the exchange of views and information among African researchers. All these are aimed at reducing the fragmentation of research in the continent through the creation of thematic research networks that cut across linguistic and regional boundaries.

CODESRIA publishes *Africa Development*, the longest standing Africa based social science journal; *Afrika Zamani*, a journal of history; the *African Sociological Review*; the *African Journal of International Affairs*; *Africa Review of Books* and the *Journal of Higher Education in Africa*. The Council also co-publishes the *Africa Media Review*; *Identity, Culture and Politics: An Afro-Asian Dialogue*; *The African Anthropologist* and the *Afro-Arab Selections for Social Sciences*. The results of its research and other activities are also disseminated through its Working Paper Series, Green Book Series, Monograph Series, Book Series, Policy Briefs and the CODESRIA Bulletin. Select CODESRIA publications are also accessible online at www.codesria.org.

CODESRIA would like to express its gratitude to the Swedish International Development Cooperation Agency (SIDA/SAREC), the International Development Research Centre (IDRC), the Ford Foundation, the MacArthur Foundation, the Carnegie Corporation, the Norwegian Agency for Development Cooperation (NORAD), the Danish Agency for International Development (DANIDA), the French Ministry of Cooperation, the United Nations Development Programme (UNDP), the Netherlands Ministry of Foreign Affairs, the Rockefeller Foundation, FINIDA, the Canadian International Development Agency (CIDA), the Open Society Foundations (OSFs), TrustAfrica, UN/UNICEF, the African Capacity Building Foundation (ACBF) and the Government of Senegal for supporting its research, training and publication programmes.

This book is dedicated to my family.

Contents

Acknowledgements

I am grateful to the following publishing companies for allowing me to use copyright material:

Taylor and Francis Group (http://www.informaworld.com)

Tabulawa, R., 1998, 'Teachers' perspectives on classroom practices in Botswana: implications for pedagogical change', *International Journal of Qualitative Studies in Education*, Vol. 11 (2), pp. 249-268.

Tabulawa, R., 2003, 'International aid agencies, learner-centred pedagogy, and political democratization: a critique', *Comparative Education*, Vol. 39 (1), pp. 7-26.

Tabulawa, R., 2004, 'Geography students as constructors of classroom knowledge and practice: a case study from Botswana', *Journal of Curriculum Studies*, Vol. 36 (1), pp. 53-73.

Tabulawa, R., 2009, 'Education reform in Botswana: reflections on policy contradictions and paradoxes', *Comparative Education*, 45 (1), pp. 87-107.

Elsevier

Tabulawa, R., 1997, 'Pedagogical classroom practice and the social context: the case of Botswana', *International Journal of Educational Development*, Vol. 17 (2), pp. 189-204, (Chapter 6 and 7) (License Number 2684261306559).

Tabulawa, R., 2011, 'The rise and attenuation of the basic education programme (BEP) in Botswana: a global-local dialectic approach', *International Journal of Educational Development*, Vol. 31 (5), pp. 433-442 (License Number 268-442).

Foreword

Why Pedagogical Reforms Fail in Sub-Saharan Africa

Few would argue that among education scholars on the African continent, Richard Tabulawa has emerged as one of the finest critics of the received wisdom on educational reform. I first encountered his work by coincidence when I discovered that we both had a well-grounded suspicion of what was then and remains a travelling wisdom of the international donor community – that the progressive ideal in education of learner-centered pedagogy did not take account of the social, cultural and political meanings of education and authority within African classrooms. This was as true of Botswana, where Professor Tabulawa does his research, as it is true in my native South Africa where I have been grappling with the political tsunami of 'outcomes-based education' which has flooded post-apartheid classrooms since the middle 1990s.

The author takes us inside what he calls the socio-cultural world of African classrooms to help us understand why prevailing practices persist despite the progressive ideal represented in one funded reform package after another. His conceptual analyses capture the best of both the sociology of education and the anthropology of education in contexts of poverty, and not a little about the politics of education as well.

There are reasons teachers dominate classroom life and rely disproportionately on didactic methods of teaching. To change that, you need to understand the conditions under which most African teachers continue to teach, and what sustains those practices.

A poorly qualified teacher teaching a class of 60 energetic children inside a classroom built for 40 children and with the scarcest of science materials, for example, available for learning, has no choice but to fall back on what has worked for generations of teachers before her – a very present in-front-of-the-class didactic posture. Anything short of such a posture risks chaos. Your first instinct, even as an experienced teacher, is to assure control. None of these conditions are factored into the otherwise noble ideal of open-ended, inquiry-driven, progressive education.

Then there is this subtle thing called authority. How does a teacher in rural Southern Africa with established patterns of adult authority and childhood obedience begin to give away or share that authority on demand from an alien curriculum? I know, this might not be the way the curriculum phrases the notion of learner-centred pedagogy, but in the mind of the teacher used to centrally-directed instruction (I use the word deliberately) this is how he or she understands the proposal for change. I have been fortunate to teach on both sides of the Atlantic, in Africa and the USA, and it is certainly true that what would pass as normative in one cultural setting (learner-centredness in a middle-class Palo Alto, California, school) would be considered outrageous in another cultural setting (a village school in a tribal authority area of rural Botswana).

It is important to make the point that African societies are not static, and that norms for teaching and learning are certainly changing across national borders – much faster these days as a result of new social media and even the now humble mobile phone. Still, announcing the progressive ideal and making it work through considered implementation strategies requires great effort and, of course, considerable resources for teacher development.

The progressive ideal often fails because of oversell. Whether intended or not, we leave the message with teachers that 'everything you know is bad' and that 'everything you are about to receive is good'. This kind of message spells the death of any reform, but especially one challenging cultural and political norms for teaching, learning and leading in classrooms. Smart implementation would affirm what works, and gradually introduce those elements in progressive pedagogy that coincide with traditional pedagogy. Teachers should, under smart implementation, not feel that their authority is being eroded but rather that it is being strengthened albeit through a different form of teaching. This takes time, and requires patience.

One thing I find useful in talking teachers (and policymakers) through the progressive ideal is the value of the didactic lecture. Teaching the history of the atom is probably best done through an excellent expository lecture that builds the drama of discovery into the oration of teaching; I have seen this done while I was in the audience, and still remember the goose-bumps felt as the professor-teacher outlined the plot. Teaching multiplication tables is probably best done, at some stage, using a degree of repetition or chorus backed up by teaching methods that deepen the meaning of those tables learnt initially through what is so easily dismissed as 'rote' learning. Of course, didactic teaching and memorization should form a smaller part of a rich mix of teaching methods and should always be judged for its capacity to advance the meaning of what is learnt. However, the mere fact that teachers recognize the familiar makes it so much easier to introduce the strange.

These potential contradictions between teacher centeredness and learner centeredness are sometimes dealt with by placing these approaches along a continuum, thus allowing for variations of emphases along the two extremes. This appears to make sense, for in the practice of teaching, neatly codified categories in teacher- or learner-dominant classrooms fail the test of complexity in real-life classrooms. Tabulawa warns against a reading of the 'continuum approach' that leaves the impression that simply by adding resources one could move the system, technically, from the less progressive to the more progressive side – to put it simply. It is precisely this 'technicist rationality' that must be displaced, the author would argue, with his preferred model of a 'socio-cultural approach' to pedagogy.

I am not sure this proposed shift towards a socio-cultural approach will be persuasive among the policy elites of some African countries. The rationale for the progressive ideal remains persuasive – it is a way of advancing democratic ideals in the classroom, it empowers learners to take charge of their own education, it relieves the teacher of having to do everything, and it empowers young children for active participation in the economy.

Moreover, as Tabulawa no doubt knows, the funding conditionalities that come with clear-minded ideals from the West leave little room for elevated deliberations on the philosophy and politics of imported pedagogies. At the same time, the author warns, we cannot assume that learners are lifeless and teachers dominant across complex systems. If I may take a setting more familiar to me, it would be hard to make the case for lifelessness in Soweto schools, the seat of a major student uprising in South Africa. This is, of course, a point taken up in relation to missionary schooling in Africa, also dubbed backwards in the Western ideal of progressive education; this Tabulawa refers to as cultural supremacy in the progressive ideal.

The collection of writings from the pen of this distinguished cultural critic of progressive pedagogy will open cans of worms from Washington to

London, and not sit easily with elites in the postcolony. That said, it would
be a mistake not to take these criticisms seriously as we continue to seek what
I would call a genuine curriculum conversation between progressive ideals,
from whatever quarter, and the hard realities of teaching and learning inside
African classrooms. If that is the goal, this is the book to help us get there.

Jonathan D. Jansen,
Vice-Chancellor and Rector
University of the Free State

Preface

The issue of pedagogical reform first attracted my attention in the early 1990s when I registered as a doctoral student with the School of Education, University of Birmingham, England. Initially, I had wanted to do my doctoral research on how best to teach map reading skills to secondary school students in Botswana. It was not long before I realized that the question I wanted to address was the wrong one: if I wanted to come up with improved techniques of teaching any aspect of geography, I would first need to establish why geography teachers approached map reading the way they did. As I worked further on re-focusing my study, I abandoned the limited area of map-reading skills in favour of the broader question of why geography teachers in Botswana schools approached the teaching of the subject the way they did.

The result was an ethnographic study entitled 'A Socio-Cultural Analysis of Geography Classroom Practice in Botswana Senior Secondary Schools'. The approach to the study was multi-disciplinary, benefitting from insights in areas as diverse as political theory, sociology, anthropology and cultural studies. The approach helped me appreciate much better the complexities of teaching, specifically that teaching is both a moral and ethical activity and that it has both temporal and spatial dimensions. In short, I got to appreciate the contextual nature of pedagogy. As I analysed the socio-cultural context of Botswana, I came to the conclusion that transferring learner-centred pedagogy to that context was never going to be easy. It had been tried before and efforts were still continuing, but none seemed to have borne fruit. That there was an important relationship between pedagogy and context became clear to me. Increasingly, I became critical of the view of pedagogy as technique, and realized that pedagogy was problematic, given its embeddedness in the social-cultural/political/economic context.

In other words, pedagogies are products of socio-cultural contexts. My research on the relationship between pedagogy and context resulted in the publication of a series of articles. 'Pedagogical classroom practice and the social context: the case of Botswana', which appeared in the *International Journal of Educational Development*, 17 (2) in 1997, was my first articulation of this social embeddedness of pedagogy. In the article, I demonstrate how teacher-centred pedagogy has been historically engendered by the enveloping Botswana social structure. In turn, the pedagogy perpetuates that social structure. That is, the pedagogy is as essential to the perpetuation of the social structure as the latter is to the reproduction of the (teacher-centred) pedagogy. Thus, the two are dialectically related. 'Geography students as constructors of classroom knowledge and practice: a case study from Botswana' appeared in the *Journal of Curriculum Studies*, Vol. 36 (1) in 2004. In this article I problematised teacher-centred pedagogy further by demonstrating how the pedagogy is co-constructed by teachers and students on the basis of their epistemological viewpoints and expectations of one another's roles. These agents work collaboratively to protect and police the boundaries of the pedagogy. The agents have vested interests in this pedagogical style, meaning that reforming the style can never be expected to be easy.

In 2003, 'International aid agencies, learner-centred pedagogy and political democratization: a critique' was published in *Comparative Education*, Vol. 11 (2). In this article, I sought to demonstrate the interface of education – through the mediation of learner-centred pedagogy – and capitalist democracy. The fall of the Berlin Wall in 1989 saw international aid agencies coming out explicitly in support of learner-centred pedagogy. Why the explicit support at that historical juncture? I contend in the article that in the 1960s and 1970s, generally, education was viewed in technicist terms. That changed in the 1980s with the ascendancy of neo-liberalism as the dominant development paradigm, a paradigm that established a necessary relationship between political democratization and economic development. Education was identified as a potent vehicle for delivering capitalist democracy across the world. And learner-centred pedagogy, given its democratic pretensions, was singled out by international aid agencies as the nexus between education and the broader principle of capitalist democracy. That set the stage for the globalization of the pedagogy, a relentless effort by international development agents to this day. Given this political/economic nature of learner-centred pedagogy, any continued treatment of pedagogy as technique has no basis whatsoever.

Neo-liberalism has entrenched itself as a dominant discourse. However, neo-liberalism is not just a political theory. Its significance lies in the fact that it is constitutive of identity. To this end, neo-liberal education is tasked with the responsibility of producing autonomous (of state provision) and self-regulating individuals. It does so by appealing to progressive education ideals and language. However, progressive education under neo-liberalism is not the same as the progressive education (of the 1960s and 1970s) of 'embedded liberalism' (Ruggie 1982). Given this ideological nature of progressive pedagogy, I now not only lament the failure of efforts to implement learner-centred pedagogy in sub-Saharan Africa, I also question the desirability of this form of pedagogy in the sub-region. Thus, mine has been an intellectual journey – from critiquing technicist models of pedagogical reform to questioning the desirability of the reforms themselves. This book reflects my thinking on the first part of the journey. However, as I show in the concluding chapter, the questioning of learner-centred pedagogy in developing countries is growing, opening a new frontier in researching pedagogy.

Rationale for and Significance of the Book

Cuban and Tyack (1995: 134-5) made the following statement, one that is as true today as it was when the two writers made it nearly twenty years ago: 'To bring about improvement at the heart of education – classroom instruction ... – has proven to be the most difficult kind of reform...' This is a world-wide problem, but one probably more pronounced in sub-Saharan Africa where there have been concerted efforts to implement pedagogic reforms in the past ten to fifteen years. Despite the reforms, instruction in schools in the sub-region is characterized by a persistent, stubborn continuity. The failure of these reforms has been largely rationalised in terms of technical problems associated with innovation delivery systems. By adopting a technicist stance towards problems of instructional reform, curriculum developers and policy makers have tended to pay scant attention to the fact that pedagogic innovations are social constructions, and as such are value-laden. Cuban and Tyack (1995) express this concern thus: 'The typical rational and instrumental assumptions of educational reformers fail to give due weight to the resilience of schools as institutions. This institutional structure probably has more influence on the implementation of policy than policy has on institutional practice" (p. 134).

In this book I critique the rational and instrumental assumptions referred to in the above quotation by Cuban and Tyack insofar as these assumptions are evident in the way pedagogic reforms have been handled in sub-Saharan Africa, using Botswana as a case study. Unlike Cuban and Tyack, however, I go beyond an analysis of the 'grammar of schooling' to embed pedagogy in the enveloping social structure. This calls for a socio-cultural approach in which the social nature of pedagogy is recognised. I argue that the failure of pedagogic reforms should not be sought solely in the inadequacies of the innovation delivery system. It should also be sought in the enveloping social structure. That is, it is essential to adopt a macro-social approach to issues of pedagogic practice if the complexity of such issues is to be comprehensively appreciated (Farquharson 1990). This, in my view, is a major departure from the norm. With this rationale in mind, *Teaching and Learning in Context* aims to:

- Demonstrate the social embeddedness of pedagogy by exposing the inadequacies of the technicist approach.
- Advance a socio-cultural explanation for the 'tissue rejection' of pedagogic reform proposals (e.g., learner-centred pedagogy).
- Provide teachers, educators and students of education with a resource book that contextualises the teaching and learning processes.

It is the case that most texts on teaching and learning used by education students and educationists in sub-Saharan Africa have been written from the perspective of the rational-technical paradigm, meaning that they are insensitive to context. *Teaching and Learning in Context* offers a different perspective on teaching and learning by grounding these activities in their local context. The book suggests that meaningful reform of instruction in sub-Saharan Africa might require major shifts in social structures, such as child-rearing practices. This might be discomforting for teachers, policy makers and international aid agencies working very hard to bring about reforms in instructional practices in sub-Saharan African classrooms. But this exactly is the intended effect of the book – to make our comfort zone less comfortable.

Although *Teaching and Learning in Context* is based largely on research carried out in the area of geography teaching in secondary schools in Botswana, its general principles could equally be applied to other school subjects. Given the non-existence of texts that approach teaching in this way, the book is aimed at subject specialists and general practitioners in the area of education, ranging from teacher educators, schoolteachers grappling with perennial problems associated with instructional reform, students of education, and education policy makers anywhere in the developing world, as well as development aid agencies and students of international and comparative education.

Outline of Chapters

Chapter One presents a critique of the way teaching and learning have been traditionally understood locally and internationally. In particular, the marginalisation of *context* is targeted for criticism. I argue that this marginalization has only served to promote a technicist approach to teaching and learning, with its attendant weakness of portraying teaching and learning as context-free, non-problematic activities. Lack of cultural sensitivity in the treatment of teaching and learning has led to the pervasive view that these are generic activities. This in turn has led to the generation of generic 'principles of teaching and learning' (presented as universals) whose application has tended to be oblivious to the context in which they are being applied. The philosophical basis of this technicist perspective on teaching and learning is traced back to the application of scientific rationality (positivism) to teaching. Given the claims of scientific knowledge to universality, models of teaching and learning derived from this form of knowledge have likewise laid claim to universal applicability, leading to the dominant (albeit tacit) view that teaching and learning are value-free activities. Having critiqued the dominant perspective on teaching and learning, a case for the alternative socio-cultural approach is advanced. It is argued that 'context matters' (Crossley and Jarvis 1999). Teaching and learning do not occur in a sociological vacuum. The shape these activities take in any given context is a function of many factors to do with that context – the political, historical, economic, social and cultural aspects of the context. No two contexts can be exactly the same. By the same logic, effective teaching can never be achieved by adopting exactly the same paradigms across contexts. Therefore, models of teaching developed in one socio-cultural context may not fit well in a different context. There is no 'one-true approach' to pedagogy (Bowers 2005).

Chapter Two questions the 'official' rationale for instructional reform in sub-Saharan Africa, in particular the preference for the constructivist learner-centred pedagogy. I argue that although the efficacy of this pedagogy is often couched in educational/cognitive terms, in essence, the pedagogy's justification is a political/economic one. This is a justification that can hardly be expected to appeal to teachers in contexts where students' performance in tests and examinations is more important than any other consideration one may think of. Where teachers and students cannot perceive an obvious relationship between a pedagogical innovation and students' performance in tests and examinations, chances are extremely slim that these agents will embrace the innovation. In other words, the perceived utility of a pedagogical innovation has implications for how it is received in the host environment. Therefore, I argue in this chapter that the apparent disconnect between the rationale for introducing learner-centred pedagogy in sub-Saharan Africa on the one hand, and its perceived utility by teachers, students, administrators and parents on the other, may be partly responsible for its 'tissue rejection'.

In Chapter Three, I invoke Thomas Kuhn's (1962) concept of 'paradigm' to demonstrate that, contrary to technical rationality, learner-centredness and teacher-centredness are informed by opposing epistemological positions, constructivism and objectivism respectively. Each position engenders in its adherents (or those socialised into it) a way of looking at the world compatible only with its own tenets. Further, each promotes its own unique orientation towards classroom architecture and desk arrangement, student-teacher relations, interactions and assessment regimes. Thus, teacher-centredness and learner-centredness constitute diametrically opposed pedagogical paradigms. A teacher or student socialised in one of the two would find it difficult to shift positions. Thus, teaching methods are necessarily value-laden. Teaching and learning, therefore, are not technical activities.

Chapter Four builds on the argument advanced in Chapter Three – that pedagogical paradigms constitute teachers' and students' taken-for-granted worlds. Findings presented in Chapter Three showed that teachers in Botswana and elsewhere in sub-Saharan Africa actively construct the pedagogical world called 'teacher-centredness'. However, it would have been an unintended outcome if the findings created an impression that teachers construct that world by themselves and of their volition. More often than not, they are 'forced' into an information-giving position by their students, a possibility not accommodated by approaches to teaching and learning informed by technical rationality. Chapter Four, therefore, factors in students as active co-constructors of teacher-centredness. A view of teacher-centredness as co-construction re-defines 'teacher-centredness' – it is not an ambiance created by the teacher acting *on* the students, as 'teacher-centredness' is often understood. Rather, teacher-centredness is constructed *jointly* by the teacher and students acting on one another. It is a classroom ambiance in which students have an interest which they are always prepared to defend should the need arise. Employing Michel Foucault's conceptualization of 'power', I present findings from a study in which students were observed forcing their teacher into an information-giving position in class. Besides being an affront to the position of teaching as a rational and instrumental activity, the idea of 'co-construction' complicates our understanding of pedagogical change in that it suggests that attempts to change classroom practices in African schools must include both the teacher and students. And yet this is rarely appreciated in extant models of pedagogic reform.

In Chapter Five, I offer an explication of the relationship between pedagogy and the social structure. I demonstrate this relationship by taking Tswana cosmology as an example. Specifically, I link the perceived authoritarianism in Botswana classrooms that research has established to aspects of Tswana social structure, in particular child-rearing practices. It is customary to explain the perceived authoritarianism in terms of culture. However, rarely is it explained how this culture promotes authoritarianism and how this in turn reaches the micro level of the classroom. Successfully linking the enveloping social structure to observed classroom practices requires a theory of socialisation. The work of Pierre Bourdieu provides such a theory. Tswana cosmology, it is argued in this chapter, embeds a theory of knowledge, learning and a view of the learner. Acquisition of knowledge is in a hierarchy between the adult and child. Internalised during primary socialization, this relationship with knowledge is carried to the classroom as the participants' (students and teacher) cultural baggage and helps to structure relationships in ways akin to authoritarianism. Bourdieu's views on education enable me to demonstrate the social embeddedness of the teacher-centred pedagogical style and, as a corollary to that, its resilience.

Chapter Six adopts a more historical approach to the evolution of teacher-centred classroom practices in Botswana. I argue that the education introduced by the missionaries in Botswana in the nineteenth century was hierarchical, bureaucratic and condescending, reflecting its social context of origin, nineteenth century Victorian Britain. However, this model of education interacted creatively with contemporary African values and ways of doing things to entrench teacher-centred educational practices. This educational model has been further entrenched in post-colonial Botswana, giving rise to an impersonal organisational structure, one that could only be expected to promote impersonal and bureaucratic social relations in the entire system, including the classroom.

In Chapter Seven, I argue that post-independence educational planning in Botswana has had an impact on classroom practices in ways never intended. It has encouraged the development of a utilitarian/instrumental view of education – the view that formal education bestows material benefits upon those who are able to acquire it. This view of education constitutes a stabilized element that permits the production and reproduction of hierarchical classroom social relations. Inadvertently, a teacher-centred pedagogical style is thereby sustained.

Chapter Eight attempts to link curriculum form to classroom practice. Rather than presenting it as an innocuous arrangement of subject-matter, the curriculum is presented as a structure that simultaneously enables and constrains teachers' and students' actions. In Botswana, the publication of the Revised National Policy on Education (RNPE) in 1994 led to the crafting of a secondary school curriculum informed by behaviourism. It is a curriculum which seeks to attune education to the workforce needs of the economy. The resurgence of human capital theory in its crudest form is obvious in this curriculum. Underpinning human capital theory is an instrumental view of education. School-acquired knowledge, as a result, is increasingly commodified and objectified. Logically, this can be expected to encourage a hierarchical pedagogical style. Ironically, this is the same policy that makes the use of learner-centred pedagogy mandatory in schools. It creates pedagogical tensions that teachers and students resolve by withdrawing into the safe cocoon of teacher-centred pedagogy.

The Conclusion brings together the central arguments of the book, urging the reader to re-think his/her comfortable assumption regarding the twin processes of teaching and learning. More importantly, the reader is urged to question the desirability of constructivist, learner-centred pedagogy in Third World contexts, given its colonizing and hegemonic tendencies.

Richard Tjombe Tabulawa
University of Botswana

1

Making a Case for a Socio-cultural Approach

Introduction

Since the 1990s, sub-Saharan Africa has experienced unprecedented attempts at reforming teacher and student classroom practices, with a learner-centred pedagogy regarded as an 'effective antidote to the prevalence of teacher-centred didactic classroom practices' (O'Sullivan 2004:585). So intense has the interest in the pedagogy been that almost all African countries are currently in the throes of instructional reform, from South Africa in the south to Egypt in the north, from Ethiopia in the east to Gambia in the west. In fact, learner-centred pedagogy has been described as one of the 'most pervasive educational ideas in contemporary sub-Saharan Africa and elsewhere' (Chisholm and Leyerndecker 2008:197). Its pervasiveness notwithstanding, the pedagogy has done poorly in terms of being institutionalized. Classroom research has tended to attribute this failure by teachers to adopt instructional innovations to technical problems such as poor teacher training programmes leading to poor teacher quality, lack of resources, and selective external examinations (see Barrett 2007; Altinyelken 2010). As a response to these problems, massive investments have been made in interventions such as in-service programmes, workshops and seminars, all aimed at changing the teachers' classroom practices in the desired direction of leaner-centredness. Still, very little visible change in the classroom interactive processes has occurred. This has led some researchers to question the emphasis that classroom researchers put on technical problems as the root cause of innovation failure. For example, King (1989:44), with reference to Africa in general, has observed that:

> What little evidence there is from classroom studies would suggest that the character of the classroom life is perhaps less determined by these material shortages than by the emergence of a teaching and learning that is not supportive of pupil participation and inquiry.

That technical problems have impeded instructional reform in Africa is beyond any doubt. But why has pedagogical change not occurred in spite of so much having been committed to such reform?

To address this question, I argue in this chapter that by being preoccupied with technical problems of innovation delivery, classroom research in sub-Saharan Africa has tended to downplay the importance of the socio-cultural context as a potential barrier to the adoption of instructional innovations. Researchers have tended to adopt what Elliot (1994) terms the 'technicist stance' to problems of pedagogical change and have ignored the wider institutional and social processes which influence the locus of change. In the present chapter I advance a critique of the approach with a view to exposing its limitations. I argue that the dominant technicist approach is in itself problematic to the extent that it can be indicted for stalling the desired pedagogical shift from a teacher-centred pedagogy to a learner-centred one. Too often, however, the approach is not subjected to questioning. It is often assumed that it is not critical to the fate of pedagogical reform.

The technicist framework has a history and has influenced teaching and research on teaching in very fundamental ways. Its limitations emanate from its philosophical basis – Positivism – with its view of professional practice, teaching included, as a value-free activity. My critique of the framework in the early pages of the chapter sets the stage for a proposal later in the chapter for embracing a socio-cultural approach, one that recognizes the political, economic, cultural, anthropological and social grounding of pedagogy. In short, the chapter makes a case for a consideration of *context*, for without an understanding of the latter, we will never be able to explain why efforts to shift to a learner-centred pedagogy have not yielded the desired results.

Defining Pedagogy

Alexander's (2008) definition of pedagogy is more comprehensive than most. He defines pedagogy as:

> ...the observable act of teaching together with its attendant discourse of educational theories, values, evidence and justifications. It is what one needs to know, and the skills one needs to command, in order to make and justify the many different kinds of decisions of which teaching is constituted" (Alexander 2008:29).

There are two critical elements in this definition: pedagogy as 'the observable act of teaching' and 'pedagogy as ideas' that inform the 'act' of teaching, i.e. the 'educational theories, values, evidence and justifications' that inform teaching.

These two elements are complementary. Notwithstanding this complementarity, the first element (the 'observable act of teaching') is often the one equated with pedagogy, in which case the latter is not distinguishable from 'techniques of teaching'. But emphasis on 'technique' de-contextualizes teaching, rendering it a primarily value-free technical undertaking. The technicist approach, with which I engage in this book, has dominated approaches to curriculum development, research on teaching and pedagogical reform.

My critique of the technicist approach to pedagogy takes off from the premise that teaching is a moral and ethical activity that is context-dependent. This resonates with the second element of Alexander's (2008) definition of pedagogy, that the latter is informed by 'knowledge, values, beliefs and justifications'. At the core of pedagogy, Alexander (2008:29) argues, are 'ideas about learners, learning and teaching, and these are shaped and modified by context, policy and culture'. In other words, pedagogy is imbued with values. To acknowledge context is to acknowledge the temporal and spatial framing of teaching. My discussion of teacher-centred and learner-centred pedagogies in this and subsequent chapters illustrates the social embeddedness of pedagogy.

Learner-centred Pedagogy: A Brief Description

A brief description of the learner-centred pedagogy is in order here. I say 'brief' because a detailed consideration of the pedagogy is carried out in Chapter Three where it is juxtaposed with teacher-centredness to highlight the two pedagogies' paradigmatic differences. For now, just a brief exposé on the nature of learner-centred pedagogy should suffice in contextualizing the argument in this chapter.

Learner-centredness has often been used interchangeably with 'participatory', 'democratic', 'inquiry-based', 'child/student-centred methods' and 'discovery' methods. All these are strands of 'Progressive Methods' whose origins can be traced to Jean-Jacques Rousseau and to the philosophical tradition of empiricism as propounded by the English philosopher John Locke. These strands differ from each other only insofar as they emphasise different degrees of learner autonomy. Connell (1987) observes that it is difficult to categorise the methods of educators who came to be known as the 'Progressives'. Because Progressive Education had many strands, it is difficult to make a short characterization of it without distorting it in the process (Stenhouse 1980). Also, no single organization has succeeded in uniting the progressive 'schools' as a single body (Punch 1977). However, these different strands are united by four common themes: (a) their wish to escape from the formal and rigid structures of nineteenth and twentieth century education systems; (b) their emphasis on activity as the central element in their methods; (c) their emphasis on the centrality of the learner in the educative process, hence the term learner/student-centred methods; and (d) their common epistemological foundation. With respect to the latter theme, there is general agreement that progressive methods are founded upon the social constructivist epistemology. As a philosophy of knowledge, social constructivism holds that 'knowledge is a product of social processes and not solely an individual construction (William 1999:205). In other words, it is a product of social interaction. As a philosophy of learning, social constructivism rejects the pervasive 'assumption that one can simply pass on information to a set of learners and expect that understanding will result' (Confrey 1990, as quoted in William 1999:207). Thus, Progressive Education views students as active participants in the learning process rather than as meek recipients of ready-made factual knowledge from the teacher. It is often placed in contradistinction to the 'teacher-centred' or 'banking education pedagogy' of Freire (1972). Although in this book I use interchangeably the different strands of Progressive Education identified above, it is the 'learner-centred' strand that I use more often than the others.

Learner-centred Pedagogy in Sub-Saharan Africa

It is now two decades since a learner-centred pedagogy (LCP) was introduced in many sub-Saharan African countries. However, it appears that not much has changed in terms of the quality of teaching; teaching in schools in these countries remains didactic and authoritarian with little or no recognition at all of the learner's potential to actively construct knowledge (see Tabulawa 1997, 1998, 2003 on Botswana; Serbessa 2006 on Ethiopia; O'Sullivan 2004 on Namibia; Jessop and Penny 1998 on South Africa and Gambia; Nykiel-Herbert 2004 on South Africa; Acheampong, Pryor and Ampiah 2006 on Ghana; Stambach 1994 Vavrus 2009; O-saki and Agu 2002 on Tanzania; Mtika and Gates 2010 on Malawi; Altinyelken 2010 on Uganda; Pontefract and Hardman 2005 on Kenya).

Botswana's experience with LCP illustrates the general experience of African countries with pedagogy. Botswana has been experimenting with LCP for almost three decades now, making it one of the oldest experiments with the pedagogy on the African continent. Its first post-independence commission on education, which produced the report *Education for Kagisano* (Social Harmony) (1977), made the observation that teaching in the country put 'excessive emphasis . . . upon abstract learning and memorization and neglect of practical studies and of acquisition and application of skills' (Republic of Botswana 1977:100). It expressed concern over the tendency of teachers to overstress traditional methods of teaching in classrooms and asserted that to be educated,

> means acquiring confidence, skills and abilities, and the capacity to persuade, organize and act; it means developing an aesthetic and moral sense [and teachers were urged to] relate to pupils as people, not just as receptacles for cognitive materials (p. 107).

What the commission was calling for in these statements was a change in the student-teacher relationship which, in the case of Botswana, has been found to be teacher dominated (Alverson 1977; Fuller and Snyder 1991; Prophet and Rowell 1990; Fuller 1991). This change could only take place if Progressive, learner-centred instructional methods were adopted by teachers. To this end, the commission urged teachers to facilitate learning:

> ...through investigations in the library, through observation in the fields or the market, and in group discussion or project work, in preference to formal instruction and written exercises. In curriculum design, the teaching approach is as important as the content (Republic of Botswana 1977:107).

To further emphasise its desire for a pedagogical shift, the commission recommended that, 'Wherever possible throughout the curriculum, instruction should include project work and an applied approach to solving problems' (Republic of Botswana 1977:113).

Given the country's economic buoyancy in the 1980s, large-scale projects were introduced, such as the Primary Education Improvement Project (PEIP) and the Secondary Education Improvement Project (JSEIP)... Both projects were committed to a learner-centred education. Consequently, teachers were specially targeted in this reform agenda and significant amounts of resources were committed to a learner-centred pedagogy. For example, in-service programmes were established for teachers, and programmes in teacher education institutions were revised to reflect the government's emphasis on learner-centred education. Evaluations of the projects in the 1990s, however, indicated that they were not living up to expectations:

> Teaching remains firmly in an authoritarian and teacher-centred mode. Students are generally passive recipients of academic verbal information (Prophet and Rowell 1993:205).

> ...teacher behaviour in Botswana classrooms is generally simple, involves fewer instructional tools, and is teacher-centred. Most communication occurs between

the teacher and the full class of students; instructional routines rely on didactic instruction (Fuller et al. 1994:152-3).

Teaching in Botswana schools remains teacher-centred and teacher dominated. 'Teacher talk' takes precedence over students talk (sic). Although students are not altogether quiet and passive, their engagement in lessons is fairly artificial and comprises short responses to close-ended teacher-initiated questions (Marope 1995:12).

Despite the commitment of the large-scale aid projects to this [learner-centred] form of teaching, in practical terms the impact on learning and teaching in the schools, and even in the teacher training institutions, has been minimal (Hopkin 1996:11).

Lamentations such as the ones above are commonplace all over Africa although there are faint voices (Croft 2002; Farrel 2002; Barrett 2007) that seem to suggest that the situation in sub-Sahara African classrooms is not as dire as the literature cited above suggests; cases of teachers applying constructivist, learner-centred principles in their predominantly teacher-centred classrooms have been observed, it is claimed. This evidence has prompted some (e.g. Nakabugo and Sieborger 2001; Brodie et al. 2002; Barrett 2007) to decry the opposition often drawn between learner-centred and teacher-centred pedagogies. Nakabugo and Sieborger (2001), for example, argue that 'Setting old and new practices in opposition to each other... obscures the reality that there is a gradual movement from one towards the other...' (p. 60). More recently, Barrett (2007:291), applying Bernstein's concept of pedagogic modes – the 'performance' (teacher-centredness) and 'competence' (learner-centredness) modes – has argued that, 'There is no contradiction between the performance and competence routes if it is accepted that the two modes can co-exist'. Given this alleged co-existence or convergence of pedagogic modes, it is argued that it is possible to talk of 'colourful variations' (Fuller et al. 1994) and a 'hybrid of traditional and reform-oriented practices' (Altinyelken 2010:162) in some African classrooms. Although this literature is certainly growing, at the moment it is still anecdotal and for this reason cannot be adduced as solid evidence of a convergence of the two 'modes' or 'paradigms'. Some of the supporters of the 'convergence thesis' are candid about the modesty of the convergence. For example, Vavrus (2009:310) observes from her Tanzanian study that student-teachers 'used inquiry-based and peer-learning activities as well as more formalistic methods *in their distinctly teacher-centred classrooms*' (emphasis added), suggesting that the observed constructivist activities were in some ways *tacked* on to the more behaviourist ones. Akyeampong et al. (2006) on their part have observed that where constructivist, learner-centred practices have been embraced, their stay has been short-lived, for ultimately teachers regress to traditional instructional practices. If anything, the evidence suggests that these newer practices are one-off occurrences, exceptions to a rule, the rule being an enduring teacher-centred pedagogy. We are not yet 'beyond the polarization of pedagogy' (Barrett 2007:273), it would seem.

I suggest that the view (espoused by Barrett 2007 and others) of teacher-centred and learner-centred pedagogies as non-contradictory and, therefore, unproblematic emanates from an unconscious adherence to a technicist approach to pedagogy. The approach views teacher-centred and learner-centred pedagogies as lying on a continuum. Figure 1.1 below taken from Bartlett and Cox (1982) is typical of the continuum representation

Figure 1.1 : **The Teaching-learning Continuum**

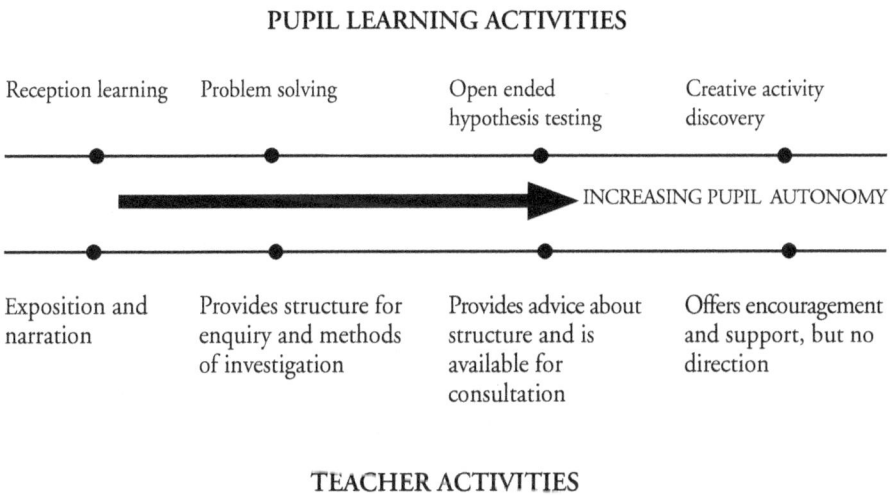

PUPIL LEARNING ACTIVITIES

Reception learning	Problem solving	Open ended hypothesis testing	Creative activity discovery

INCREASING PUPIL AUTONOMY

Exposition and narration	Provides structure for enquiry and methods of investigation	Provides advice about structure and is available for consultation	Offers encouragement and support, but no direction

TEACHER ACTIVITIES

Source: Bartlett and Cox, 1982.

On the left-hand side of the continuum are teacher and student activities that are associated with the teacher-centred pedagogy while the right-hand side represents the learner-centred pedagogy in which students' autonomy is enhanced. Between the two extreme ends of the continuum is an area where the mixing of the two pedagogies is possible, that is, the area where 'colourful variations' or a 'hybrid' of traditional and new practices can be found. It is in this area that we can locate the studies carried out by Nakabugo and Sieborger (2001), Brodie et al. (2002) and Barrett (2007) mentioned above.

However, there are problems with representing the two pedagogies as lying on a continuum. In the first place, the very concept of 'continuum' in this context is itself problematic – it suggests that the two pedagogies do not differ *fundamentally*. As is clear from the representation in Figure 1.1 above the pedagogies differ mainly in terms of the degree of student autonomy, which autonomy increases as one moves from the teacher-centred side of the continuum to the learner-centred side. Secondly, and following logically from the first assumption, the continuum representation of the pedagogies implicitly suggests that pedagogical reform involves a non-problematic, effortless 'shift' by teachers and students along the continuum from the left-hand side to the right-hand side. This is captured in Nakabugo and Sieborger's (2001) quotation above. Thirdly, the model cannot accommodate a view of pedagogy as value-laden. And following from the latter, context does not matter in pedagogical change. This is the technicist approach I have referred to above. More shall be said about this approach in the remaining sections of the chapter.

Taken together, these assumptions lead to the adoption of a simplistic view of the process of pedagogical change – that resources are sufficient to effect pedagogical reform. Typically, lack of change is rationalized in terms of insufficient time and resources, high teacher-student ratios and defective teacher education programmes resulting in poorly trained teachers. This invariably gives the impression that if resources were made available in relative abundance, pedagogical change would most likely occur in sub-Saharan Africa. Barrett (2007:292), for example, attributes the predominance of teacher-centred approaches to 'economic scarcity, which leads to insufficient preparation, development, supervision and monitoring of teachers as well as working and living conditions that spread demoralization through the teaching force'. More recently even, Altinyelken (2010:168) has attributed the limited presence of child-centred pedagogy in Uganda to a '[l]ack of human and material resources, capacity shortages and shortcomings in curriculum design'. The economic scarcity thesis, while by and large true, is not a sufficient reason for pedagogical reform failure. Take the case of Botswana where resource scarcity, until the advent of the global credit crunch of 2008, was not an acute problem, at least not to the extent it was, and still is, in other parts of Africa. Botswana has been experimenting with learner-centred pedagogy since the early 1980s, far longer than most sub-Saharan African countries. Yet the resilience of teacher-dominated classroom practices is still being reported today. This seems to suggest that perhaps there is more to pedagogical reform than just the (non)-availability of resources.

This emphasis on the primacy of technical issues when attempting to make sense of pedagogical reform is what has been referred to at the beginning of the chapter as the technicist approach. The implicit assumption in the technicist approach seems to be that pedagogical change is mainly a matter of injecting resources in a deficient system. Typically, when change fails to be institutionalized, teachers and/or their conditions of work are blamed. The solution is to pour more resources into the interventionist programmes to help teachers change. If there is still no change, more resources have to be mobilized. This becomes a cycle, with costs escalating with each attempt. This is not to say that technical issues are not important in pedagogical change. They are undoubtedly important, but they are not a sufficient condition for change to take place.

The limitation of the technicist approach to understanding change is that it does not go beyond the technical. Invariably, the remedies recommended also tend to be technical – make more resources available and improve teacher training. We know that the latter is a recurring recommendation in reports on improving teacher quality. We also know that the more we try to improve teacher training along the lines recommended, the less things seem to change. Why then are classroom practices so intractable with respect to reform efforts? I suggest that the intractability of teacher-centred pedagogy derives from a superficial conception of pedagogy and of the process of pedagogical change. Pedagogical change involves more than just the injection of resources into a system that is perceived as deficient. There is need to treat learner-centred and teacher-centred pedagogies themselves as problematic, something that the technicist approach overlooks. These pedagogies have been engendered and are supported by particular contexts. Ignoring these contexts the way the technicist approach does can only lead to a distorted appreciation of the nature of pedagogic change. If context indeed matters, then pedagogical change does not take place in a sociological vacuum. The context in which a particular pedagogy originates acts as the latter's support structure, ensuring in the process the pedagogy's stability, constancy and resilience. Beyond resources, there is need to look deep into the structures that support, for example, teacher-centred pedagogy in the sub-Saharan African context and, by implication, that also repel learner-centredness. A comprehensive theory of pedagogical change would have to acknowledge these structures.

Technical Rationality as an Epistemology of Practice

As pointed out above the technicist approach implies that teaching is a value-free, objective activity whose problems are solvable through the application of the rigorous procedures of the scientific method. This approach is deeply rooted in technical rationality, an epistemology of practice based on the empiricist/positivist tradition (McNiff 1988; Schon 1987; Smyth 1991). Schon (1987) has this to say about positivism:

> The positivist epistemology of practice rests on three dichotomies. Given the separation of means from ends, instrumental problem solving can be seen as a technical procedure to be measured by its effectiveness in achieving a pre-established objective. Given the separation of research from practice, rigorous practice can be seen as an application of instrumental problems of research-based theories and techniques whose objectivity and generality derive from the method of controlled experiment. Given the separation of knowing from doing, action is only an implementation and a test of technical decision (p. 78).

Elsewhere, Schon (1983:21) refers to technical rationality as the 'view that.... professional activity consists in instrumental problem-solving made rigorous by the application of scientific theory and technique'.

Positivism is traceable to the works of Enlightenment thinkers such as René Descartes, Francis Bacon, John Locke, Isaac Newton and others. Interest in science in the seventeenth century did not grow out of sheer curiosity; the interest was political in that the aim was to overthrow the intellectual and cultural fashions of previous centuries (Bowen 2003). For this reason, the second half of the eighteenth century witnessed a number of revolutions – industrial, social and political – that changed the West. So profound was the impact of science that it is claimed:

> 'The scientific milieu in the latter half of the nineteenth and early twentieth centuries was dominated in part by Darwinian ideas, deductive approaches, and an acceptance of the concept of Newtonian cause and effect relationships' (Grossman 1977, as cited in Bowen 2005).

Use of the (particularly Newtonian) mechanistic cause and effect paradigm, was extended to the study of almost everything. In science, the paradigm led to the search and subsequent discovery of laws governing the operation of the universe. Emphasis was on formulating theory, that is, 'lawful relationships amongst variables' (Tom 1980:16). The same paradigm, it was surmised, could be employed to discover the laws that governed human society, laying the foundations for the evolution of the discipline of sociology. Even human thinking could be studied scientifically using this paradigm, laying the foundations for psychology, the discipline that has more than any other dominated teacher education. So profound was the influence of this paradigm that it was declared as the ultimate aim of science to construct:

all of science, including psychology on the basis of physics, so that all theoretical terms are definable by those of physics and laws derivable from those of physics (Rudolph Carnap, as cited in Holt-Jensen 1980:77).

Teaching as professional practice did not escape the influence of the scientific method. In an effort to build what Gage (1978:41) termed a 'scientific basis for the art of teaching', researchers on teaching adopted cause and effect analysis, which analysis in turn gave birth to the process-product paradigm of research on teaching. This conception subsequently led to a flurry of studies seeking law-like relationships between such variables as teacher behaviour and student learning, the so-called 'teacher effectiveness' research. Gage, the representative of this conception, had this to say about the nature of research on teaching:

> Research on teaching is aimed at the identification and measurement of variables in the behavior and characteristics of teachers, at discovering the antecedents or determinants of these central variables, and at revealing the consequences or effect of these variables (Gage 1963:vi cited in Donmoyer 2006:18).

Not only does this conception put the teacher at the centre of the educative enterprise, it also defines the teaching and learning relationship as a cause-and-effect relationship, where the teacher causes some response in the learner. Brophy (1984:91, cited in Pearson 1989:25), in an apparent reference to the then evolving research on teacher effectiveness, stated that:

> For the first time there is available a developing scientific data base . . . about linkages between teacher behavior and student outcome.

From teacher effectiveness research is derived propositional statements about teaching which, if implemented by teachers, will improve the achievement of students (Pearson 1989:24). As Gage (1978:38) states, these statements must be 'relatively specific, objectively observable and require relatively little extrapolation from terminology to what is to be done'. Thus, just as in the physical sciences, teaching and teacher education programmes should be based on facts, not opinions; that is, teaching is a value-neutral activity. The influence of behaviourism (an issue we discuss in Chapter Three) is self-evident in this thinking.

One of the deleterious effects of the technicist approach, with its stress on value-neutrality, is that it tends to ignore the role of agency (e.g. that of teachers) in pedagogical change. In Botswana, for example, the Department of Curriculum Development and Evaluation of the Ministry of Education and Skills Development is responsible for developing curricular and teaching strategies, with little input from the practicing teachers (Maruatona 1994). The role of teachers is simply to adopt and implement pre-packaged, standardized and almost teacher-proof content and teaching strategies 'developed' by bureaucrats. In other words, the teacher's job is that of executing laws and principles of effective teaching (Tom 1980). Because thinking (conception) is removed from implementation (execution), the model of the teacher 'becomes that of the technician or white-collar clerk' (Giroux and McLaren 1986:220). In these circumstances, the ideal model of teaching and learning is one in which learning is the memorization of discrete facts that are easy to measure and evaluate, with lecturing being the most efficient way of covering the prescribed syllabus.

A statement on the metaphor 'teacher-as-technician' is apt here. To the extent that it is about how we see the world, it is 'a compressed, imaginative expression of a perspective' (Boolstrom 1998:397), a metaphor is expressive of a particular perspective on power and power relations. The metaphor 'teacher as technician' makes hierarchical the relationship between the teacher and students, thus implicitly sustaining a teacher-centred approach to teaching and learning, an approach which paradoxically simultaneously deskills teachers. Because of the way in which it hierarchically structures social relations, this model has been termed the 'top-down' model, the 'centre-periphery' model, the 'input-output' model, and what Hoyle (1988) terms the 'maintenance paradigm'. With its emphasis on educational change as a rational technical process, the model typically conceptualizes pedagogical change as a process that is:

> .... initiated at the macro level from a central position and passed down to the micro level of classrooms where deficiencies in curriculum materials can be remedied, which leads to improvement in teachers and teaching styles (Prophet 1995:129).

Thus, in this model of change management, the teacher essentially plays a passive and dependent role and can change his or her practice only by adopting teaching practices and curricula 'mandated by those who are external to the setting in which the teaching is taking place' (Richardson 1994:6).

One other aspect of the technicist approach is that in educational policy making the teacher is often singled out as the most important change agent, to the exclusion of other participants, such as students. Whenever change is thought desirable in educational practice, interventionist programmes are usually established for teachers. Improving the quality of teachers is usually viewed as a prerequisite for quality learning. The role students (the real consumers of curriculum initiatives) play in curriculum implementation is largely viewed as inconsequential. Students are rarely involved in any meaningful way in curriculum decision-making, in spite of the fact that they are central to the process of schooling. That students are perceived as inconsequential in curriculum matters is also self-evident in the work of classroom researchers, who tend to focus almost exclusively on what the teacher does in class, rather than on what students also do to influence classroom practices. In Chapter Four, I demonstrate the fallacy of this approach.

Finally, on the basis of its value-free assumption, technical rationality holds that there is 'no value conflict and that there are no competing paradigms of practice' (Pearson 1989:28). This position leads to a very important conclusion, that solutions to problems can be standardised. Effectively, this means that since values in professional practice (such as teaching) are out of question, *context* is irrelevant. This point is illustrated by the way learner-centred pedagogy has been portrayed – as a one-size-fits-all pedagogical approach (Reyes 1992), that is, it is universal pedagogy, one that works with equal effectiveness irrespective of the context. However, the pedagogy is value-laden since it expresses a view about the world, about the kind of people and society we want to create through education. This ideological/political nature of the pedagogy is masked by the technicist view. If there are no competing paradigms of practice, and if teacher-centred and learner-centred pedagogies do not represent competing paradigms of teaching, then it should be possible to present the two as lying on a continuum.

Where context is rendered irrelevant, standardized techniques of solving problems are considered possible. However, since teaching is a value-laden activity, in the words of Crossley and Jarvis (1999), 'context matters', meaning that standardized solutions to problems of teaching and learning are not only undesirable, they are impossible. Neglect of context resulting from the dominance of the technicist approach to pedagogical change might, therefore, be responsible for the failure of the institutionalization of the learner-centred pedagogy and conversely, for the resilience of the teacher-centred pedagogy. No amount of resources will change teaching and learning in sub-Saharan Africa in a significant way when we fail to problematise the context in which the twin processes (of teaching and learning) occur. This calls for a socio-cultural approach to pedagogical change to replace the technicist approach.

Towards a Socio-cultural Approach to Pedagogy

There is a growing dissatisfaction with the technicist approach to pedagogic change. McGrath (2008:3), in an implicit reference to the technicist approach, for example, observes that 'the main approaches taken to teacher development are failing to deal with the complexity of teachers' knowledge, work and identity and lack sufficient grasp of the nature of change processes and the way that these are mediated by cultural, political and economic environments'. Vavrus (2009) has been bold in attempting to develop a framework she terms the 'cultural politics of pedagogy' in her examination of the multi-faceted environment of teacher education and pedagogical change in Tanzania. The latter attempt is an effort to eschew the technicist approach to pedagogic change by including the 'economic and political dimensions of pedagogical theory and practice in aid-dependent African states' (Vavrus 2009:305). Through this book, I intend contributing to this emerging debate by considering in more detail than has been attempted before the cultural, epistemological, political, economic, social and religious bases of pedagogical practice, not only in aid-dependent Africa but Africa as a whole.

A socio-cultural approach takes off from the basic premise that teaching is inherently value-laden and context-specific, that is, teaching does not take place in a sociological vacuum. Teaching shapes and is shaped by the social, cultural, historical, political and economic contexts within which it occurs. No two contexts can be exactly the same. By the same logic, teaching can never be exactly the same across contexts. While it is possible to identify 'constants' in teaching, these must be understood as tentative, that is, subject to change as and when the context changes. Pedagogical approaches such as learner-centred and teacher-centred approaches have social origins and are, therefore, socially grounded. This position puts the basic premises of technical rationality on their head. First, contrary to the logic of technical rationality, a socio-cultural approach presents pedagogical styles (teacher-centred pedagogy (TCP) and learner-centred-pedagogy (LCP) as problematic and representing competing paradigms of practice. Not only are they grounded in radically different epistemological foundations, they are also supported by different structures in the contexts in which they find expression. Thus, TCP and LCP are fundamentally different pedagogical styles, in fact, paradigms. Following from the above, their transfer from one context to another is problematic. These two repudiations of the technicist approach imply that there can never be a one-size-fits-all pedagogical style. In short, a socio-cultural approach (a) problematises the pedagogical styles themselves; they are not taken for granted as is the case in the technicist approach; (b) problematises the transfer of pedagogies from one context to another; and (c) takes seriously the influence of the wider enveloping social structure in its attempt to explain the shape teaching and learning take in any context.

Tissue Rejection: An Analytical Tool

> A basic problem in educational change is that of 'tissue rejection' whereby an innovation
> . . . does not become an effectively functioning part of the system (Hoyle 1970:2).

Another way of appreciating the significance of context in teaching and learning is to use the medical metaphors of 'tissue rejection' and 'immunological condition' (Hoyle 1969). Tissue rejection refers to the rejection of a transplanted organ by its host because of the latter's immunological condition. A transplanted heart, for example, may be rejected by the patient's body because it does not fit well in the latter's immunological state. It makes no sense to attempt an organ transplant on a body whose immunological condition is not designed to accommodate the organ. If the immunological condition did not matter, it would be possible to transplant any organ to any body without regard to the latter's condition. Applied to educational settings, Hoyle (1969) argues that tissue rejection occurs when there is a discrepancy or incongruence between the innovation and the 'pedagogical code' of the school, and I would add, of the enveloping social structure. The implanted innovation is rejected by the host environment (e.g. the school/society) because it is incompatible with the latter's values and past experience. Hoyle observes that many current innovations (e.g. learner-centred pedagogy) are underpinned by a 'code' which is radically new as far as the adopting unit is concerned. In the case of learner-centred pedagogy, this code places emphasis on classroom openness, flexibility and learner empowerment. The 'message' carried by this pedagogical code may require a switch in code on the part of the host. It is at this juncture that the fate of the innovation is decided. Where this code is already shifting towards classroom openness, for example, support for an innovation carrying a 'radical' message is likely to be forthcoming. On the relationship between innovations and social structure, Hoyle and Bell (1972:19) say that, 'An innovation will diffuse through a social structure if it is congruent with the central values obtaining in that structure'. In such a case, the institutionalization of an innovation underpinned by the openness code will be relatively easy to accomplish. On the other hand, where this code is not shifting, or is shifting, but in the opposite direction, institutionalization becomes difficult, and the innovation is rejected. In short, it is necessary to evaluate not only the context in which pedagogy is being introduced but also the nature of the pedagogy itself to establish its fit or lack thereof with its 'host' context. Such an approach is a world apart from the technicist one.

Conclusion

The main conclusion to be reached from the above is that adoption, implementation and institutionalization of pedagogy would be greatly facilitated by a social structure whose code is compatible with that of the innovation. This calls for an approach to pedagogic change that not only accommodates analysis of the enveloping structure to determine the latter's 'readiness' for the proposed pedagogic innovation, but also one that treats the pedagogy being introduced as problematic. The technicist approach, as argued above, has no room for this. Certain features (e.g. child-rearing practices) of the social structure may act as support structures for the sustenance of a particular form of pedagogy. Thus, to understand the resilience of TCP in the sub-Saharan African context we need to isolate and then analyse the structures that support it. Conversely, to understand the tissue rejection being suffered by LCP, it is necessary to analyse the code that it embeds and judge its fit with the host context.

It is precisely these two concerns that are the focus of the remaining chapters of the book. The next chapter looks at what I consider to be the 'true' rationale for introducing LCP in sub-Saharan Africa. The rationale is a politico-economic one. I treat the rationale as problematic in its own right since it cannot be expected to appeal to sub-Saharan Africa teachers, students and education administrators whose preoccupation is improving the test/examination scores of their students, not imbuing learners with the skills and attitudes needed to navigate today's political and economic world. To mask its ideological nature, sponsors of LCP in sub-Saharan Africa initially presented it as a one-size-fits-all pedagogical approach, a universal pedagogy that had no respect for context. Its technicist nature, combined with its irrelevance to the tasks of teachers and students in sub-Saharan Africa, render the pedagogy 'uninstitutionalisable' in the sub-region.

2

Why Learner-centred Pedagogy in Sub-Saharan Africa?

Introduction

The rationale advanced in this chapter for contemporary interest in learner-centred education is very different from the one often advanced by proponents of the pedagogy, mainly that learner-centred pedagogy improves the 'quality' of teaching and learning. The proponents rarely unpack the concept of 'quality teaching and learning' – despite the fact that 'quality' is a contentious concept (see Barrett et al. 2006) – but for us to appreciate it better, they give us occasional glimpses of what they understand by quality in this context. Tabulawa (2003) and Vavrus (2009) surmise that contemporary interest in pedagogical reform in sub-Saharan Africa is largely based on economic and political rationales – the need to improve the sub-region's human capital base as a way of stimulating economic growth and the West's desire to globalise a liberal democratic ethos. In this context, Vavrus (2009:304) concludes that 'quality' 'means constructivist approaches to teaching that privilege active, inquiry-based learning and student-centred teaching'. In other words, although the efficacy of the pedagogy is often couched in cognitive/educational terms, in essence, its perceived efficacy lies in its political and economic nature. On the basis of this understanding of quality teaching and learning teachers are told that their students' performance will improve if they adopt this form of teaching.

However, this often unstated rationale for the constructivist learner-centred pedagogy might in fact be contributing to the failure of pedagogical reform in sub-Saharan Africa. Political/economic rationales for the pedagogy can only promote a technical understanding of teaching. Furthermore, the rationales have very little relationship with student performance *as understood* by teachers in sub-Saharan Africa (where 'quality' is understood predominantly in terms of student performance in tests and examinations). Pedagogical innovations whose utility in this regard is not obvious to teachers and students are unlikely to be embraced. The perceived utility of an innovation has implications for how it is received in its host environment. Teachers and students in the sub-Saharan African context are mostly likely to evaluate the utility value of a pedagogical innovation in terms of whether it is likely to enhance students' performance in tests and examinations, not in terms of whether it is likely to produce students with the character traits preferred for contemporary political life and the economy. Would teachers and students be ready to adopt and implement a pedagogy that has no apparent and immediate utility value to them? In the context of Africa, the answer is a clear 'No'. Thus, the very rationale for the learner-centred pedagogy might be its Achilles' heel. If this argument is admissible, then the pedagogy must be treated as problematic, instead of assuming, as the technicist approach does, that it is only technical issues to do with the innovation delivery system that matter.

The economic/political rationale for the constructivist, learner-centred pedagogy cannot be appreciated without first recognizing the role of international aid agencies in its propagation. The fact that these agencies' interest in the pedagogy intensified after the fall of the Berlin Wall in 1989 is in itself significant. The apparent 'lack' of interest in the pedagogy before 1989 may be attributed to the very central hypothesis of the modernization theory of development which became enshrined in policies of aid agencies soon after the latter were created. The hypothesis, coupled with human capital theory, viewed education in technicist terms. However, the ascendancy of neo-liberalism as a development paradigm in the 1980s and 1990s elevated political democratization as a prerequisite for economic development. Education, then, assumed a central role in the democratization project. Given its democratic tendencies, learner-centred pedagogy was a natural choice for the development of democratic social relations in the schools of aid-receiving countries, the majority of which are in sub-Saharan Africa. International aid agencies, now operating in a unipolar, geopolitical environment, could afford to be explicit about their preference for the pedagogy. Therefore, besides being an import, learner-centred pedagogy is a worldview intended to develop a preferred kind of society and people. In short, the pedagogy in sub-Saharan Africa is significant less for its educational/cognitive value than for its political and economic utility. However, the latter is of little interest to teachers and students.

Why Learner-centred Pedagogy now?

Answering this question is a prerequisite for an understanding of the pervasiveness of the learner-centred pedagogy. Is it not intriguing that the surge in interest in the pedagogy coincided with a political development of global significance, being the fall of the Berlin Wall, with all that it symbolized – the end of the bipolar world order? Is it not intriguing that the pedagogy has been sponsored and popularized by international agencies such as the World Bank and the International Monetary Fund (IMF), a role that they started playing much more actively and boldly soon after the demise of the Soviet Union? Is it not also interesting that in countries such as South Africa and Namibia, learner-centred pedagogy assumed prominence with the countries' attainment of political independence?

Justification for adopting the learner-centred pedagogy is usually expressed by the aid agencies in benign and apolitical terms. For example, the justification is often couched in educational and cognitive terms, such as 'the pedagogy leads to improvements in learning outcomes' and that it is 'more effective'. Pertinent questions, such as 'what learning outcomes?' and 'effectiveness for what?', are rarely posed or addressed. Also rarely questioned is the assumption of equating change in the quality of teaching with change in teaching styles, especially with the constructivist, learner-centred pedagogy. Guthrie (1980) argues that there is no causal relationship between the two and that, to date, there is no study that has conclusively established that learner-centredness is necessarily superior to traditional teaching in Third World countries in terms of improving students' achievement in test scores. In his comparative study of progressive and non-progressive methods, Anthony (1979:180) concluded that 'progressive methods are not generally superior to non-progressive methods for the teaching of reading and English, and that progressive methods are generally inferior to non-progressive methods for the teaching of arithmetic'. On his part, Bennett (1976) in his seminal study, *Teaching Styles and Pupil Progress,* argued against the permissive classroom atmosphere in progressive schools, calling for more teacher direction and clear sequencing and structuring of learning experiences.

There seems to be unanimity among both international aid agencies and educational researchers that learner-centred education can be effective in inculcating 'affective, moral and philosophical values about desirable psycho-sociological traits for individuals and for society' (Guthrie 1990:222). What character traits or attributes are these and where do they come from? The traits include creativity, versatility, innovativeness, critical thinking, problem solving, tolerance of divergent views and independence of thought. Constructivist, learner-centred approaches are seen as the appropriate approaches to deliver these character traits. In this discourse, 'quality' teaching is defined as teaching that adopts constructivist approaches 'that privilege active, inquiry-based learning and student-centred teaching' (Vavrus 2009:304). Privileging these attributes can be traced to political and economic developments since 1989. This is not to suggest that before the fall of the Berlin Wall these attributes were not considered important to the education enterprise. On the contrary, the Progressive Education Movement of the 1960s and 1970s purported to promote these qualities in learners (Silcock 1996:200). Partly because of the bipolar, global geopolitical configuration of the pre-1990s, the West and international aid agencies were constrained to openly associate education (and by extension, learner-centred pedagogy) with the imperatives of political democratization and promotion of free-market economy. The collapse of the Soviet Union (symbolized by the fall of the Berlin Wall), leading to a unipolar world order (dominated by the United States of America), emboldened the West and international aid agencies to publicly declare their preference and support for Western liberal democracy and the free-market economy, and together with these, education that promoted character traits congenial to both democratization and the free-market economy. The position of aid agencies on this matter has been summarized by Burnell (1991:7):

> [T]he ascendant assumption now seems to be that political pluralism is essential for development. Put another way, a movement towards greater political accountability will enable a robust and free-market economy to flourish.

'Political pluralism' in effect refers to 'liberal democracy' and 'free-market economy' to 'competitive capitalism'. Thus the promotion of liberal democracy is necessarily the promotion of competitive capitalism, as far as aid agencies are concerned. For the agencies, economic development is perceived as only possible under liberal democracy, so that promoting the latter should be a priority for any country serious about development. It is, therefore, not surprising that aid agencies have made the adoption *of* multi-party democracy by aid-receiving countries a condition for giving aid. This condition was integrated in the structural adjustment programmes that many sub-Saharan Africa have endured since the 1980s.

The aid agencies have cited the democratisation of education as one of the most important ways of promoting liberal democracy at the macro level. For example, consider the following policy statements from the bilateral aid agencies of the United Kingdom (UK) and Norway. In the UK, the Overseas

Development Administration (ODA) and its successor, the Department for International Development (DfID) have stated clear positions:

> Citizens who have been exposed to learning styles which require the questioning of assumptions, empirical styles of studying and the exploration of alternatives are seen as likely to have more chance of participating fruitfully in a pluralistic political process than those who have not. (Overseas Development Administration 1994:3)

> The relationship between education and the political process is well illustrated in Eastern Europe and the former Soviet Union, where the process of democratisation is seen to be hampered by outdated curricula and teaching methods (Department for International Development 1997:7).

In Norway, the position has been illustrated by the Ministry of Foreign Affairs:

> For the growth and consolidation of a democratic system, it is important that the attitudes and values of such a system, like respect for human rights, should be expressed and reflected in different contexts. For example, in the educational system information about democracy and human rights needs to be imparted from the elementary level onwards (Royal Norwegian Ministry of Foreign Affairs 1993:19).

Similar statements have also been made by other bilateral aid agencies in the USA, Canada and Denmark. All the statements stress the perceived significance of the relationship between education and politics, specifically that education has the potential to contribute significantly towards the democratisation process. As Harber (1997:22) has noted in the African context:

> Western governments and aid agencies not only seem, in principle at least, to favour democratisation of African political systems, they also see education playing an important part in the process.

Often singled out (as in the UK statements above) as the nexus between education and the broader principles of democracy and economic development is the learner-centred pedagogy. That this should be the case is not surprising, as Shukla (1994:11) observes: '*[D]emocracy in relation to education cannot but be an extension of child-centred-ness (paedocentrism) to the social dimension*'. Likewise, the desirability of learner-centred pedagogy today is couched in the discourse of international economic competitiveness (Tabulawa 2009). Thus, since 1989, there has been a tightening of the relationship between politics and economics, leading to a politico-economic theory i.e. neo-liberalism, which development aid has since enshrined in its programmes, including development aid to education. Neo-liberalism is delivered in sub-

Saharan African countries by aid agencies through educational projects and consultancies funded by the aid agencies, and learner-centred pedagogy forms the nexus between neo-liberalism and education. In Botswana, this pedagogy was heavily emphasised in both the Primary Education Improvement Project (PEIP; 1981-1991) and the Junior Secondary Education Improvement Project (JSEIP). These projects were largely financed by the United States Agency for International Development (USAID). In Uganda, learner-centred pedagogy was promoted by, among others, the Aga Khan Foundation and USAID (Altinyelken 2010). In Tanzania it was the International Monetary Fund (IMF) and the World Bank through the Secondary Education Development Programme (SEDP) (Vavrus 2009), while in Malawi the international agendas of Education for All (EFA) and the Millennium Development Goals (MDGs) have been the main carriers of the pedagogy (Mtika and Gates 2010).

It is important to appreciate, though, that interest in the learner-centred pedagogy is not a twentieth-century phenomenon. It arose in the context of the so-called Enlightenment or Age of Reason, an era in which the desire to reconstruct society was evident – a project in which education was expected to play a pivotal role. By turning to science and the scientific method (the latter defined as 'a systematic and careful way of observing natural phenomena' (Gutek 2005:136), Enlightenment theorists sought to turn the supernatural order upside down. By turning to nature for lessons on how to organize society, these thinkers were challenging divine authority; and emphasis on the natural propensities of the child was an attack on the notion of original sin. Jean-Jacques Rousseau's theorization (as discussed in Chapter Three) on education not only called for a new social order, it also specifically called for the construction of an egalitarian and democratic society. The association of the learner-centred pedagogy with democratization is a theme that has continued to reverberate around the world, lately with renewed fervour. The pedagogy is a view about the world, about the kind of people and society we want to create through education. However, this political/ideological nature of the pedagogy is often not recognised. This is because it is often presented as if it were value-free and merely technical. Its implementation is often informed by the ideology of technical rationality with its stress on value neutrality (Tabulawa 1998). This explains why it is often presented as a one-size-fits-all pedagogical approach (Reyes 1992), that is, it is a universal pedagogy, one that works with equal effectiveness irrespective of the context. It is this technicist view of the pedagogy that masks its ideological/political nature.

Contrary to justifications of the learner-centred pedagogy based on educational grounds, the interest of aid agencies in the pedagogy is part of a wider design on the part of international aid institutions to facilitate the penetration of capitalist ideology in periphery states, this being done under the guise of democratisation. Adopting a world systems approach, I argue that the hidden agenda is to alter the 'modes of thought' and practices of those in periphery states so that they look at reality in the same way(s) as those in core states. This process is being accelerated by the current wave of globalisation, which is a carrier of conservative, neo-liberal ideology.

Aid to Education from a World Systems Approach

The world systems approach conceptualises the contemporary world as integrated but dominated by the capitalist economic system of the USA, Western Europe and Japan (Clayton 1998). These countries constitute the 'core' zone and are characterised by a higher level of industrialisation, while the less industrialised nations of the world constitute the 'periphery' zone (Wallerstein 1984). The two zones are characterised by unequal economic and power relations. The world economy differentially rewards these zones, with a disproportionate flow of surplus to the core zone. In addition to supporting the dominant (capitalist) classes (oriented towards the world market), the economic structure of each zone also supports states which operate in the interests of those classes. These states tend to be weaker in the periphery and stronger in the core zone of the world system. As Stocpol (1977:1077) states:

> the differential strength of the multiple states within the world capitalist economy is crucial for maintaining the system as a whole, for the strong states reinforce and increase the differential flow of surplus to the core zones.

Stronger states assist their dominant (capitalist) classes to manipulate and enforce terms of trade in their favour in the world market. This ensures the exploitation of periphery states.

However, the privileged position in the world system of core states cannot be guaranteed, for their relations with periphery states are dynamic, Thus unlike dependency theorists, who tended to adopt a deterministic stance on the issue of core-periphery relationship, world system theorists do not regard periphery states as doomed to their subordinate position in global power relations. This fact alone means that there is tension between the two zones, and the privileged zone would naturally want to perpetuate and preserve the status quo. In the past (for example, during colonial conquest) this tension would manifest itself in open warfare (Magdoff 1982). Today the preferred means of legitimising global power relations is through the inculcation of what Wallerstein (1984:117) terms 'modes of thought and analysis'. Largely used to carry out this function are aid agencies. Through the aid agencies, core states use their funds in 'many different ways to promote their versions of Third World improvement' (King 1991:25), and one of those versions is that of a capitalist South. This is least surprising since the agencies are 'dominated by capitalist ideologies' (Bray 1984:13). Their aid, which comes in the form of grants, loans, equipment and personnel, promotes the conditions necessary for the reproduction of capitalism (Hayter 1971).

Education as the 'dominant Ideological State Apparatus' (Althusser 1971) is a tool used by core states to disseminate those ideologies supportive of their interests. After all, education is a political and moral activity and, by its very nature, embodies cultures and ideologies (Ginsburg *et al.* 1992). It can, therefore, be used to transmit modes of thought and practice. Development aid agencies are particularly well placed to transfer these cultures and ideologies from core to periphery states. Education aid, just like all foreign aid, 'represents a transfer not only of resources and technologies, but of culture and values as well' (Stokke 1995:21). Clayton (1998) conceptualises the effects of educational assistance to periphery states in terms of its ideological effects which take place through what Samoff (1993) terms 'intellectual socialization'. This form of socialisation takes place through being taught by 'core' teachers, attending core institutions, and through reading books and curricular materials produced by core enterprises. All these are imbued with core values, ideas, and structures' (Clayton 1998:151). Teaching methods (such as learner-centredness) transferred from core to periphery states also transmit a way of thinking, or what Bourdieu (1971) terms 'habit of thought'. Some of the central values learner-centredness purports to promote are individual autonomy, open-mindedness and tolerance for alternative viewpoints. All these are in line with the individualistic Western culture and are also character traits deemed necessary for an individual to survive in a pluralistic, liberal democratic, capitalist society. Thus, by purporting to promote democracy, learner-centredness invariably promotes the reproduction of capitalism in periphery states. It is, therefore, not surprising that aid agencies have shown so much interest in the pedagogy. However, it should be recognised that learner-centredness relates to capitalism in an indirect and non-causal way.

To appreciate the interest of aid agencies in the learner-centred pedagogy, it is important to look at how ideas about development have changed since the emergence of development aid in the late 1940s to the point where democratisation is now viewed as a condition for economic growth. This helps to put aid agencies' current interest in the learner-centred pedagogy in perspective. More specifically, the historical perspective shows how capitalist democracy (as an ideology as well as a political-economic system) permeated and became enshrined in the policies of aid agencies when the latter emerged in the 1940s and 1950s. However, it was during the 1980s that the aid agencies' interest in liberal democracy, and consequently in the learner-centred pedagogy, became explicit. Before looking at the changes that have occurred in ideas about development, the democracy-capitalism nexus must be explained.

Liberal Democracy and Capitalism: The (In)separable Marriage?

There is a general misconception that the association of economic development with liberal democracy is a post-1989 phenomenon. On the contrary, this view of the inseparability of development (here understood as the spread of the free-market economic system) and political pluralism (liberal democracy) now enshrined in aid agency policies has a history far older than that of the aid agencies themselves. There is unanimity among scholars of liberal democracy that the latter emerged in the wake of capitalism, and that there is concordance between the two. However, there is less agreement on the question of how liberal democracy evolved from capitalism. Those in the neo-liberal camp (such as Lipset 1959; Friedman 1962) aver that capitalism produced a complex and differentiated economy. This in turn produced a 'complex and differentiated political system where there [were] multiple centers of power' (Dryzek 1996:25). Decentralised power is conducive to liberal democracy. For Lipset (1959), capitalist prosperity increased the size of the middle class – that class committed to liberal virtues. Thus, it was the capitalists themselves who produced democracy because they wanted it. So, capitalism is inseparable from liberal democracy, a point emphatically stated by Friedman (1962:8) who asserts that there exists an intimate connection between economics and politics, that only certain combinations of political and economic arrangements are possible, and that in particular, a society that is socialist cannot be democratic, in the sense of guaranteeing individual freedom.

This liberal version of history is vehemently contested by radical historians/ scholars (such as Macpherson 1973; Rueschemeyer et al. 1992; Boron 1995; Dryzek 1996). While these scholars agree that liberal democracy was born in the wake of capitalism, they however oppose the view that it was the emerging capitalist class that ensured the 'flourishing' of democracy. Boron (1995), for example, argues that capitalism led to liberalism and the emergence of a working class. It did not lead to democracy. The latter only emerged as a result of the actions of the almost disenfranchised working class. It was the plight of this class that precipitated 'popular mobilizations and workers' struggles' (Boron 1995:11) which gave birth to liberal democracy. Otherwise, he argues, the American and the French revolutions of the eighteenth and nineteenth centuries would have easily 'crystallized as sheer oligarchical domination barely disguised under some restricted liberal institutions...." (Boron 1995:11). Thus, democracy and capitalism are inherently antagonistic to each other. As long as capitalism thrives, there will always be a working class which has more to gain from democracy, and will always push for democratisation (Rueschemeyer et al. 1992). In effect, capitalist development necessarily entails a curtailment of political freedom.

This debate notwithstanding, the view of the inseparability of capitalism as an economic system and liberal democracy as a form of political organisation has always been ascendant in much of the capitalist world. With the demise of communism in 1989, the legitimacy of this view has gained even greater credibility in the West.

When they emerged in the late 1940s and early 1950s, aid institutions (the World Bank, IMF, United Nations organisations, and bilateral agencies) were informed by the modernisation theory of development – a theory that implicitly celebrated the inseparability of liberal democracy and capitalism.

The Modernisation Paradigm: 1950-1980

Capitalist democracy as both an ideology and a political-economic system formally entered the global stage in the 1950s and 1960s. These decades witnessed the formulation by US social scientists of the modernisation paradigm. This paradigm was subsequently 'enshrined in the policy of the US Government and multilateral aid agencies' (Dryzek 1996:18). The modernisation paradigm of development was closely associated with Rostow's (1960) stages of economic growth. Rostow's 'non-communist manifesto' held that the stages of economic growth would 'culminate in a liberal capitalist economic system with the political characteristics of the Western democracies' (Dryzek 1996:18). It was thus a re-statement of the inseparability of capitalism and liberal democracy thesis. The implication of this was clear: societies that needed to develop could follow the core nations of Europe, America and Japan as models. Third World countries, as Peet (1991:33) states, could,

> 'encourage the diffusion of innovation from the centre [Euro-America and Japan], [could] adopt capitalism as the mode of social integration and [could] welcome United States aid and direction'.

That the modernisation theory of development was Eurocentric is beyond doubt. The theory's basic assumption was that the West's experience with development was the norm for historical progress and had to be emulated by the rest of the world, not least by developing countries. With its basis in structural functionalism, modernisation theory stated that for Third World countries to modernize, they needed to erode and break old social, economic and psychological commitments. This could be done by introducing structures of capitalism into those countries. Western education (as one of the structures of capitalism) in periphery states was aimed at eroding traditional modes of thought. It was envisaged that economic growth in developing countries would ultimately lead to a more differentiated political system (liberal democracy) in those countries.

Much of development aid to developing countries until the 1980s was underpinned by this belief, although this ideological and political mission of aid was rarely explicitly expressed. It is this belief and its implicit nature that explains why until the 1990s, aid agencies and multilateral institutions extended aid even to some of the most brutal and authoritarian regimes in the world (such as Chile and Malawi) without conditions. Of course there were many instances when such regimes were sustained by core states because of their strategic location as buffers to the spread of communism. However, on the whole, development aid was premised on a basic hypothesis of the modernisation theory of development – that economic growth (that is, the spread of capitalism) moves authoritarian regimes towards liberal democratic values. For this reason, political conditionalities were unnecessary.

We can now understand why Western governments and aid agencies could stand tall and argue that their assistance was benign, philanthropic and politically neutral – because they did not explicitly prescribe any favoured political system (such as liberal democracy) to the recipients of aid. After all, this political system would emerge automatically once the structures of capitalism had been introduced. Thus, underpinning the modernisation theory of development enshrined in the policies of aid agencies was an ideology – capitalist democracy.

Educational Aid and the Modernisation Project

Education occupied a special position in the modernisation project. As an agent of social change, education was expected to promote 'individual modernity', defined as the 'process by which individuals supposedly change from a traditional way of life to a rapidly changing, technological way of life' (Gottlieb 2000:161). At its conception, educational aid to periphery states was based on this perspective. In those states, Western education was expected to erode old social and psychological commitments. It was expected to produce educated elites with Western values and enterpreneurial attitudes. These elites would then lead their states on the path to modernity.

Thus, just like 'development', education was viewed as a technical undertaking. This technicist view of education was accentuated by human capital theory which, 'more than any other theoretical construct, had a profound influence on concepts of the place of education in Third World modernisation and development' (Gottlieb 2000:161). Woodhall (1985:2312) defines human capital as the investment human beings make in themselves 'by means of education, training, or other activities, which raises their future income by raising their lifetime earnings'. The central tenet of human capital theory is that educated individuals are more economically productive than less educated ones. Studies of the economics of education mushroomed in the 1960s and 1970s. These studies concentrated on both the social and private rate of returns to educational investment (Psacharopoulos 1981).

This view of education was subsequently adopted by multilateral and bilateral aid agencies such as the World Bank. The Organisation for Economic Co-operation and Development (OECD), for example, was unequivocal in its approval of human capital theory:

> The development of contemporary economies depends crucially on the knowledge, skills, and attitudes of their workers – in short on human capital. In many respects, human capital has become even more important in recent years (OECD 1987:69).

The pedagogical implications of human capital theory have been analysed by Baptiste (2001). After a lengthy interrogation of the basic assumptions of the theory, Baptiste reaches the conclusion that individuals described in human capital theory resemble what he terms 'lone wolves' (Baptiste 2001:196). The kind of education that suits these 'lone wolves' would be 'apolitical, adaptive, and individualistic' (Baptiste 2001:198). Pedagogically, educational activities of lone wolves are determined by 'technical considerations . . . rather than by any ethical or moral philosophy of the educator or program' (Baptiste 2001:196); being adaptive, lone wolves are mechanical beings who are only spectators in their universe; and, being rugged individuals, as learners they lack a collective purpose. Being wedded to the view of education as apolitical, adaptive and individualistic (in short, to human capital theory), it could hardly be expected that aid agencies would show much interest in pedagogical matters. The technicist view of education treats pedagogy as value-neutral and, thus, non-problematic (Tabulawa 1997).

However, the aid agencies view of pedagogy as benign and apolitical was to change in the early 1980s with the rise of neo-liberalism in the West, displacing the modernisation theory of development. This paradigm shift led to a re-conceptualisation of education in the service of the economy. All aspects of education, from curricular content to classroom practices, were affected. In the section that follows, I account for the rise of neo-liberalism (free-market capitalism), its impact on the role of education in economic development in periphery states, and how it ultimately helped to shape the pedagogical orientation of aid agencies thereby leading to their current interest in learner-centred pedagogy. Explication of these developments will demonstrate that 'educational practice is profoundly influenced by theories of human and social behaviour' (Baptiste 2001:184) and that teaching is inherently a political and value-based activity.

The 1980s: A Shift in Emphasis

In the 1970s, the modernisation theory of development came under attack from dependency and world systems theorists. Although in academic circles dependency and world systems theories seemed to displace modernisation theory, in aid agencies the displacer was neo-liberalism, first introduced in the domestic policies of core states in the late 1970s. To justify their policies theoretically, aid agencies turned away from development sociology to neo-classical economics, particularly monetarism. This paradigm shift was to have a profound impact on how aid agencies presented themselves as it, in practice, required them to be explicit about development aid's political and ideological mission. It also led to a re-conceptualisation of the role of education in the development of periphery states. It is thus important to look in more detail at how this occurred.

In the economic and political spheres, the 1970s witnessed two very significant events: (i) an enduring economic recession which in itself was an indictment of the Keynesian economics that underpinned welfare state capitalism; and (ii) the rise of neo-conservative governments in the USA (the Reagan administration), Britain (the Thatcher government) and Germany (the Kohl government) which presided over the demise of communism, symbolised by the fall of the Berlin Wall in 1989. These events are largely responsible for the current dominant view among Western aid agencies that political pluralism (liberal democracy) is a necessary condition for economic development. It is, therefore, not surprising that democratisation should have such a high priority on the educational agenda of aid institutions for periphery states. The basic premise is that learner-centred pedagogy will promote democracy, a necessary condition for the development of a free-market economy. Thus, learner-centred pedagogy is perceived as conducive to capitalism although, as already indicated, the relationship between the two is an indirect one.

The Economic Crisis of the 1970s

The severity of this economic crisis prompted some (for example, Gamble and Walton 1976) to talk of a 'crisis of capitalism'. The crisis led to hyper-inflation and stagnation in production. It also led to high and rising unemployment. To many neo-liberals it soon became clear that the capitalist system needed re-ordering. The 'answer' to the crisis was to be found in the works of neo-liberal economists, amongst them Friedman, the winner of the 1976 Nobel Prize in Economics, and Hayek, whose writings influenced the policies of the New Right in Britain. Friedman's views deserve some detailed consideration here because his influence is so far unsurpassed and has penetrated every part of the globe, mainly because his economic formulations have, by and large, been adopted by core states and multilateral aid agencies. The same formulations have subsequently been thrust upon periphery states.

Friedman saw the economic crisis as resulting from state interference in the economic arena, which in turn tended to stifle the 'creative and liberating potential of the market' (Boron 1995:33). The only way out of the crisis, in Friedman's view, was through monetarism:

> an economic policy which sees the control of the money supply as crucial to the control of inflation and which, by implication, condemns government attempts to regulate the economy through public spending...' (Scruton 1982:304)

In short, Friedman wanted drastic cuts in government spending and the promotion of private enterprise. This would involve the removal of government subsidies, dismantling the welfare system and privatizing state-owned enterprises, all of which had characterised the 'Keynesian consensus' of the post-1945 period. These ideas coincided with the rise of neo-conservative governments in the USA and Britain which, desperate for a solution to the economic crisis, took some of Friedman's ideas on board. As Boron (1995:34) states:

> ...Friedman's ideas are at the core of the prevailing neo-liberal orthodoxy and have been the rationalizing principles of the neo-conservative governments all around the world.

My interest in Friedman's theory is that not only is it an economic theory, it is a political theory as well. This is one reason why it was so appealing to neo-conservative governments. The notion of the 'market' is central in Friedman's political and economic formulation. In his view, the market involves voluntary co-operation among individuals. It has two qualities: it resonates with (i) the idea of no government interference; and, resulting from this, (ii) individual autonomy. Friedman sets the market against the state, treating the two as inherently antagonistic. The state represents coercion and authoritarianism, while the market is the cradle of freedom and democracy (Boron 1995). So where the state is heavily involved in economic activities, there cannot be talk of individual autonomy and freedom. Not only is the market important for good economic performance, it is also at the same time the 'fundamental sanctuary that preserves economic and political freedoms' (Boron 1995:36). Thus, freedom can only be defined in terms of the struggle between the state and the market. The latter is about competition, and this competition impacts positively on the state and democracy. The dominance of the market necessarily ensures contraction of state activities in the economy, in itself a desirable situation in Friedman's view. Furthermore, since the market limits the expansion of the state, a situation is avoided where political power is concentrated in a few hands. Devolved political power favours liberal democracy. In this way, without a market and free-market enterprise, there cannot be liberal democracy, nor can a free-market system thrive where there is no liberal democracy. This is a re-statement of the inseparability of capitalism and democracy thesis, whose origins, as we saw earlier on in the paper, are to be found in eighteenth-century liberalism.

This synopsis of Friedman's political/economic theory identifies the ideological nature of the theory. It must be inferred, too, that socialism, because it is the antithesis of free-market enterprise, cannot be democratic. Only competitive capitalism is compatible with political freedom/liberal democracy. Friedman (1962) himself is frank about it:

> ...the kind of economic organization that provides economic freedom directly, namely, competitive capitalism, also promotes political freedom because it separates economic power from political power and in this way enables the one to offset the other (Friedman 1962:9).

When this reasoning is followed to its logical conclusion:

> [D]emocracy simply becomes the political organization proper of capitalism – competitive ex definition – and capitalism is posited as the sole structural support congruent with the specific needs of a democratic state (Boron 1995:6).

Thus, free-market capitalism and liberal democracy are two sides of the same coin; you cannot advocate one without necessarily advocating the other.

The Rise of Neo-Conservative Governments in the West

It is clear from the above that the apparent failure of Keynesianism in the 1970s set the stage for the revival of neo-classical economics. This revival coincided with the rise of neo-conservative governments in the West. These were the years when the Thatcher government, the Reagan administration and the Kohl government swept into power in Britain, the USA and Germany respectively. No sooner had these neo-conservative governments come into office than they started administering Friedman's prescriptions (albeit modified) to their ailing economies. International aid agencies under the control of the West, such as the World Bank and the International Monetary Fund, followed suit. The Reagan administration and the Thatcher government spearheaded economic deregulation and the privatisation of state-owned enterprises, thereby limiting the role of the state in direct economic activity. These economic reforms were subsequently thrust upon periphery states by core governments and aid agencies.

Periphery states since the early 1980s have been told to cut government spending if they wish to foster economic growth. Under Structural Adjustment Programmes (SAPs) these states are told to remove subsidies on essentials (a very bitter pill often accompanied by riots) and to privatise public-owned enterprises. In short, they are being pressurised to adopt the free-market system of competitive capitalism. Simultaneously, periphery states are told to democratise, that is, to adopt liberal democracy. This is made a condition for foreign aid. The assumption is that efforts to implement a free-market economic system would not yield the desired results where there is no liberal democracy. This contrasts with the earlier view informed by modernisation theory that economic growth (i.e. the spread of capitalism) in periphery states would ultimately yield democracy.

This paradigm shift, as already indicated, resulted from the ascendancy of the political theory of monetarism as well as the demise of communism in 1989. The latter event signaled the end of the 'bipolar international system which had dominated international relations and world politics since World War II' (Stokke 1995:9). This has led to the much discussed 'New World Order'. This is a world order in which Western governments now feel freer than ever before to pursue their political concerns in relation to periphery states. The political norms and interests being pursued by core governments relate to governmental organisation and economic concerns, that is, democratisation and the adoption of free-market economics. Thus behind the clarion call for democracy in periphery states by core states and aid agencies is the ideology of market capitalism. Nevertheless, in general, free-market capitalism is not really penetrating the developing world in accord with the Western model.

Education and Democratisation in Periphery States

It was inevitable that education in periphery states would be affected by all these economic and political changes. With emphasis now on political democratisation in periphery states, education as the dominant ideological state apparatus has a significant role in the process. Its mandate has been expanded. Whereas in the past education in periphery states largely focused on inculcating the skills, attitudes and knowledge deemed necessary for economic development, today it has the additional task of promoting the neo-liberal version of democracy. For this to be achieved, schools themselves are expected to be democratic communities if learners and their teachers are to 'acquire those qualities of mind and social attitudes which are the prerequisites of a genuinely democratic society' (Carr 1991:185). In periphery states, this democratic ethos can only be developed if schools function in 'ways which challenge the conformism of students and teachers and the society around them' (Meyer-Bisch 1995:15). The authoritarian climate of classrooms of Third World schools is seen as inimical to the development of liberal democracy. For democratic social relations to be promoted in the classroom, democratic teaching methods have to be employed. Because it is 'more democratic than authoritarian teaching' (Baker 1998:173), the learner-centred pedagogy emerges as the natural choice for the cultivation and inculcation of a liberal democratic ethos.

We can now appreciate why aid agencies, such as DfID, USAID and the Norwegian Aid Agency (NORAD), now emphasise the democratisation of classrooms through the adoption of a learner-centred pedagogy. The pedagogy is expected to break current authoritarian practices in periphery schools so as to produce individuals whose mindset would be compatible with the political conditions deemed necessary for the penetration of the free-market economic system. Interestingly, the aid agencies are exporting the pedagogy at a time when the same pedagogy is being denigrated in the very same donor countries that are exporting it.

That a pedagogical style can be used as a political instrument should not be surprising at all because education is a political activity, and to make curricular choices, such as adopting a particular pedagogy, is to engage in a political activity. Ginsburg et al. (1992:424) contend that the way educators organise their classrooms and the way they relate to and interact with their students is a form of political activity:

> different forms of classroom social relations facilitate or impede the developments (sic)
> of students' political efficacy and orientation to public forms of political involvement.

Ginsburg and his colleagues conclude that adopting pedagogies that are authoritarian or democratic may either reinforce or contradict the political structures obtaining nationally or globally. Thus, there is a close affinity, say, between a democratic pedagogy (such as learner-centredness) and political structures associated with democratic practice. It is, therefore, reasonably safe to conclude that aid agencies' interest in learner-centred pedagogy is intended to reinforce liberal democracy in periphery states.

To illustrate this point, I shall take the Primary Education Improvement Project (PEIP) in Botswana as an example. This was a USAID-funded project (1981-1991) whose aim was to 'provide technical assistance to the GOB [Government of Botswana] in the areas of primary pre-service and in-service education improvement' (United States Agency for International Development 1986:6). Analysis of some of the instructional interventions that were implemented during the project reveals that embedded in the interventions was a form of classroom practice akin to the constructivist, learner-centred pedagogy. Following the concentration so far on highlighting the political dimensions of the learner-centred pedagogy, it is logical to consider the economic dimensions of learner-centredness.

Learner-centredness and Economic Development

As argued above, the democratization imperative was intertwined with the economic imperative of spreading free-market capitalism. The global economic crisis of the 1970s and 1980s led to a questioning of the efficacy of the then dominant Fordist forms of economic production and organization. New patterns of production were needed, and with them a new kind of worker. This new worker approximates to Castells' (1997) 'self-programmable' worker. This worker is a lifelong learner, one who constantly redefines his/her skills for a given task. The call in the new patterns of production is for a multi-skilled, adaptable, and flexible workforce. The 'self-programmable' worker is contrasted with the 'generic' worker (Castells 1997) who acquires his/her skills through what Clegg (1999) terms 'exploitative learning', associated with a more traditional manufacturing economy. As a result, education the world over is being reformed to endow learners (defined as future workers) with the attributes (such as creativity, versatility, innovativeness, critical thinking, problem-solving skills, and a positive disposition towards teamwork) that the new 'flexible economy' (Rassool 1993) requires.

Commentators have observed that work in the industrialized world has in the past two decades undergone fundamental structural reorganization leading to 'significant changes in the practices, ethos, values and discourses of the world of work' (Johnson et al. 2003:20). New patterns of production driven by technological and organizational changes have emerged. Some have termed these new patterns 'post-Fordism' (Brown and Lauder 1992) and some 'fast capitalism' (Gee et al. 1996). Brown and Lauder (1992:3) have described post-Fordism as a system of production 'based on adaptable machinery, adaptable workers, flatter hierarchies, and the breakdown of the division between mental and manual labour and learning'. It is a matter for debate (see Brown and Lauder 1992; Muller 2000; Johnson et al. 2003) as to what exactly caused this shift from Fordist to post-Fordist production patterns. However, there seems to be consensus on hyper-competition in the global market resulting from deregulated national markets as a major cause of the shift.

Technological changes have led to unpredictability, uncertainty and constant change in the labour market. Skills, therefore, cannot be fixed for any particular job. As Silcock (1996:200) observes, 'the best workers, like the best learners, are those whose understanding transcends situationally gained skills'. Due to constant technological changes, knowledge has become ephemeral. This constant state of flux means that workers are forever learning. One-off training is no longer adequate. Hence, the renewed interest in the concept of lifelong learning. This discourse of global competitiveness 'means that economies require a well-qualified population and that they require workers with flexible, generic and constantly up-gradable skills" (Muller 2000:95), that is, self-programmable workers.

Unlike self-programmable workers, generic workers follow directions in hierarchically organized work environments. These workers do not have to demonstrate initiative, innovativeness and creativity since they are 'hired from the neck down' (Gee *et al.* 1996). In fact, they are discouraged from demonstrating these qualities. Their work is alienating and deskilling. But as Hickox and Moore (1992) observe, deskilling work processes, centralized decision making, and celebration of the dichotomy between conception and execution, all of which characterized Fordist forms of production, are being challenged.

The World Bank (1999:2) captures succinctly the nature of the worker suited to the 'new' economy:

> Tomorrow's workers will need to be able to engage in lifelong education, learn new things quickly, perform more non-routine tasks and more complex problem-solving, take more decisions, understand more about what they are working on, require less supervision, assume more responsibility, and – as vital tools to these ends – have better reading, quantitative, reasoning, and expository skills."

Windschitl (2002:135) avers that the 'new' economy places 'a premium on employees who can think creatively, adapt flexibly to the new demands, identify as well as solve problems, and create more complex products in collaboration with others'. Gee et al. (1996:12) observe that this paradigm shift in the kind of worker now required in the capitalist workplace has 'major implications for the nature of schools and schooling, as well as for society as a whole'. The dominant view is that only nations with education systems that are attuned to the changed patterns of production are the ones that are mostly likely to survive in a global market place characterized by hyper-competition. In response to this likely scenario, nations all over the world are restructuring their education systems in an effort to improve their economic competitiveness. A view of how workers of the future are to be educated is also emerging (Hartley 2003); de Clercq (1997:156) captures the direction in which education should move:

> The education system has [. . .] to shift from a system that differentiates and socializes students for the rigid hierarchical division of labour of modern industrial societies, to a system producing high-ability quality [sic] products with the ability to solve problems, think critically and apply new skills and techniques to different situations.

It is now the task of education to deliver this kind of learner/worker. More specifically targeted for reforms are the extant social relations in the classroom, that is, pedagogy. A constructivist, learner-centred pedagogy has emerged as the preferred pedagogy for the production of the self-programmable learner/worker.

This view of the new role of education in a hyper-competitive economic environment has been 'embraced' by bilateral aid organizations, their governments and the world financial institutions such as the World Bank and IMF. It has been integrated in their aid/loan/grant packages, and through these packages, it is propagated around the world, especially in aid-dependent sub-Saharan Africa. Aid to education invariably insists on the pedagogy. Even aid-independent countries (such as Botswana, Namibia and South Africa) but which nonetheless depend on multilateral organizations for economic advice, are told to target education, especially pedagogical styles for reform.

Discussion of contemporary interest in constructivist, learner-centred pedagogy would be incomplete without a comment on the role played by the digital revolution in general and the computer, in particular, in the resurgence of progressive education ideals. The Internet has democratized access to knowledge, diminishing the traditional 'fountain-image' of the teacher. As Seymour Papert (1980) has argued, learners' interaction with the computer boosts self-directed learning, which eventually facilitates the construction of new knowledge. In his /her interactions with electronic media, the learner ceases to be an imbiber of received wisdom and becomes an active constructor of knowledge. The computer, therefore, is transformative: '[I]n teaching the computer how to think, children embark on an exploration about how they themselves think. The experience can be heady: Thinking about thinking turns the child into an epistemologist' (Papert 1980:19). In this sense, the computer has a 'liberating' effect in that it 'rescues' the learner from the overbearing authority of the teacher: 'The teacher becomes a partner in a joint enterprise of understanding something that is truly unknown because the situations created by each child are totally new' (Papert, as cited in Robins and Webster 1999:189). To the extent that the computer puts the learner in a position of control in the learning process, it facilitates the disintegration of teacher-centred pedagogies and empowers the learner. Thus, there is affinity between computer literacy and progressive education traditions, of which the constructivist, learner-centred pedagogy is a part.

The attractiveness of the constructivist, learner-centred pedagogy, therefore, emanates from its promise to deliver political democracy, economic development and individual freedom. Chisholm and Leyendecker (2008:202) observe that in sub-Saharan Africa 'learner-centred education is considered the vehicle to drive societies and economies from mainly agricultural bases into modern and knowledge-based societies with the attendant economic benefits'. If indeed the quality of a country's human resource base is the determinant of its economic performance and learner-centred pedagogy is perceived as the most appropriate pedagogy to produce the self-programmable worker, then no country would like to lag behind in upgrading its human capital base, hence the education reform stampede we are witnessing. Take Botswana as an example. In 1994, and against the backdrop of a harsh global economic reality, Botswana unveiled a new policy, the Revised National Policy on Education (RNPE), which, in many ways, was a response to perceived changes in global patterns of production and industrial organization. Its main thrust was the development and sustenance of a 'workforce which can apply advanced technology and respond competitively to the changing demands of the international economy' (Republic of Botswana 1993:xii). In short, the RNPE aimed at producing the learner-equivalent of the self-programmable worker.

Illustrating the general point about the relationship between learner-centredness and liberal democracy is the case of the Primary Education Improvement Project (PEIP) (1981-1991), a USAID-sponsored project in Botswana whose aim was to increase access and improve the quality and relevance of primary education in the country. Three instructional innovations were implemented through PEIP, namely the Breakthrough Project, the Project Method and the Botswana Teaching Competency Instruments (BTCI). Embedded in these innovations were certain social values and forms of participation related to political orientation that the project wanted students to develop. There is scant evidence to support the view that the project aimed at improving teaching and learning. What is clear is that the project aimed at developing democratic social relations in both the classroom and the school. Thus, the project's purpose should be understood in political and ideological terms, not in cognitive/educational ones. And this is not unique to Botswana. Citing Leyendecker (2003) and the Ministry of Education and Culture of Namibia, Chisholm and Leyendecker (2008) state that in Namibia, learner-centredness was chosen as the vehicle to drive the process of political reform and to achieve access to education for all, equity, education for democracy, and democracy in education. The following comes from *Toward Education for All* (1993:41), a book published by the Namibia Ministry of Education and Culture:

> To develop education for democracy we must develop democratic education . . . Our learners must understand that democracy means more than just voting.... [and] ... that they cannot simply receive democracy from those who rule their society. . . To teach about democracy our teachers – and our education system as a whole – must practice democracy.

PEIP and the Consolidation of Democracy in Botswana: The Role of USAID

PEIP emanated from the influential *Education for* Kagisano (*Social Harmony*), the report of the 1977 National Commission on Education, which was set up to look into ways of improving both the qualitative and quantitative aspects of the Botswana education system. The report identified primary education as being terminal for almost half of the children completing Standard Seven (Republic of Botswana 1977). It was thus crucial to increase access and improve the quality and relevance of primary education. The government subsequently set out to address these concerns, but was faced with severe shortages of human and financial resources to execute its plan. To circumvent this challenge, the government sought assistance from the USA. The result was the GOB-USAID collaboration which gave birth to the PEIP.

When the project ended in 1991, its accomplishments included the establishment of a fully functioning Department of Primary Education at the University of Botswana (UB), a Master of Education Degree programme in primary education at UB, curriculum and institutional development at the primary teacher training colleges, and an In-service Education Network (Evans and Knox 1991). The ultimate goal of all these developments was to improve the quality, relevance and effectiveness of teaching and learning in primary schools. However, it is not explicit what terms like 'quality', 'effectiveness' and 'relevance' really meant, all the more so when their meanings are relative. Nevertheless, one can glean the image of quality teaching and learning the project was intended to promote from the nature of the interventions that were put in place. It is clear from the interventions that there were certain social values and forms of participation related to political orientation that the project wanted students to develop. Through the interventions, the project sought to promote democratic social relations through a constructivist and co-operative approach to teaching and learning. To illustrate this, I will briefly discuss three instructional innovations that were implemented through PEIP with the aim of altering teachers' and students' classroom practices. These are *Breakthrough to Literacy in Setswana: The Project Method*, and the *Botswana Teaching Competency Instruments*. The first two were initially British-sponsored, but on realising that they could contribute 'markedly to the achievement of the stated PEIP objectives' (Evans and Knox 1991:56), USAID materially supported the innovations.

Why would USAID be interested in a democratic pedagogy in Botswana? Its interest in a democratic pedagogy can be understood in the context of the USA's foreign policy. The US government funds projects aimed at promoting democracy globally as part of its wider foreign policy. This legislative mandate has existed since 1961. In the 1980s and 1990s, the US government initiated two projects, Project Democracy and the Democracy Initiative respectively. Both were aimed at integrating democracy into the USAID programme. As Crawford (1995:105) observes, through the Democracy Initiative, for example, democracy was to be 'incorporated in all development projects and programmes both as a desired end in itself and as means to increase effectiveness'. It is, therefore, not surprising that PEIP, as a USAID-funded project, aimed at democratising classroom social relations ostensibly through learner-centred pedagogy.

Breakthrough to Literacy in Setswana

This innovation was based on the Breakthrough to Literacy approach that was developed and first used in England. It was introduced in Botswana in the 1980s. As a method of teaching it was aimed at improving Standard One children's reading and writing abilities. As a philosophy of teaching, it is anchored in the ideology of learner-centredness. It involves children taking some control of their learning and co-operating with each other in the learning process. It intends to change the prevailing authoritarian student-teacher relationship to a more democratic one in which the teacher is a facilitator of the students' learning, not an arbiter of all knowledge. For example, it emphasises a shift from whole class teaching to group and individual teaching, from competition to co-operation, from students as followers to students as leaders, and from students working in isolation to co-operative and differentiated learning in which students freely discuss their work. The approach recognises the value and legitimacy of students' existing knowledge and daily experiences (Horgan et al. 1991). Breakthrough aims to develop questioning individuals, capable of carrying out empirical investigations and arriving at rational conclusions. One criticism of African education systems is that they produce people who cannot think independently and critically (Bassey 1999). These are people who, for example, unquestioningly accept authority. Such a character trait is seen as inimical to democracy. It is, therefore, not surprising that PEIP, as a USAID-sponsored project, supported the Breakthrough Approach since it aimed at eroding traditional habits. There is evidence that the innovation is succeeding in this regard. In her study of the Breakthrough Approach in Botswana, Arthur (1998:320) pointed out that it has:

> prompted expressions of concern on the part of parents that children in these classrooms are being socialized . . . into culturally inappropriate behaviour such as approaching adults (for help or showing off their work), instead of waiting at a respectful distance.

Thus, Breakthrough challenges the hierarchical social relations that characterise the Botswana culture.

The Project Method

Just like Breakthrough, the Project Method is a child-centred method of teaching and learning. It was incorporated in primary schools to consolidate the successes of the Breakthrough Approach. As already stated, one objective of the latter was to produce individuals capable of investigating and discovering the world around them. The Project Method was an attempt to achieve this objective. With this method, students work independently as individuals or in groups to investigate an identified problem. Working together in groups, students share ideas and listen to the views of others, in the process evaluating these views in relation to their own. Also important is that students become less dependent on their teachers. This empowers them, giving them the freedom to exercise choice, an important aspect of liberal democracy (Komba 1998). Thus, in the process of carrying out investigations, students develop psycho-social skills that are relevant to a liberal democracy.

The architects of PEIP also realised that altering classroom practices through the two innovations discussed above would not succeed without a democratic supervision model. School inspection activities in Botswana could best be described as fault-finding and oppressive by emphasising the expert-inexpert dichotomy, thus perpetuating the teacher's dependency on the inspector. These hierarchical social relations in effect mirror the hierarchical organisation of schools in the country. The hierarchical organisation is also expressed in the classroom in the form of the authoritarian, teacher-centred methods of teaching and learning. The latter point is taken up in Chapter Seven for more detailed discussion.

Thus it would be a futile exercise to attempt to alter classroom social relations while the enveloping school social structure remained oppressive. As Smyth (1986:143) rightly points out:

> Where the possibilities for genuinely unconstrained communication are limited because of hierarchical relationships, it is not difficult to see how more democratic means of learning can be thwarted.

The architects of PEIP were clearly aware of this fact and consequently proposed a mode of instructional supervision, the Botswana Teaching Competency Instruments (BTCI), which would, if properly implemented, diffuse a democratic ethos throughout the entire school social structure.

The Botswana Teaching Competency Instruments (BTCI)

This was based on the Teacher Performance Assessment Instrument (TPAI) developed by the University of Georgia, Department of Education. The BTCI comprised two sets of competencies which fell into two main categories: Classroom Procedures and Interpersonal Skills. Yoder and Mautle (1991:33) state that, 'The instrument identifies characteristics of good primary school teaching; focusing in general on what could be broadly termed child-centred teaching methodologies'. The instrument sought to democratise supervision by emphasising the notion of 'collegiality', defined as:

> the genuinely non-threatening state of mind that exists between teachers who are prepared to assist each other in arriving at a joint understanding of their own and each other's teaching; in other words, the development of a shared framework of meaning about teaching' (Smyth 1984:33)

This collegiality was to be exercised in a variety of ways; head teachers observing teachers teach and vice versa; education officers observing teachers and vice versa; and teachers observing one another. In all these settings the observer was not to act as an expert, but rather as a partner in an attempt to improve teaching and learning in the classroom. Using the BTCI required the supervisor and the supervisee to agree in advance on what was to be observed and when. After the lesson the partners had to discuss the observations, giving feedback to each other, ultimately coming up with a product each felt they had an opportunity to produce. This conceptualisation of instructional supervision represented a fundamental shift from the authoritarian and manipulative approach prevailing then.

It is not difficult to see the effects a mode of instructional supervision such as the BTCI, if properly implemented, would have on social relations in the school. It would break the hierarchical relationships between the education officers, head teachers and class teachers. It would bring class teachers closer to each other, breaking the marked isolation and privacy that characterise teaching (Denscombe 1982). A democratic school environment can greatly facilitate institutionalisation of innovations (such as the Breakthrough Approach and the Project Method) aimed at democratising classroom social relations. No wonder PEIP found it necessary to support and co-ordinate the implementation of the three innovations discussed above.

Thus, it is not difficult to see the kind of image of quality and effective teaching these PEIP instructional innovations intended promoting: it would appear that the basic criterion for judging improvement in the quality of teaching and learning in primary education was to be the presence of democratic social relations in the classroom. That is, in the view of PEIP, promotion of democratic social relations was a desired end in itself. If it were anticipated that democratic classroom social relations would then lead to improved student achievement, one would question the research basis of such an expectation. Any positive correlation between the two might simply be incidental. Bantock (1981:63), commenting on studies carried out by Anthony (1979) and Bennett (1976), concludes that the 'superiority of discovery methods cannot at present be justified on grounds of empirical research'. Thus, PEIP's version of quality and effective primary education should be understood in non-cognitive terms. Its intentions were political and ideological. It is clear that the learner-centred pedagogy that was embedded in PEIP was aimed at inculcating social and political values of individual autonomy, open-mindedness and tolerance for other people's views, all these being essential character traits required for an individual to operate effectively in a liberal democratic political environment. Given Botswana's own concern with nurturing its nascent democracy and the USA's official policy of spreading democracy globally through its international aid programmes, it is not surprising that PEIP emphasised learner-centred pedagogy which was aimed at democratising the school ambience.

Conclusion

This chapter aimed to demonstrate the political and economic basis of the learner-centred pedagogy. This objective is to be understood in the context of the argument (advanced in the preceding chapter) that learner-centred pedagogy is a political and economic artifact which can never be said to be value-neutral. Its contemporary efficacy is more political/economic than educational/cognitive. Interest in learner-centred pedagogy was spurred by the rise of neo-liberalism in the 1980s as the dominant economic/political ideology. Neoliberalism became enshrined in the policies of bilateral and multilateral aid agencies, displacing modernisation theory. In terms of Third World development, neo-liberalism surmised that economic development was only possible where there was liberal democracy. Education, as a change agent, had an indispensable role to play in both the democratisation and economic development processes in those countries. To achieve this, aid agencies identified the learner-centred pedagogy (because of its democratic tendencies) as the appropriate pedagogy in the development and dissemination of democratic social relations in Third World schools.

The example of PEIP is a specific example of the general point that learner-centredness as introduced in sub-Saharan Africa is more of a political/economic artifact than an educational innovation. Essentially, aid agencies saw the pedagogy's efficacy as lying in its ability to promote values associated with both liberal democracy and the knowledge-based economy. It was envisaged that the pedagogy would help to break authoritarian structures in schools and that through its erosion of traditional modes of thought, it would produce individuals with the right disposition towards a liberal democracy and a changed workplace. It is for this reason that I have argued in the chapter that aid agencies' primary interest in the pedagogy is political and ideological, not educational. It is in this context that learner-centred pedagogy's much-praised capacity to promote 'quality' and 'effective' education should be understood. Given that there is no compelling empirical research evidence that there is a positive (and causal) relationship between the pedagogy and students' cognitive learning, couching its efficacy in cognitive/educational terms at best appears to be an attempt to disguise its ideological mission.

What is emerging from this chapter is that there is a need to treat learner-centredness as a form of education that is laden with political and economic values. Its current dominance in sub-Saharan Africa and around the world can be sufficiently explained only if its political and economic contexts are appreciated. In the same vein, this very same political/economic context of its evolution is significant in understanding the pedagogy's failure to be institutionalized in sub-Sahara African classrooms. This failure might be a result, not so much of resource scarcity as it is of the very political/economic origins of the pedagogy. Teachers and students rationally choose pedagogical styles that fit their purposes, which, in the sub-Sahara African context, is to produce good examinations results. The latter are what define 'quality' teaching in this context. So, teachers and students tend to judge the efficacy of pedagogical innovations on the basis of their educational value and not their economic/political value, which latter value is, in any case, seldom made explicit to them. If teachers, students and administrators cannot ascertain the educational value of learner-centred pedagogy, the chances are high that they will reject or resist its introduction. This might be what is happening to the pedagogy in sub-Sahara Africa. Now, explaining this failure of the pedagogy to be institutionalized solely in terms of technical problems associated with the delivery processes (e.g. large student-teacher ratios, shortage of teaching materials, defective teacher education programmes, etc.) is simplistic and inadequate.

3

Learner-centredness and Teacher-centredness: Pedagogical Paradigms?

Introduction

Instead of seeing teacher-centredness and learner-centredness as lying on a continuum, this chapter argues that the two pedagogies are diametrically opposed to each other. This is because the two are based on value systems that are so different from one another that it is difficult to see how they can possibly be viewed as compatible. In other words, learner-centredness and teacher-centredness represent 'pedagogical paradigms'. By employing Kuhn's (1970) concept of 'paradigm', I demonstrate the fundamental differences between the two pedagogies. In more specific terms, the two pedagogies are founded on incongruent epistemological assumptions. These assumptions give a particular orientation to classroom architecture and internal organization, student-teacher and student-student interactional patterns. As research evidence has shown (see Chapter One), teacher-centredness is the paradigmatic location of teachers and students in sub-Saharan Africa. To demand that teachers shift from a teacher-centred paradigm to the learner-centred one is to demand that they make a 'paradigm shift'. Given the fundamental differences between the two, this shift is never easy to accomplish, for basically the shift is a request for teachers to vacate their taken-for-granted world for a 'world' they know very little about. This chapter should be seen as a further repudiation of the view of teaching as a technical, rational activity as discussed in Chapters One and Two.

Concept of Paradigm

Kuhn (1970:viii) defines 'paradigms' as,

> universally recognized scientific achievements that for some time provide model
> problems and solutions to a community of practitioners.

Scientific knowledge, Kuhn argues, is characterized by its dynamic nature since science's conceptual structure and knowledge get transformed over time. Within a particular paradigm, practitioners set legitimate parameters within which their activities take place (Esland 1971). A paradigm has four basic properties: it contains (1) the prior knowledge of the discipline; (2) the projected legitimate problems to be addressed; (3) the methodological rules to be employed to find solutions to the problems; and (4) the criteria of truth and validity of the generated knowledge. In addition to defining what can be legitimately studied by its advocates, a paradigm also specifies what is necessarily excluded from the list of permissible topics (Shulman 1986). Practitioners operating within the same paradigm share an entire constellation of values, assumptions, goals, norms, language beliefs, techniques and ways of perceiving and understanding the world (Kuhn 1970). The shared values permit inter-subjectivity among the adherents of a paradigm. For as long as the paradigm continues to provide model solutions to the practitioners' problems, it constitutes *normal science*, that is, it is the taken-for-granted world of the practitioner. However, because of the dynamic nature of knowledge, more problems may emerge that may no longer be solved within the framework of the dominant paradigm, thus necessarily putting the latter in a crisis. A new paradigm may emerge. Practitioners in the dominant paradigm may resist shifting to the emerging paradigm and thus continue working within the parameters of the old one. However, if the new paradigm proves more promising than their own, they may shift to it. The idea that a scientific community 'adopts new values, norms, assumptions, language, and ways of perceiving and understanding its scientific world' when it shifts to a new paradigm gives credence to the realists' view that scientific knowledge does not 'represent universal truth that is true in all contexts... but instead represents a socially agreed upon theoretical and contextual truth...' (Tuthill and Ashton 1983:8). Thus, the paradigm concept negates any claim of science to value-neutrality.

Because a new paradigm makes the old one with all its paraphernalia obsolete, the tendency is for adherents of the reigning paradigm to resist the 'invading' one. This makes paradigm shifts difficult to achieve (Chalmers 1978;

Pogrow 1996). The disintegration of the dominant paradigm represents a disintegration of the practitioners' taken-for-granted world and a concomitant loss of psychological support. For the practitioners, this experience may be anomic since it leads to a disruption of the existing cognitive order. Naturally, this has a deskilling effect on the advocates of the paradigm under threat, and they may, through philosophical and methodological debates, attempt to disprove the emerging paradigm. They may also resist the emerging paradigm for fear of loss of prestige which they may have earned as occupants of the paradigm under threat.

The aim here is not to provide a critical appraisal of Kuhn's theory of scientific revolutions, but rather to sensitise the reader to the potential of the concept of 'paradigm' as an analytical framework for explaining educational/pedagogical change. For a detailed critique of Kuhn, see Masterman (1970).

Although Kuhn used the paradigm concept to explain developments in science, particularly theoretical physics, the concept has also been applied to the social sciences and education. In educational research, for example, researchers often see themselves as adhering to one or more of the well-known research paradigms – the positivist paradigm; the interpretive paradigm; the qualitative paradigm and so on. All these paradigms are ways of looking at the world, that is, they are world-views, mindsets, frames of reference or conceptual frameworks. Each views phenomena differently from the others. Each claims to be producing more reliable and dependable knowledge than the others. Thus, social practice is characterized by competing paradigms, contrary to what technical rationality tells us.

The same could be said of teaching, which is also a social practice. Teacher-centredness (also variously referred to as 'banking education' (Freire 1972) or 'transmission-reception pedagogical style' (Mac an Ghaill 1992) and learner-centredness could be looked at as constituting pedagogical paradigms (Farquharson 1990). In the arena of educational practice the two compete for recognition and supremacy. They hold assumptions about the social world, the nature of reality and about the learner which are diametrically opposed. Both pedagogical paradigms have distinct and incompatible views of what constitutes legitimate knowledge, how that knowledge should be transmitted and how it is subsequently evaluated. In short, the two are based on incongruent epistemological assumptions and values. One of the weaknesses of educational debate is the failure to recognize that pedagogical styles such as teacher-centredness and learner-centredness are informed by distinctive and particular epistemologies. The result has been that pedagogical issues have been treated as non-problematic. It is precisely (though not solely) this neglect of epistemological issues that has largely promoted the technicist approach to pedagogical change, leading to the failure of many pedagogical innovations in the African setting.

The pedagogical paradigm within which students and teachers appear to be operating in a given context constitutes their taken-for-granted classroom world which gives their classroom practices stability and constancy. The literature on classroom research in sub-Saharan Africa reviewed in Chapter One clearly locates teachers' and students' classroom practices within the banking education/teacher-centred pedagogical paradigm. To propose that they shift from this paradigm to a learner-centred one is necessarily a proposal that they fundamentally change their views of the nature of knowledge, of the learner and his/her role, and of classroom arrangement in general. But this also calls for the disintegration of the reigning paradigm, thus of the practitioners' taken-for-granted classroom world. As has been pointed out above, abandoning familiar territory is never easy for practitioners. The result might be the practitioners' rejection or subversion of the proposed pedagogical innovation. Furthermore, a paradigm shift must be preceded by a paradigm crisis or general dissatisfaction with the reigning paradigm, in which case change would be initiated from within the paradigm itself. In other words, the community of practitioners (e.g. teachers and students) must themselves feel and see the need for change. In such a situation, a paradigm shift is more likely to occur than in a situation where the change is imposed.

This raises an important question: 'Do teachers, education officials, parents and students (what one might term the pedagogic community) in sub-Saharan Africa experience that inner urge to shift from the banking-education pedagogical paradigm to the learner-centred one?' In other words, is there dissatisfaction with the banking-education pedagogical paradigm? From what we have seen as the rationale for pedagogic change in Chapter Two, there can be no doubt that the change is being initiated by outsiders, namely international aid agencies. One is yet to come across evidence of both teacher and student dissatisfaction with the pedagogical paradigm in the sub-Saharan African context. Available evidence points to a situation in which both teachers and students work hard to maintain and sustain the teacher-centred paradigm. The latter point is the subject of Chapter Four.

The concept of paradigm as applied in education in general and teaching in particular, however, is not without controversy. Gage (1989) observes that since the 1980s, the field of research on teaching has been characterized by

'Paradigm Wars' occasioned by the polarization between positivist/behaviourist and interpretive paradigms. Positions were hardened in the 1980s when supporters of the emerging naturalistic/qualitative paradigm (e.g. Lincoln and Guba 1985) maintained that this paradigm was not only incommensurate but also incompatible with the traditional positivist paradigm, while supporters of the latter paradigm (e.g. Gage 1963/1989) argued that the paradigms were complementary. In addition to being resilient, paradigms have also proliferated (Donmoyer 2006). Efforts have been (and continue to be) made to end the paradigm wars, but with very little success. For example, Donmoyer (2006:30) has made a passionate plea to educational researchers to abandon the paradigm talk on the grounds that the field of education is a 'public policy field and [that] public fields require that issues be examined from public perspectives and considering different, and, at times, even contradictory criteria'. However, pleas such as this one are yet to be accompanied by what Gage (1989:148) refers to as 'pragmatic philosophical analysis [which might show] an honest and productive rapprochement between the paradigms'. Thus despite efforts to transcend them, paradigms in research on teaching persist to date.

Similarly, the teacher-centredness versus learner-centredness debate has not been able to reconcile the epistemological differences between the two pedagogies, and yet it is these differences that are at the root of the polarized view of pedagogy decried by Barrett (2007) and others. It is difficult to see how the polarized view can disappear before epistemological differences are resolved. And the question, therefore, is, 'Are these epistemological differences resolvable?' The response is that at the moment such resolution is nowhere in sight, meaning that pedagogical paradigms are enduring and that perhaps there is something about the differences that demands closer attention than has been accorded thus far. To use the terms of Broadie et al. (2002), unless and until epistemological differences between the two pedagogies have been resolved, it will not be possible to utilize the 'substance' of learner-centred pedagogy. Only its 'form' (use of techniques) would be possible. Unfortunately, it is the evidence of the teachers' utilization of the 'form' of the pedagogy that Barrett (2007) and others have mistaken for (and conflated with) its 'substance'.

The remaining sections of this chapter demonstrate that teacher-centredness and learner-centredness are pedagogical paradigms that are neither commensurable nor compatible. They hinge on views of the nature of knowledge that are diametrically opposed, and call for classroom practices that, logically, are equally opposed. Unless and until this substantive element of pedagogy is addressed in teacher education and in-service programmes, no amount of resources poured into interventions will bring about durable changes in teacher classroom practices in sub-Saharan countries. The objectivist/positivist view of knowledge constitutes the support structure of teacher-centred pedagogy. Before we can expect a paradigm shift, teacher education and other interventions need to be oriented to function in ways that challenge this structure.

Epistemology and Pedagogical Paradigms

According to Dupre (2007:7) epistemology is that 'area of philosophy concerned with knowledge: determining what we know and how we know it and identifying the conditions to be met for something to count as knowledge'. The view of knowledge we hold influences the way we approach teaching and learning. Two epistemological perspectives have had more influence on teaching and learning than any other perspectives. They are *objectivism* and *social constructivism*. The former is closely associated with teacher-centredness while the latter is associated with learner-centredness. Explication of these epistemological positions might highlight the fundamental differences between the two pedagogical paradigms.

> ... where views of education have been derived from different epistemological traditions and thus have been built on different epistemological assumptions, the existence of these different traditions and assumptions has not been recognized... many of the critics of "progressive" theories of education.... have failed to recognise the distinctive and particular form of epistemology upon which such theories are based, or even that there is a different epistemology... (Kelly 1986:xv).

This failure to appreciate epistemological bases of pedagogical paradigms invariably results in the technicist approach to teaching (see Chapter One). A socio-cultural approach to teaching and learning recognizes these bases as important not only in the classroom practices of the teachers and students but also to pedagogical change. Introducing, for example, learner-centred methods in an educational environment that has known nothing else but banking education requires an appreciation of these epistemological differences, in the absence of which tissue rejection is inevitable. If we accept that teacher-centred and the learner-centred pedagogies are fundamentally different, to the extent that they are incompatible, we would be inclined to view them as ideological views founded on incongruent epistemological assumptions. As Thompson (1972:64-5) states, "...the difference between the two views [lies] in deep underlying differences between their assumptions on the nature of knowledge." This makes the differences between these views fundamental.

Teacher-centred Pedagogy: Epistemological Foundations

Teacher-centredness as a pedagogical paradigm is deeply entrenched in the objectivist epistemology which views knowledge as 'detached from the human subjectivity in which it is constituted, maintained and transformed' (Esland 1971:75). Reality under this epistemology is viewed as being 'out there'. It is a commodity that is fixed, static and unchanging. It exists independently of the learner, that is, it is objective. Objectivism, in turn, is founded upon the philosophical tradition of rationalism (a tradition in the theory of knowledge closely associated with the seventeenth-century French philosopher, René Descartes, but dating back to Plato), with its basic premise of knowledge as existing *a priori*, that is, knowledge is a certainty and has a status independent of the knower. Rationalists emphasise the primacy of reason as a source of knowledge. Their basic premise is that knowledge is independent of sensual experience and perception, that what is contained in the human mind cannot be accounted for in terms of our senses' contact with the external environment. In extreme cases, God is seen as the source of all knowledge. This means that rationalists see knowledge as certain, with a status quite independent of the knower, indicating that there exists 'intrinsically worthwhile knowledge' (Peters 1965:11). This epistemological tradition also became the orthodox view of knowledge of the Christian theology which also stressed the certainty of knowledge and played down the sensual and emotional aspects of human existence (Kelly 1986:35). As Thomson (1947:83-4) states:

> Truth was conceived of as something knowable in its completeness, and so-mething, therefore, which was fixed; static, unchangeable. It was found in the realm of 'ideas' or universals which were free from the chances and changes of this mortal world – were immutable, complete and perfect.

The stress on the certainty of knowledge leads to the search for a 'right' form of knowledge with which individuals must identify. Kelly (1986) extrapolates this view of knowledge to the political realm. He argues that rationalism necessarily leads to totalitarianism in many spheres of life – moral, political and even the educational sphere. This should be the case because if knowledge is certain, absolute and more or less unchanging, then there cannot be legitimate alternatives to it.

In education, rationalism leads to a stress on knowledge/subject matter rather than on the learner. Because there exists a 'body of knowledge', education becomes the initiation of learners into intrinsically worthwhile activities leading to the acquisition of this knowledge. The epistemology puts children 'in the position of the barbarians outside the gates' who must be taken 'inside the citadel of civilization' (Peters 1965:107) through the process of education. Much of curriculum development today is informed by this rationalist epistemology.

This view resonates with the medieval, Calvinist doctrine of 'innate depravity' (Rusk 1954:158) and the Catholic belief in original sin. In terms of these doctrines, human beings were born evil and corrupt. Only training could improve this innately bad state. The doctrine of innate depravity meant that seventeenth-century Europe had no conception of childhood; it was a 'stage' to be grown out of as quickly as possible; the child was an imperfect adult who had to be quickened to adulthood. As Bowen (2003:186) states, 'In everything, adult models were forced upon the child. The constant companion was fear of the rod, and the maxim of "Spare the rod and spoil the child" was universal'. This significantly influenced child-rearing practices and education. Invariably, both processes involved removing the 'badness' out of the children before 'goodness' could be poured in. Because of the theological doctrines mentioned above, the treatment of children was harsh, and teachers were expected to act as authoritarian disciplinarians. Corporal punishment in the West, therefore, had its roots in Christian theology. When this model was imported into Africa by the missionaries, it found an equally authoritarian cultural environment. This often ignored convergence of Western and native culture is discussed in Chapter Five.

Besides its implications for discipline and curriculum arrangements, the rationalist conception of knowledge has obvious implications for the form in which it (knowledge) is transmitted. Everhart (1983:239) puts it this way:

> ...what 'counts' as knowledge affects the process by which knowledge comes to be 'known' which in turn affects the type of activity engaged in as a result of the knowledge existing.

For example, where knowledge is understood in objectivist terms, learning involves an unproblematic authoritative transference of portions of knowledge from the teacher to the student. In this transference, the teacher is viewed as the 'expert' and the students as passive recipients of ready-made knowledge. Education, as Freire (1972) states, becomes an act of depositing in which the teacher is the depositor and the students the depositories. Such a conception of education turns students into 'containers' or 'receptacles' to be filled by the teacher. Students' scope for action is limited to receiving and storing the deposited 'commodity'. Thus the objectivist, epistemological viewpoint engenders certain assumptions about the learner; a passive receiver; an 'empty vessel' to be filled by the teacher.

This view of the learner has further implications for the definition of a 'good' and a 'poor' student. A 'good' student is one who is 'cognitively docile and deferential' (Esland 1971:89) towards the teacher. This is the student who meekly permits the teacher to deposit knowledge. The learner, Esland (1971:89) further observes, 'is a novitiate in a world of pre-existing, theoretical forms into which he is initiated and which he is expected to reconstitute'. The teacher's mastery of the subject matter is beyond question. His/her role is to organise the depositing of the objectively existing 'body of knowledge' (subject matter content) for the learner to learn and reproduce on demand. Their job is a technical one, involving the selection of means by which the ends can be achieved. It is, therefore, not surprising that teachers operating within this pedagogical paradigm tend to be preoccupied with 'right answers'. Learners become answer-producers, not thinkers. In fact the whole process of teaching-learning becomes answer-centered. The following observation by Holt (1964:154) is still as relevant today as it was four decades ago:

> Practically everything we do in school tends to make children answer-centred. In the first place, right answers pay off. Schools are some kind of temple for "right answers", and the only way to get ahead is to lay plenty of them on the altar. The chances are good that the teachers themselves are answer-centred. What they do, they do so because this is what the book says to do (sic), or what they have always done. One consequence of this is that children are too busy to think.

Consider the following example of what typified general lesson progression in the lessons observed by the author. The topic in the Geography lesson was 'Weathering':

Teacher: What is weathering?

Student: The erosion of rocks?

Teacher: No, you are confusing weathering with erosion. Who can give us the correct definition?

Students: It is the breaking up of rocks.

Teacher: Correct. But who can put it in a more sophisticated geographical language?

Student: It is the breaking up or disintegration of rocks by chemical or mechanical processes.

Teacher: Good. (He writes the definition on the board)

[I later found out that this was a verbatim recitation of the class textbook definition of 'weathering'.]

The teacher then continued:

Teacher: How many types of weathering are there?

Student: Two

Teacher: Which are they?

Student: Chemical and mechanical.

Teacher: What is the difference between the two?

Student: Chemical weathering changes the chemical composition of the rocks unlike in mechanical weathering.

Teacher: Good. (Writes the answer on the board)

This interrogative style of questioning exhibits three characteristics. First, the teacher's questioning style was geared towards eliciting from students what the teacher considered to be the 'right' answers. It would appear that when the teacher asked questions, he already had preconceived 'right' answers that he expected students to produce. But right-answerism tends to have the inadvertent effect of reproducing the authoritarian teacher-centered methods of teaching.

Second, answers that are perceived as incorrect are ignored, thereby depriving the learner of the opportunity to 'learn' from the wrong answers. By stressing the production of correct answers, the teachers ignored the perceived incorrect answers. On the surface, this might appear as a trivial observation. At a deeper and hidden level, however, the teacher's ignoring of 'incorrect' answers may be viewed as an unconscious strategy to define, legitimize, and augment the prevailing classroom power and authority relations in which she or he plays a dominant role. Prophet and Rowell (1993) capture these effects in these words:

> From the teaching-learning perspectives, the rejection of answers precludes opportunities for cognitive development by the students. . . Ignoring student responses reinforces a behaviourist approach to teaching with rote learning as the model and right answers as the outcome (p. 202).

Third, the questions are closed ended. By unwittingly allocating 'turns at speaking' and asking closed-ended questions, which demanded definite and precise answers, the teacher made sure that he always remained in control of the interactional situations. The danger with open-ended questions is that they may yield unpredictable answers that may put the teacher 'off-balance', resulting in a possible loss of classroom control. Thus, the strategy of asking closed-ended questions and allocating turns at speaking helps the teacher to 'shape the meaning of what is said in the desired direction' (Edwards and Furlong 1978:17), and helps them to maintain a strong grip on interactional processes. All this tends to work towards the reproduction of an authoritarian pedagogical style.

The objectivist epistemology has the other effect of developing a schism between *teaching and learning* as distinct but inextricably related activities, with one becoming meaningless without the other. Not only does this teach-learn converse place the teacher in a very powerful position, 'it also serves to demarcate role boundaries between the teacher and the students; the teacher teaches and the students learn' (Tabulawa 1997:201). This sentiment is nicely captured by the title of an article on Tanzanian secondary schools by Stambach (1994, as cited in Vavrus 2009:304): 'Here in Africa, we teach; students listen'. Thus, whether or not one is an 'effective' teacher becomes a function of how well one carries out those activities associated with teaching. Likewise, whether one is a 'good' or 'nice' student becomes a function of how well one carries out those activities associated with learning. This schism helps in constituting students' and teachers' identities (i.e. it tells them who they are and what they can or cannot do). Possible and permissible practices are delineated. Once these boundaries have been demarcated, each group is expected to play its role. The effect of this is the narrowing of the range of possible and permissible practices and actions. Furthermore, the teach-learn schism leads to the view of school knowledge as a commodity out of the students' reach. And because the teacher's duty is seen in terms of executing prescribed subject matter, his or her work is cast in terms of 'optimizing efficient performances' (Pignatelli 1993:419). Teachers then become mere technicians who 'pass along a body of unproblematized traditional "facts"' (Kincheloe 1997:xxix). All this fits the definition of the term 'technical' by Bartolome (1994:173), which is:

> the positivist tradition in education that presents teaching as a precise and scientific undertaking and teachers as technicians responsible for carrying out (preselected) instructional programs and strategies.

The teacher's effectiveness is then judged by how well he or she transmits the ready made knowledge. By their very nature, '[t]echnicist practices sustain and exacerbate asymmetrical relations of power in the schools' (Pignatelli 1993: 422) and, by extension, in the classroom.

Perhaps the most ubiquitous manifestation of the objectivist epistemology is in school architecture and the internal arrangement of classrooms. Classrooms in many African schools are oblong in shape. Inside the classroom, desks are arranged in rows all facing the front (usually the chalkboard) part of the class. A diagramme of this arrangement is shown below as Figure 3.1.

Figure 3.1: Typical desk arrangement in many public schools

All the students sit facing the front part of the class. Typically, the teacher's desk is at the front part of the classroom. How did teachers make sense of the arrangement?

Teacher 1: I always feel psychologically in control of the class when they are all facing me, and again I can also detect instances of playfulness in class when they are all seated facing me.

Teacher 2: It becomes easier to bring order in class in the sense that you are able to see who amongst your students is not listening attentively, is falling asleep, or is doing something different from what the whole class is doing.

These comments illustrate the extent to which teachers were concerned with control (which they equated with learning). Except in group discussions, student-student interactions were conspicuously absent. Perhaps such interaction would not have been in tune with the teachers' understanding of a classroom atmosphere most conducive to learning. When asked to comment on what they considered to be a classroom atmosphere most conducive to learning, two of the teachers had this to say:

First teacher: This is a classroom atmosphere in which there is maximum concentration and where the teacher has as much control as is possible to make sure that the students do not get out of hand.

Second teacher: First of all, a friendly one where there is no fear. In terms of control it all depends. When you break them into small groups, you should allow them to talk among themselves. But if you are teaching, you are not going to allow them to chat among themselves. That must stop.

Thus, any form of student-to-student talk is only considered purposive so long as the classroom activity for that time allows for it, as, for example, during group discussions. As the teachers' comments show, there exists a difference between group discussions and teaching. Group work, it appears, is not teaching proper. Teaching proper seems to be when the teacher is talking or when activities over which the teacher has full control are taking place.

Observation of lessons showed that teaching and learning was characterized by the absence of pedagogical differentiation, that is, students were involved in one task, at one given time, carrying it out at the same pace. All students had to be involved in one activity at a time before moving on to another, en masse. Indeed, the teachers did not see the need for a differentiated pedagogy. In the words of one of them, 'There is no point in having each student working at his/her own pace. After all they are going to sit for the same examination at the same time and on the same day'.

Activities, therefore, tended to be routinised, and this routinization of classroom activities inevitably leads to predictable patterns of behavior. Once this is achieved, it becomes easier for the teacher to manage the class, thereby enforcing and re-enforcing his/her authority. Teaching and classroom management become almost indistinguishable from social control.

Conformity to these interactional patterns needed to be enforced. 'Teaching by surveillance' ensured that no student did something different from what the whole class was expected to be doing. All students had to conform to one common goal. According to Foucault (1979), the classroom design was 'Panoptic' in that it facilitated the extension of the teacher's 'disciplinary gaze', which gaze ensured that students conformed to the 'norm'. Doing something other than what the teacher expected all students to be doing did not constitute 'doing school work.' By 'mass processing' the students, the teachers made sure that they (teachers) were always in control. At a deeper level, though, the classroom arrangement was an indication of the implicit assumptions the teachers held of the nature of knowledge – the objectivist view of knowledge. The classroom arrangement facilitated the unidirectional transmission of this knowledge to the students. This required a classroom environment that was conducive, which the teachers described as one where there was maximum student concentration. One teacher summed up the rationale for the classroom arrangement thus:

> Well, it is reminiscent of the church situation where the priest stands there to impart the knowledge of the Scripture. So, basically the role of the teacher is like that of the priest. The teacher has all the knowledge and the students must get it from him.

This accurately defines the transmission-reception pedagogical style.

How, on their part, did the students make sense of the internal organization of the classroom described above?

Student 1:   I think the intention is that students have to be attentive.

Student 2:   It is a good arrangement because students have to face the teacher. Since they have to get the information from the teacher they must face him and be attentive.

An important aspect of the objectivist view of knowledge in the context of teaching is *teacher visibility*, where the teacher is the centre of most classroom processes. When students are seated facing the front part of the class, they are not facing empty space or the chalkboard, which is just a part of the four walls. They are facing the front part of the class which is the *teacher*. In light of the prevailing view of the nature of knowledge, a class without a teacher may not have a 'front' or 'centre'. Since it is the teacher who is the centre, she or he must never be out of sight. Students protest when this 'centre' is not visible, such as when the teacher is teaching seated. Teacher dominance/surveillance, therefore, is also *demanded* by the students. Thus, far from being an orchestration by the teacher acting on the students, teacher dominance is a demand from students themselves. This issue is taken up in more detail in Chapter Four.

The desk arrangement in the diagramme above facilitates the mobility of the 'centre' (teacher) within and around the classroom, thus facilitating the disciplinary gaze. As long as the visibility of the centre is maintained, activities may progress relatively unhampered. In situations where there is mass teaching i.e. no pedagogical differentiation, monitoring to ensure that students are doing the same task at the same pace and time becomes very important. Teacher visibility, facilitated by the arrangement of desks in rows, becomes an effective way of making sure that students conform to one common goal. This way the teacher's gaze is extended and made even more effective.

Now, all these effects of the objectivist epistemology tend to lead only to the entrenchment of asymmetrical power relations and, subsequently, to a congruent, authoritarian classroom pedagogical style.

Scientific Legitimation of Teacher-centred Pedagogy

The banking education pedagogical paradigm has its scientific backing and legitimation in behaviourist psychology which adopts a:

> view of man as a passive creature, of learning as a modification of behaviour, of the study of human learning and behaviour as not qualitatively different from the study of animal behaviour and learning (Kelly 1986:91).

As pointed out in Chapter One it is difficult to think of any discipline that has escaped the pull of the scientific method. In the field of psychology, behaviourism emerged in the nineteenth century as a direct result of the application of Newtonian cause-and-effect analysis in the study of human behaviour. Represented by the likes of Ivan Pavlov (1849-1936), Edward L. Thorndike (1874-1949), John B. Watson (1878-1958) and Burrhus F. Skinner (1904-90), behaviourism became the most influential branch of psychology in the twentieth century. The basic premise of the behaviourists was that human behaviour was basically patterned (just like the natural world) and, therefore, governed by pre-existing laws which, once discovered, would make human behaviour predictable and controllable. In the words of Tuthill and Ashton (1983:12), psychologists of the behaviourist mould 'believe that behaviour can be understood and explained by physically observable (and measurable) stimuli and response'. When applied to teaching, the behaviourist conception 'assumes that learning is caused by teachers' behaviour and that, consequently, teachers must be in total control of their classrooms' (Donmoyer 2006:22). Behaviourism, therefore, supports the mechanical transfer of knowledge from the teacher's head to the students' head. In short, behaviourism scientifically justifies teacher-centred pedagogy. This pedagogy, therefore, constitutes a pedagogical paradigm, one in which those who have been socialized share a common language, assumptions, values and goals. They inhabit a common world, one in which their thinking and actions are taken for granted. After a period of decline in the 1970s behaviourism is making a major come-back in the form of competency-based models of curriculum design. This is the subject for discussion in Chapter Eight. In the meantime, let us juxtapose teacher-centred pedagogy with learner-centred pedagogy in order to further illuminate the paradigmatic differences between the two.

Learner-centred Pedagogy: Epistemological Foundations

In Chapter One, I described learner-centred pedagogy briefly. In this section I now take a much closer look at it, the aim being to demonstrate that the pedagogy differs fundamentally from the teacher-centred one we have just discussed in the preceding section. Learner-centred pedagogy is a pedagogical paradigm whose adherents share common values, norms, beliefs and assumptions, but these differ fundamentally from those shared by the adherents of the teacher-centred pedagogical paradigm.

Learner-centred pedagogy is based on the epistemological notion of knowledge as a social construction, and that the learner plays an active role in the construction of knowledge. Such an epistemology engenders views on the classroom roles of both the teacher and the student and classroom organization that are different from those identified with banking education. In more precise terms, the learner-centred pedagogy is based on the social constructivist epistemology. Constructivism is an elusive concept precisely because its definition has a number of variants (see Nola 1997; Windschitl 2002; Terhart 2003). Its key features as summarized by Hyland (1994) are:

> ...emphasis on learning as a continuous process grounded in experience, on the idea of a holistic process of adaptation through the resolution of conflicts and opposing viewpoints, and on the notion that learning needs to be regarded as a means of creating knowledge rather than merely the regurgitation and reinforcement of existing norms and traditions (p. 54).

The implications of social constructivism for teaching and learning are immense, and Terhart (2003:32) succinctly captures them in the following words:

> Learning should not be directed from the outside: it does not consist of "processing" pieces of information or knowledge which – kept ready and available outside – are actively "taken in" by the learner.... There can be no more teaching in the sense of transmitting prepared packages of knowledge divorced from concrete situations – nor can such teaching be morally justified.

With its emphasis on the 'situatedness' and 'constructedness' of knowledge, social constructivism turns the objectivist epistemology on its head: knowledge and truth cannot be absolute and certain. Furthermore, to the extent that it aims to assist learners 'lead a self-determined existence, and live in tolerant and relaxed togetherness with other human beings and nature' (Terhart 2003:33) constructive pedagogy resonates with democracy, hence international aid agencies' interest in the pedagogy.

As a view of knowledge, constructivism is informed by the empiricist philosophical tradition (of which Francis Bacon and John Locke are among its renowned representatives) which was born out of the criticisms of the rationalist theory (Sharpes 2002). It arose as a direct challenge to the central tenet of rationalism: it did not accept the rationalist notion that all knowledge comes a *priori* from the rational mind (Kelly 1986:7). In its most extreme version, empiricism rejected the notion of innate ideas and knowledge and only saw the human mind as a *tabula rasa*, a clean slate, when the individual is born. Knowledge only comes into the human mind through the human senses. Locke, for example, proposed that where there is no experience, there is no knowledge. Because knowledge cannot be independent of the knower, there is no way in which it can ever be a certainty and thus an end in itself. For this reason, knowledge is tentative and hypothetical, and, as Kelly (1986:7) puts it, 'knowledge is procedural... a means to coming to learn'. Because it is created by human beings, knowledge is a social construction and therefore can only exist a *posteriori*. Thus, on the basis of its assumptions derived from the empiricist philosophical tradition, learner-centered pedagogy refutes the rationalists' notion that there exists a body of knowledge 'out there', independent of the learner, into which the latter must be initiated.

In the sphere of education, empiricism led to priority being given to the concept of the individual, not the concept of knowledge, in educational planning (Sharpes 1988). Because of the tentative, uncertain and problematic nature of knowledge, educational planning cannot take a knowledge-centred stance; it has to be learner-centred. As Kelly (1986:7) points out, educational planning has to 'see the development of the individual as the central concern of education and the selection of knowledge content as subsidiary and subordinate to that'. Bacon and Locke laid the foundation for the 'progressive' learner-centred view of education. It was left to Rousseau (1712-1778) to develop Lockeian thought in particular into a theory of education at the centre of which was learner-centred education. This he did in the Emile. However, it was John Dewey who gave learner-centredness its current philosophical basis, and it found its scientific justification in the developmental psychology of Jean Piaget, Lev Vigotsky and Jerome Bruner. A brief discussion here of the views of Rousseau will illustrate the nature of learner-centredness. Rousseau forms the watershed between theories of the Middle Ages and those of the 'modem era'.

Rousseau was one of the first theorists of *Individualism* and his writings signaled change in philosophy and education (Sharpes 1988:28). Whereas rationalists believed in innate depravity, Rousseau believed in the innate innocence or goodness of the child. It is society that corrupts the child and that inhibits individual freedom and liberty. He thought it essential that children ought to escape from the inhibitions of society and learn in the freedom of nature. Not only did this view challenge rationalism, it also challenged the Church's doctrine of original sin. It was for this reason that Rousseau was seen as anti-social, anti-establishment and a 'revolutionary'. Rousseau saw education's aim as to foster the liberty and happiness of the child. Education was only education through things, as he emphasises:

> I am never weary of repeating: let all the lessons of young people take the form of doing rather than talking: let them learn nothing from books which they can learn from experience (quoted in Sharpes 1988:28).

Experiencing, therefore, was to be the cornerstone of education. By rejecting the then prevailing rationalist belief that knowledge alone constituted the structure of what individuals know, Rousseau was placing the learner at the centre of curriculum planning. He proposed that the structuring of learning experiences be in accordance with the child's stage of development. This psychological standpoint was as much a harbinger of developmental theories of psychology as it 'was the acceptance of the participation as opposed to the preparation view of education' (Rusk 1954:156). One can only create the learner's interest in tasks if those tasks are adapted to the learner's capabilities. Thus, education for Rousseau becomes a matter of guiding the learner rather than imposing knowledge on him/her. Rousseau, therefore, was the first to shift the centre of gravity from the curriculum (knowledge) to the learner (Rusk 1954:165), and herein lay the seeds for the 'progressive' theories of education. All the other disciples of Rousseau (e.g. Pestalozzi, Herbart, Froebel and Montessori) emphasised certain aspects of his view of education (Kelly 1986:107). Zemiles (1987:204) has this to say about 'progressive' methods:

> Calling for openness to experience, and pointing to the importance of personal choice and free expression, progressive education negated the traditional emphasis on achieving inner control by inhibition, and competence by adult modeling.

The pedagogical implications of this educational paradigm are clear: knowledge cannot be studied employing traditional methods such as teacher-telling and lecturing. Since knowledge resides in the individual, it cannot be transferred intact from the 'head of the teacher to the heads of students' (Wildy and Wallace 1995:145). The absence of any 'bodies of knowledge' to be assimilated by the learner means that knowledge can only be gained by 'involvement in the process of knowledge-using and thus of knowledge-getting, by the experience of developing knowledge in order to solve problems' (Kelly 1986:54). Thus the constructivist perspective holds a view of the learner as an active and purposeful being in class. This is in stark contrast to the passive view of the learner that is promoted by the objectivist perspective of knowledge. The starting point of educational planning from the constructivist perspective, therefore, is the learner and *not* the subject matter to be learnt.

Constructivist epistemology calls for school and classroom design and internal arrangements that are different from those designed with an objectivist view of knowledge. To illustrate this point, I present findings from a study I carried out in a private, independent secondary school located in an exclusive suburb of the capital city of Gaborone, Botswana (for details see Tabulawa 1995). The school's pedagogical credo was undoubtedly constructivist.

Instead of oblong-shaped classrooms, this school had hexagonally-shaped classrooms. Inside the classrooms, instead of desks for single students, were tables long enough to be shared by two or three students. Although these tended to be arranged in a more or less haphazard manner, students generally faced the teacher. The important thing, however, is that the arrangement did not appear to be formally enforced. Figure 3.2 below illustrates a typical classroom arrangement.

Figure 3.2: Desk arrangement

Going through the school's official documents, it emerged that this classroom arrangement reflected the school's philosophy. The school offered a course called 'Language, Logic and Learning' to its Form One students (the first year of secondary schooling in Botswana). Two of the course's aims were:

1. To give students confidence in the fact that they have skills in themselves that they can develop;
2. To reduce the students' dependence on the teacher, teacher notes and the textbook as a ....path to examination success.

These aims recognize learners' existing knowledge – that they are not clean slates; that self-confidence and assertiveness are valued; and, that students need to be independent, i.e. they should construct knowledge and not just depend on the 'objective' sources of knowledge such as textbooks and teachers. From what we now understand by learner-centredness, there is no doubt that these aims reflect this pedagogical credo. Right from conception, the founders of the school wanted it to be an independent institution:

> They felt strongly that such a school would need a freedom in the conduct of its affairs that could only be assured and safeguarded by making the school indepen-dent of public funds (School Yearbook 1992:4).

The school's commitment to a democratic ethos was not merely rhetoric. It was reflected in a number of its organizational features. First, the school's layout was designed with democratic practice in mind. This is confirmed by the school's Principal in his/her Foreword to the school's 1993 Yearbook: 'There is no central administration building and no claustrophobic classroom blocks' (p. 3). This decentralization of the administration was an attempt to democratize the school's structures. In terms of students' involvement in the running of the school, the school's Principal had this to say: 'The school has eschewed from the start any kind of prefect system, opting instead for an elected Student Council' (School Yearbook 1992:3). The prefect system is what prevails in almost all public schools in Botswana and functions more or less as the eyes and ears of central administration in the dormitories and other corners of the school. Although we should be careful not to exaggerate the role of the Student Council in the day-to-day running of the school, there can be little doubt that its mere existence symbolised democracy-in-action. This is not to suggest that there was no hierarchy of authority in the school. Hierarchy existed, but it was mediated by features such as the decentralized administration and the unique Student Council. The results of these features were relaxed and informal teacher-student relationships as well as democratic classroom practices. The following came from teachers during interviews:

Here, student-teachers, relations are pretty good. Only a few students find it difficult to approach a teacher. I think this is one thing that distinguishes this school from the rest.

This school's students have an independent mind. They view the teacher in a different light altogether. To them the teacher is just one of them. There is no barrier between them and the teacher.

These sentiments were corroborated by the school's 1992 Yearbook:

Relations between younger and older members of the community are easy and informal. The reserve and submissiveness that one often finds in student-faculty relations in America is almost absent at [this school]. Instead, we share a special sense of humour that helps us with such otherwise sensitive topics as politics, religion and race (p. 9).

Regarding classroom practices, lesson observations showed that emphasis was less on the product of learning and more on the process of learning. I will illustrate this by taking a snapshot of one of the teachers' lessons (Mrs. Smith – a pseudonym), on the Okavango Delta of Botswana with her Form Four class.

Although there was ample published material on how the Okavango Delta and other lakes in northern Botswana evolved, Mrs. Smith made no reference to the material. Instead, she based the entire lesson on an extract, entitled *The Return of the Lakes,* from a local newspaper by the columnist Cliff Meyer. The extract is a fairy story of how the lakes in northern Botswana were formed, how most of them disappeared, and how they might reappear in future. In it he writes of 'raging fires', 'cities turning into rubble', 'the Kalahari sands burning with fires', and rivers 're-emerging in the Kalahari Desert' (of course there is geological evidence that the Kalahari Desert once had flowing rivers). Geographical concepts such as 'earthquake', 'epicentre' and 'depression' feature in the extract.

After introducing the topic, Mrs. Smith starts reading out the extract. Each student has a copy. Along the way students interrupt her by asking questions, talking loudly among themselves and giggling. The teacher ignores all this. One student comments:

Student: There is nothing like this. This is frightening (Class laughs).
Mrs. Smith: Quiet please. This is just a hypothetical situation. Could you please wait until I have finished reading the extract?
Student: Why does the writer use a hypothetical situation? This sounds unrealistic.

The teacher ignores the comment. Having heard the whole extract, the class starts to isolate and discuss concepts of geographical interest. For example, she asks:

Mrs. Smith:	How would you describe an earthquake in the context of this extract?
Student:	Mm . . . It is a destructive movement of the earth.
Mrs. Smith:	Why destructive movement in particular?
Student:	Because in the extract the writer talks of raging fires, cities being destroyed and the desert burning.
Mrs. Smith:	Is that a convincing answer, Tau?
Tau:	Yaa! I think so. It has to be destructive. Remember that when we talked about the earth's position in the solar system we said that it rotates and revolves. That is earth movement but it is not destructive. So, an earthquake has to be destructive.

[There is laughter and shouting. The teacher manages to quieten down the class and continues]

Mrs. Smith:	What is the epicenter?
Student:	The earthquake is underneath. But the point at which it starts, that is, the focus, is the epicenter.

Typically, the lesson progresses in this dialogue form. There are no attempts by the teacher to impose answers. When the class has exhausted defining and explaining the important concepts, Mrs. Smith poses the following question:

"Is the scenario presented by Cliff Meyer in this extract a realistic view of a possible future?"

She requests them to discuss the question among themselves. Students can be heard and seen arguing intensely.

Worth noting is that the question posed is open-ended, giving students relative autonomy in answering it and rendering inappropriate the search for wrong or right answers. It demands that students apply geographical concepts such as 'earthquake' and 'epicenter' to explain the geological evolution of the delta and other lakes in that region of the country. During the discussion there is little interference from the teacher, except for the constant reminder to minimize noise. By the end of the discussion it is clear that students have failed to reach any sound conclusions. There are shouts of: 'This is impossible', 'It is unrealistic'. Mrs. Smith then rephrases the question:

'Would you imagine an earthquake one day devastating the whole of southern Africa, leading to changes in climate, and rivers re-emerging in the Kalahari sands?

One of the students, seemingly off-handedly, remarks:

'No way. Not when we are still alive. It might happen in future, say 100 years to come.

This seemingly off-handed remark becomes the basis for the discussion of the importance of *time scale* in geological evolution. It is agreed that since geological processes take millions of years, the scenario depicted by Meyer, though exaggerated, is a possibility.

The teacher had the easier option of asking the students to name factors that influence geological evolution – *time scale* being one of them. Instead, she decides on a more elaborate, longer route to the answer. The questions posed and their contexts are such that they leave little room for the mere recall and memorization of isolated facts. Mrs. Smith does not tell the students the answer. All she does is set a context or framework within which students work their way to the answer. She harnesses the students' natural curiosity by basing the lesson on a fairy tale which she knows is going to arouse interest, thus motivating the students. When the motivation is induced and the learning context developed, students start to produce classroom knowledge. The whole learning context (of open-ended tasks and problem-solving) forecloses rote learning and opens up opportunities for dialogue, requiring students to apply concepts and principles.

It can be deduced from this extract that the school, teachers and students did not favour transmission of knowledge from the teacher to the students. In interviews with both the teachers and students, it was very clear that lecturing at the students, as one teacher put it, 'can't work with these students'. It was an elite school of students of middle-class background. There was no doubt in my mind that pedagogical processes in the school approximated learner-centredness.

ScientificJustification of Learner-centered Pedagogy

Just like teacher-centred pedagogy, learner-centered pedagogy has its own scientific justification – in developmental psychology, of which the most famous representatives are Piaget, Vygotsky and Bruner. This branch of psychology emerged as a reaction to behaviourism's neglect of mental operations. These psychologists were not only concerned with the way children learnt, they were also concerned with the way children developed. They stressed the distinction between learning and cognitive development.

Developmental psychology posits that children develop intellectually by structuring and restructuring their perceptions of the environment and by active forms of interaction with that environment. Intellectual development, therefore, cannot take place through a passive process; it has to take place in a process characterised by physical and motor activity. Thus the developmental psychologists' view that true learning comes from the experience of genuine interaction with the environment can be considered a scientific justification of the views on learning expressed by Rousseau and later developed John Dewey.

The fact that the two pedagogical paradigms are each scientifically justified by two opposing schools of psychology only serves to highlight their fundamental paradigmatic differences.

Conclusion

I have attempted in this chapter to demonstrate the potential of the concept of paradigm in helping us understand the nature of pedagogical change. Seeing teacher-centred and learner-centred pedagogies as two incompatible paradigms, given their diametrically opposed epistemologies, helps us to appreciate the problematic nature of change, contrary to the view promoted by the dominant, technical rational model. Thus, learner-centered and teacher-centered pedagogies are a world apart from each other. They differ fundamentally, and therefore treating them as if they form a continuum (along which teachers and students can be moved from one end to the other) and are informed by the same underlying assumptions about knowledge is erroneous. Thus, the expectation by curriculum developers in many African contexts that teachers and students change from their teacher-centered pedagogical style to learner-centered one is necessarily to expect them to make a paradigm shift. History, however, testifies that it is never easy to shift from one paradigm to the other. Pogrow rightly observes that '[w]hile paradigm shifts are important in the evolution of knowledge, they are extremely rare; most fields do not even have one per century' (Pogrow 1996:659). Education is one such field. Thus it takes more than mere advocacy and in-service training to convince teachers to shift from one pedagogical style or value-system to the other. To change from one pedagogical paradigm to the other necessarily requires that teachers abandon their taken-for-granted classroom world for another world with which they are not familiar. This has serious implications in terms of their accumulated skills and knowledge used for solving the practical and often unpredictable classroom dilemmas they encounter on a day-to-day basis. It is, therefore, not surprising that teachers tend to resist such change. The problem with the technicist approach is that it does not view the shift from a teacher-centered to a learner-centered pedagogy as necessarily entailing radical change. Sarason (1990:90) made an instructive observation that '[c]hanging the regularities in the classroom is a very complex, demanding, and personally upsetting affair'. Inherent in the concept of paradigm shift is the notion of radical change. But radical change is never easy to accomplish.

In the next chapter, I present study findings that demonstrate that teacher-centredness as the paradigmatic location of students and their teachers in public schools in most sub-Saharan African schools is constructed not by teachers alone acting *on* the students, but rather by teachers acting together *with* students. Through a process of *co-construction,* both teachers and students jealously guard their teacher-dominated ambiance because it is their taken-for-granted world. It imbues their actions with meaning and intelligibility. The concept of *co-construction* directly challenges the often implicit assumption in classroom research that it is the teacher acting *on* the students who constructs the teacher-centred classroom environment. The rendition complicates further pedagogical change in that contrary to what technical rationality preaches to us, students are an important factor in pedagogical change.

4

Teacher-centred Pedagogy as Co-construction

Introduction

In Chapter One, I observed that one of the effects of technical rationality on research on teaching has been the tendency to focus almost exclusively on what the teacher does in class, rather than on what students also do to influence classroom practices. Students, it appears, do not matter really in classroom processes and curriculum implementation. This thinking suggests that their behaviour will change as and when that of the teacher changes. The thinking is perfectly in line with the logic of both process-product research and behaviourism – typically, students are portrayed as 'passive recipients of academic verbal information' (Prophet and Rowell 1993:205), which implies that they do not make any worthwhile contribution towards the shaping of the observed classroom practices. Where students' contributions are accepted, they are described as 'fairly artificial [comprising] short responses to closed-ended teacher-initiated questions' (Marope 1995:12). To use a popular metaphor, students are 'pawns' that merely respond, in a rather mechanical manner, to the teacher's actions.

This chapter makes a critique of this position through the presentation of findings from a study in which students were observed employing both subtle and overt strategies to keep their teachers in an information-giving position. The findings challenge the pervasive view that 'teacher dominance' of classroom activities is a product of the teacher acting *on* the students. Rather, teacher dominance results from teachers and students exercising power on one another. To this end, I argue that students make great input in classroom processes to the extent that they significantly influence the way a teacher carries out his or her teaching tasks. At the centre of this argument is the notion of classroom reality as a social construction jointly constructed by both the teacher and students. Doyle's (1992:509) suggestion that 'the study of teaching and curriculum must be grounded much more deeply than it has been in the events that students and teachers jointly construct in the classroom settings' is undoubtedly apt. Thus, the classroom reality dubbed 'teacher-centredness' is a co-construction involving both students and the teacher. In Chapter Three, I discussed some of the strategies teachers used to keep themselves in an information-giving position. In the present chapter, I demonstrate how students kept themselves in an information-receiving position. The result of these actions was a teacher-centred ambiance.

The concept of 'co-construction' is potent in three main ways. First, it validates the view that as an immunological condition, teacher-centredness is antithetical to learner-centredness, a condition that increases the possibility of tissue rejection of learner-centredness where attempts to introduce it in a predominantly teacher-centred environment are made. Secondly, the co-construction concept rhymes with the concept of pedagogical paradigm as presented in Chapter Three in that adherents (teachers and students) of a paradigm tend to behave in ways that reproduce the paradigm. They are unlikely to behave in ways that challenge the fundamental bases of the paradigm.

Thirdly, the concept portrays the classroom as a living social system, and like all social systems it is a creation of human beings acting on one another. The meanings this social system imbues in both teachers and students make them purposeful sense-makers who constantly construct ideas in order to understand situations and events. This teacher and student-empowering position has spurred interest in research on *teacher thinking*, and this research has flourished since the 1980s. The research is premised on the assumption that teachers' thoughts, beliefs, judgments, and decisions guide their classroom behaviour (Stern and Shavelson 1983; Richardson, Tidwell and Lloyd 1991). The assumption implies a view of teachers as active and autonomous agents whose role is shaped by their classroom experience (Elbaz 1983). Thus, in opposition to the sterile and dependent view of the teacher promoted by the technicist approach, research on teacher thinking views the teacher as capable of mediating ideas and constructing meaning and knowledge. Unfortunately, not as much attention has been paid to research on *student thinking*, yet, as this chapter seeks to demonstrate, attempts to radically reform teaching and learning practices (e.g. by introducing a 'radically' different innovation such as learner-centred pedagogy) are surely likely to be resisted, not only by the teachers but also by the students.

This raises an interesting definitional problem – that of how we define teacher-centredness. Because in the technical rational model, the student-teacher relationship is hierarchised, invariably, teacher-centredness as a classroom ambiance is an orchestration of the teacher acting on the students. It makes sense, therefore, that attempts to change this ambiance must target the teacher, not the student. A view of classroom ambiance as co-construction, on the other hand, yields a definition of teacher-centredness that is radically different from the one engendered by the technical rational model. Co-construction assumes 'hierarchically flattened' relations between the teacher and students, meaning that the latter also influence the former. Followed to its logical conclusion, this line of thinking would define teacher-centredness as a 'joint project' of the teacher and his/her students, implying that students have 'interests' in the classroom ambiance. They will use every 'tool' at their disposal to police its boundaries. This position complicates pedagogical change in that it suggests that attempts to change classroom practices in African schools must include both the teacher and students.

To develop the argument for taking students seriously in pedagogical change, first I critique the 'power-as-sovereign' conception (Popkewitz 2000, as cited in McEneaney 2002:104) that undergirds technical rationality and, by extension, studies on classroom research that privilege the teacher in the construction of classroom reality. I offer an alternative analysis of power based on the ideas of Foucault. This alternative analysis portrays students as at once objects and subjects of power. Secondly, and on the basis of the alternative analysis of power, I advance an argument for viewing classroom reality as a co-construction. To illustrate these two positions, I present findings from an empirical case study in which students latently and manifestly contributed to the construction of the classroom reality that has been dubbed 'teacher-centredness'. Finally, I offer a set of conclusions derived from my analysis.

Power and Power Relations: A Foucaultian View

Orner (1992:82) recommends that researchers abandon what she terms the 'monarchical conception of power'. This is the conception of power as a commodity, as 'property' possessed by individuals or groups of individuals, which can be acquired or seized. For example, it is often taken for granted that teachers possess power and that students lack it. Talk about 'student empowerment', e.g. through a learner-centred pedagogy, often implies teachers giving some of their power to students. This view of power as property to be exchanged inevitably leads to the 'identification of power with repression'

(Cousins and Hussain 1984:230), and to a definition of power as primarily a negative force that serves the interests of domination. Aronowitz and Giroux (1985:154) have characterized this perspective of power as follows:

> Treated as an instance of negation, power becomes a contaminating force that leaves the imprint of domination or powerlessness on whatever it touches. Thus, social control becomes synonymous with the exercise of domination in schools… The question of how power works in schools is almost by intellectual default limited to recording how it reproduces relations of domination and subordinacy through various school practices.

As McEneaney (2002) observes, this conception of power implicitly informs much educational research. In classroom research, such a conception has led to the understanding of classroom power relations in terms of dominators (teachers) and the dominated (students); teachers possess power and use it to dominate students, hence the description of students as passive actors in class. Studies that describe classroom practice as 'teacher-centred' or 'teacher-dominated' are informed by this monarchical conception of power.

The problem with this conception of power as it relates to classroom power relations is that it denies the classroom its character as a site for struggles and contradictions. Teaching is characterized by gaps, ruptures, and contradictions occasioned by the interactions between teacher and students (Orner 1992). This means that the students are active agents who exercise power to produce classroom practice. However, this is not conceivable in the 'monarchical conception of power' paradigm. An alternative conceptualization of power (one that recognizes students as active agents) is necessary.

Foucault's (1980) analysis of power is instructive in this regard. His view is that power cannot be a commodity. It is 'neither given, nor exchanged, nor recovered, but rather exercised, and… only exists in action (Foucault 1980:89). It is only when people interact in relationships that power comes into existence. That is, power is a productive social dynamic. In Foucault's view, it is not power that differentiates between those who possess it (e.g. teachers) and those 'who do not have it and submit to it' (e.g. students). Rather,

> Power must be analysed as something which circulates, or rather as something which only functions in the form of a chain. It is never localized here or there, never in anybody's hands, never appropriated as a commodity or piece of wealth. Power is employed and exercised through a net-like organisation. And not only do individuals circulate between its threads; they are always in the position of simultaneously undergoing and exercising this power. They are not only its inert or consenting target; they are always also the elements of its articulation. In other words, individuals are the vehicles of power, not its points of application. (Foucault 1980:98)

In Foucault's (1982) view, a power relationship, as opposed to a 'relationship of violence' (which characterizes a slave/master relationship), has two features. It requires, first, that the person over whom power is exercised 'be thoroughly recognized and maintained to the very end as a person who acts', and secondly, that, 'faced with a relationship of power, a whole field of responses, reactions, results, and possible inventions may open up' (Foucault 1982:220). That is, a power relationship is an open-ended relationship in which the exercise of power is a 'way in which certain actions may structure the field of other possible actions' (p. 222). An important element of any power relationship is freedom. Where action is completely constrained, one may not talk of there being a relationship of power. As Foucault himself states, '[p]ower is exercised only over free subjects, and only insofar as they are free (p. 221). In other words, the person over whom power is being exercised (e.g. the student) is also simultaneously a person who acts, and whose actions in the process transform the one exercising power. In Dreyfus and Rabinow's (1982:186) words, 'power is exercised upon the dominant as well as on the dominated'. Thus, the exercise of power is never unidirectional. It is never the 'province of one group and not the other' (Kincheloe 1997:xxiii). It is in this sense that power is seen as a productive force; it implies the capacity to act. Kincheloe (1997:xxvi) summarizes the argument in this way:

> If power is not a unitary force with unitary effects or unidirectional hierarchy, then we can be alert to different ways oppressed people elude control. If we are all em-powered by our particular capacities and skills and we are all unempowered by our inability either to satisfy our wants and needs or express our living spirit, we begin to understand that power is exercised by both dominant and subordinate forces.

Thus, in the classroom the teacher exercises power over students and the latter also exercise power over the teacher. While one may not deny that there exists a power hierarchy in the classroom between teacher and students, one must, nevertheless, not be tempted to believe that total domination is possible. Oppression elicits resistance, and this may be manifest or latent. Far from being an imposition by the teacher, classroom reality is *negotiated* (Delamont 1976) and, as such, is a dynamic process in that it is constantly defined and redefined. Inasmuch as teachers employ certain strategies to influence students' learning, the latter also devise, consciously or subconsciously, strategies to influence the teacher's classroom behaviour:

> A new class is not a clean slate passively waiting for the teacher to inscribe his will on it. It is an ongoing social system with very definite expectations about appro-priate teacher behaviour. If these are not confirmed the pupils will protest and

the renegotiated patterns of behaviour may not prove to be just what the teacher intended (Nash 1976:94).

This observation is echoed by Riseborough (1985:209) when he states that pupils can be 'overt curriculum and hidden curriculum decision makers'. He adds:

> [T]he lesson does not simply belong to the teacher, children can and do make it their own. They put so much on the agenda of the lesson, to a point where they are the curriculum decision-makers. They make a major contribution to the social construction of classroom knowledge. Children actively select, organize and evaluate knowledge in schools. (p. 214)

Similarly, Doyle (1983:185) cites a study in which Davis and McKnight (1976) reported '[meeting] with strong resistance from high school students when they attempted to shift information-processing demands in a mathematics class from routine or procedural tasks to understanding tasks. The students refused to co-operate and argued that they had a right to be told what to do.'

Research that portrays teachers as dominators of the classroom and students as mere pawns is flawed because it fails to capture the complexity of the ways power works both on and through people. The description of classroom practice as 'teacher-centred/dominated' requires problematization. Often it creates the impression that students have made no contribution in the construction of that reality. This is misleading, for the reality called 'teacher-centredness' is itself a co-construction, that is, there is a sense in which students are involved in the construction of their own 'domination'. The appreciation of classroom practice as a dialectical co-construction assumes a pivotal position in understanding classroom dynamics. How, then, is this co-construction to be understood?

Classroom Reality as Co-construction

The classroom as an arena for human activity has an inherent structure (Doyle 1992). This structure is constructed by teachers and students so as to make classroom social interaction possible. I borrow at this point Arnold Gehlen's twin concepts (as developed by Berger and Kellner 1965) of *background* and *foreground* to explicate the dialectic of the classroom as a co-construction.

Human life requires a stable background of routinized meanings. This background 'permits "spontaneous", barely reflective, almost automatic actions' (Berger and Kellner 1965:112). Life would be unbearable if it did not have a background of routinized activities, the meaning of which is taken for granted. This background becomes a reference point for future actions and practices.

The classroom, as an arena for human activity, requires a background of routinized practices. Without that background there cannot be stability, and by extension, no teaching and learning. Both teacher and students know very well that stability is essential if learning is to take place; but because social stability is never a biological provision they have to 'construct' it. They accomplish this by developing common-sense images of the nature of teaching and learning. Such images and their accompanying roles are then routinized, and hence taken for granted. In their routinized form they come to constitute the classroom background. However, if human life only had a background, society would be static, because by its very nature the background constrains action. Social actors would then be reduced to 'choiceless' actors, pawns who are at the mercy of the overly oppressive social structure. As Giroux (1980:234) observes, this structuralist view of human action 'seals off the possibility for educational and social change'.

The coming into being of the background automatically 'opens up a foreground for deliberation and innovation' (Berger and Luckmann 1967:71) which permits 'deliberate, reflective, purposeful actions (Berger and Kellner 1965:112). Thus, the existence of the foreground ensures that the background does not become a 'determining' instrumentality. Rather it becomes a structure that 'mediates' human action.

The dialectical relationship of the background and foreground ensures the possibility of reflexive human action. Because it guarantees 'freedom' of acting agents, the foreground opens up a whole field of power relations. It is here where meaning is negotiated and renegotiated by the actors. In the processes of negotiation and renegotiation a 'definition of the situation' emerges. Thus, classroom social interaction 'can be viewed as "negotiated" between participants [teachers and students] on the basis of a mutual "agreement" to sustain a particular "definition of the situation"' (Jones, 1997:561). Because it has both a background and foreground, the classroom situation is at once stable and unstable. The stability occasioned by the classroom's background permits the reproduction of practices, while the foreground permits their production. In this sense, the classroom situation is simultaneously a constraining and an enabling field: it permits common participation (engendered by the existence of an agreed-upon 'definition of the situation') while at the same time allowing for tensions, contradictions, and contests. In other words, students' and teachers' classroom practices are neither completely constrained nor completely free. Viewed this way, the classroom becomes a dynamic system in which teachers and students are not 'pawns' but are instead active agents operating within contextual constraints. In this situation of relative freedom, teachers and students exercise power on one another, leading to the co-construction of classroom reality.

The strength of the idea of classroom practice as co-construction lies in its difference from the views expressed by theorists (such as Anyon 1980) who see classroom practice as mechanistically determined by wider structural and economic forces. It also rejects the phenomenological (subjectivist) view of a structurally unconstrained agent. What remains, therefore, is the view that '[p]raxis is only possible where the objective-subjective dialectic is maintained (Freire 1985:69).

The study findings reported below illustrate the co-constructedness of teacher-centredness. The basic premises of the empirical study were that power and power relations are central to an understanding of classroom practice, and that students are capable of exercising power in the classroom, that is, they are co-constructors of classroom practice. The study, therefore, concerned itself with establishing the manifest and subtle strategies that students employ and the role of power and power relations in shaping those strategies. Because these strategies are under-researched, we do not have a clear understanding of how much of an impediment students may be to efforts to alter teachers' classroom practices. This chapter attempts to move closer towards such an understanding.

Findings and Discussion

Observed Classroom Dynamics

The findings of the study confirmed the findings of earlier studies on classroom dynamics: teachers play a 'dominant' role in the classroom, with teaching and learning being primarily based on information transmission by the teacher. As reported in the preceding chapter, teachers employed strategies that ensured sustenance of their dominance. For example, they ignored what they considered to be students' incorrect answers (conversely, they emphasized 'right' answers); mass teaching was the norm; and they asked closed-ended questions. All these techniques, I suggest, ensured the maintenance of the teacher's dominance in class; hence the description of lessons as teacher-centred/dominated.

Conventional interpretation of such findings tends to portray the teacher as the embodiment of the oppressive structures; he or she is presented as the one who possesses power which he or she uses for purposes of social control. The students are, therefore, cast as passive and powerless. The implicit view of power here is that of power-as-sovereign. However, in this study, teacher dominance was not necessarily seen as a product of the teacher's inherent desire for social control. The interviews and observation data showed that in many instances, teachers were 'forced' into the dominant position by the students themselves. Teacher dominance, far from being a teacher imposition, is a negotiated product resulting from students and teachers exercising power (within the limits of the constraints set by their context) on each other. In other words, students do contribute towards the classroom reality called 'teacher-centredness'. The question, therefore, is 'how was this accomplished'?

Construction of Teacher Dominance: The Role of Students

Student Expectations of Teacher Behaviour

Students had certain expectations of both their teachers' and fellow students' behaviour. These expectations regulated the participants' classroom behaviour. In particular, the expectations positioned students as 'gatekeepers' to the teachers' reputation. From the interviews with the teachers it was clear that they were aware of this powerful position of students. The students, however, were not as conscious of the power of their own position as the teachers were. Nevertheless, they had certain expectations of teacher behaviour. It was these expectations, which the teachers were fully aware of, that influenced how they conducted their lessons.

Whether the teacher was described by the students as 'good' or 'poor' depended on how well he or she carried out responsibilities that essentially had to do with imparting school knowledge (and not deviating from that role). Characteristically, a 'good' teacher was described by students in the following ways:

Student 1:   A competent teacher, I think comes to class prepared and has a good mastery of subject content. It must be clear that he knows what he is talking about. Whenever we get a new teacher we 'test' him to find out if he knows his stuff. Depending on how he or she impresses us we either call him or her the 'deep' one or the 'shallow' one.

Student 2: Notes are very important to us as students. We cannot pass our tests and examinations if we do not have notes for revision. Some teachers just give you what is in the textbook. A good teacher must prepare and give detailed notes. Yes, we can make our own notes but ... we don't have time.

Student 3: I like a teacher who satisfactorily answers students' questions. Some teachers have this habit of ignoring questions by students or ridiculing students who ask questions they themselves feel are stupid.

Student 4: A good teacher keeps order in class and makes you do your work. You see there are students who always want to challenge the teacher by making noise. The teacher must be able to control those. Homework must be checked by the teacher.

The teachers' act of satisfying these qualities was described by the students as *go tshologa*, a Setswana equivalent of 'to pour out' – in this context, 'pouring out' knowledge. Metaphorically, the teacher was viewed as a fountain of knowledge. If teachers were perceived in this way, then probably the most important thing for students was how effectively the teachers transmitted that essential commodity, knowledge, and it was their ability to do so (or lack thereof) that determined if they were any 'good'. A teacher who did not live up to these expectations was labeled a *majesa*, a term developed by students in Botswana which, literally translated, means 'an incompetent' teacher. Students felt that a majesa displayed the following qualities:

> This is the teacher who gives notes without explaining them clearly or does not give notes at all. We have protested against such teachers before by reporting them to our class teacher.

> Some teachers, particularly female teachers, like teaching while seated on their front chairs. They also often speak very slowly. We do not respect such teachers. When students feel that the teacher is not watching them they tend to play. When the teacher is a slow speaker we doze off. It's like the teacher is not confident about what he or she is doing.

> Some teachers have the tendency to come late to class and to not mark homework and tests on time. As a student you need to know how you are performing. But some teachers take too long to give us feedback and we often wonder if these are not the lazy ones.

The label of majesa was one that every teacher dreaded, and all of them confessed that in their teaching they consciously and deliberately attempted to avoid it. How?

Teacher 1: I make sure that I am prepared when I go for my lessons, and if I am not prepared I tell the students so.

Teacher 2: Every time I am in class I avoid habits that would make me appear a majesa – habits like not being well prepared. I collect their notebooks and check if they write notes, and I also give them quizzes at the end of the lesson.

Teacher 3: I make sure that I have my facts right. I try to mark their work on time and to give them feedback on time. I make sure that I am familiar and conversant with my material.

All these measures were taken by the teachers to appear 'effective' and 'efficient' in the students' eyes. In the comments above, teachers emphasized mastery of subject matter and preparedness. One may ask if these are not qualities expected of any teacher anywhere? The answer of course is, 'Yes, they are'. However, how teachers demonstrate possession of these qualities will differ, depending on the context. The teachers observed were aware that they had to demonstrate visible possession of these qualities by assuming an information-giving position. This would ensure that they 'effectively' executed their mandate of imparting knowledge or 'delivering the goods' to the students. Efficient transmission of information to students formed the cornerstone of almost all lessons observed in the school. Not all the teachers would have liked to approach their lessons in this fashion; but all were aware of the dangers of deviating from the norm.

Adhering to the 'norm', in Foucault's view, has the effect of disciplining human subjects. He terms this *normalization,* the internalization of correct behaviour. Through normalization, students and teachers internalize norms and rules that ensure consistency in their behaviour. Deviation from what is considered 'normal' is punishable, whereas adherence to the 'norm' is rewarded. One effect of normalization is self-regulation. Self-regulation is 'achieved through discourse practices that provide validation for behavior' (Anderson and Grinberg 1998:335). Being described as a 'good/competent' teacher is normalizing in that the label tells the teacher what kind of behaviour is rewarded. On the other hand, being called a *majesa* tells the teacher what kind of behaviour is unacceptable. The fact that the students are the 'primary source of the teacher's reputation among colleagues, administrators, and in the community, as well as among [other] students' (Schlechty and Atwood 1977:286) ensures that the teacher is continually under a disciplinary/normalizing gaze, a kind of surveillance that makes unnecessary constant reminding about the 'proper' way of behaving. The teacher, therefore, self-regulates his or her own behaviour. The 'social order' of the classroom (characterized by asymmetrical power relations between the teacher and students) is reaffirmed and reproduced.

Students, too, are under a normalizing and controlling gaze, not from the teacher as such, but from themselves. It is the students themselves who serve as the source of validation for their own behaviour. This is achieved, as will be discussed later, through such factors as peer pressure and humiliation of those who may be inclined to deviate from the constructed value system.

This analysis shows that in the classroom, power is not a monopoly of any one group. Rather, power is embedded in the relations among students and teachers. These relations are not static. Nor are they unidirectional. In other words, there is no imposition; as Butin (2001:168) puts it, a "good" student... is not simply made. Nor is a teacher simply the "authority" in control'. Butin contends that these identities are not simply inscribed upon these classroom participants: rather 'the individual does this to herself, one might say under duress, one might argue unwittingly, one might confess with scant choice, but it is not something done to her; it is something done with her'.

The point is that both the teacher and the student are involved in their own subjectification. That is, while they 'create' one another's identities they are at the same time involved in self-creation. This constitutive quality of power would not be possible if 'some individuals [were] active and control power while others [were] passive and controlled by power (Butin 2001:168). If classroom events, including the subjectification of individuals and groups, cannot be an imposition, researchers are left with only the view of classroom events as co-constructions.

Student silence: 'playing possum'?

Students also constructed classroom practice through 'silence'. Student 'refusal' to participate in classroom activities is interpreted in several ways. For some, it is idiosyncratic student behaviour, a sign of laziness: it is deviant behaviour. This interpretation is shallow and prejudiced. At a more sophisticated level, student silence is explained in terms of students' lack of 'voice', which is associated with powerlessness. The weakness of this interpretation is that it is anchored on the monarchical conception of power, a conception of power that (as noted above) positions students as 'pawns' in classroom practices. The view of power as relational yields a radically different interpretation of students' silence. In this view of power, student silence is not a manifestation of powerlessness or lack of voice. It is the 'active' exercise of power and construction of classroom practice. Silence is an important means of communication in some cultures (see Darnell 1979 and Chambers 1992 on the Cree and Dene of North America respectively, and Alverson 1978 on the Tswana of Botswana).

Goldberger (1996:343) urges researchers not to dismiss silence as lack of power, but rather to search for what lies 'underneath silence'. If researchers were to follow Goldberger's advice, they would, as the 19th century English novelist George Eliot imagines, 'die of that roar which lies on the other side of silence' (cited in Belenky et al. 1986:3). In other words, researchers need to theorize silence.

As Hurtado (1996:382) suggests, 'Silence is a powerful weapon when it can be controlled. It is akin to camouflaging oneself when at war in an open field; playing possum at strategic times causes the power of the silent one to be underestimated. The second sentence in this quotation clearly captures the general stance adopted towards silence in classroom research. This is what appears to be happening with student silence. In the episodes below, students constructed classroom practice (teacher dominance, in particular) through silence.

Episode 1:   The teacher walks into a geography class and introduces his lesson by the usual way of the question-and-answer sequence:

Teacher: What is tourism? [There is no answer. He repeats the question but till there is no answer.]

Teacher: I will rephrase the question. What factors affect the development of tourism? [Still there is no response.]

Teacher *[Looking dejected]:* I am sure that you know the answer. Expressing yourselves is the problem.

The teacher continued for almost three minutes asking the same question and trying to give students clues to the answer. In so doing, a 'stand-off' develops between the teacher and the students. Students are resisting the teacher's attempt to move them into his own world of meaning.

Realizing that students were not 'willing' to answer his questions, he remarked, 'Well, I will do the talking since in the afternoons people are too tired to answer questions'. The teacher then abandoned the question-and-answer session and started lecturing on tourism and the factors that affect its development. While he was 'lecturing', the students listened attentively and caused no disruptions to the flow of information. Thus, the students succeeded in moving the teacher into their own frame of reference or world of meaning. Perhaps the attentiveness was possible because the students' game of possum was yielding the desired results.

Episode 2:   Another teacher in a Form 4 class organizes students for a group discussion on 'The importance of the mining industry to the economy of Botswana'. The discussions are to be carried out in

English. The majority of students are observed doing nothing related to the task at hand. In another lesson, the same teacher asks students to discuss in groups five disadvantages of hydroelectric power. Only eight students (four pairs) out of a total of 23 are observed working. The rest are either doing nothing or reading the class textbook. In these episodes students appear to be 'refusing' to participate in certain classroom activities. This is what one teacher had to say in connection with the students' behaviour:

> Even if you give them group work, they do not have the motivation to do the group work. Only one or two students will do the work. In this way you find yourself compelled to lecture at them if they are to gain any school knowledge.

The way these students seem to express their refusal is through silence. How then is the phenomenon of student silence to be explained?

In this context, the post-structural feminist attempt to demonstrate the gendered nature of classroom practice may be helpful (e.g. Belenky et al. 1986; Orner 1992; Maher and Tetreault 1994; Goldberger 1996; St. Pierre 2000). These feminists, following Foucault, understand power as a dialectical force. This understanding predisposes them to adopt a contrary stance towards modernist dichotomies such as powerful/powerless, voice/silence, man/woman, subjectivity/ objectivity and many others, preferring instead to see these categories as being in a dialectical relationship, that is, as being relational. Seen in this way, one category is not privileged over the other, as is the case in the ordinary binary system. Post-structural feminists would, for example, deconstruct the voice/silence dichotomy so that the two end up, not as opposites, but as 'definitionally interdependent (Anyon 1994:119). They would argue that as voice constructs knowledge, so, too, does silence, in that silence is resistance; it is the exercise of power, and thus the construction of knowledge (Goldberger 1996). In other words, silence is voice; it is power. Thus, the students in the episodes above were exercising power when they refused to participate (by keeping quiet) when their teachers wanted them to participate. In the process they actively constructed classroom practice, as indicated by one teacher's remark that when students 'refuse' to participate 'you find yourself compelled to lecture at them if they are to gain any school knowledge'.

Why did the students 'choose' to exercise their power through silence? Maher and Tetreault's (1994:165) observation is instructive:

> The construction of voice is also partly a function of position. Students fashion themselves in terms of their awareness of others in their particular classroom and institution, and in terms of their individual or group relation to the dominant culture.

Indeed, whether or not students participate in classroom activities depends on a number of factors, one of which is the position they occupy in relation to (a) other students, and (b) their teacher. This factor of positionality could explain the silent refusal of students to participate. Positionality factors (such as age, race, class, etc.) have 'an influence on teaching and learning, on instructors' and students' construction of knowledge, and on classroom dynamics' (Tisdell 1998: 147). Age, as a positionality factor, is pertinent to the understanding of student silence in the lesson episodes above. The significance of age in African classroom interactional patterns is treated in-depth in the next chapter.

Henry (1996:377) observes that 'refusal to participate is a kind of oppositional stance'. It is an action embedded in the classroom relations of power, and has an effect on how the lesson progresses. The effect of the students' 'refusal to act' is that asymmetrical power relations in the classroom are exacerbated and teacher dominance is perpetuated. Thus, students are accomplices in the production and reproduction of asymmetrical power relations in the classroom. Student silence (as resistance), therefore, may not be a manifestation of powerlessness or lack of voice. In effect, it is the active exercise of power and construction of classroom practice. Student passivity, so much reported in classroom research, is therefore, an illusion.

Teachers' Deficit View of Students

The teachers I worked with held a deficit view of their students. The view was linked to the perceived deficient social, cultural, and economic background of the students. Two factors related to students' backgrounds contributed to this perception: the students' poor mastery of English and their rural background. These factors were linked to each other in a somewhat causal relationship – poor mastery of the English language, the medium of instruction in Botswana's secondary schools, was attributed to the students' rural background. I observed that students were not eager to respond to questions posed by their teachers, nor were they prepared to participate in group activities organized by their teachers. Although the teachers interpreted this behaviour as 'unwillingness to participate', they acknowledged at the same time that students' poor self-expression hindered them from fully participating in planned activities. Indeed, I observed on several occasions students struggling to express themselves.

As I have noted, this deficiency was linked to their rural background, a background, it was believed, that did not include learning resources such as television and libraries that students could use to improve their English. This deficiency was not envisaged with students in towns. As the teachers said:

> If you compare these two groups of students [i.e. urban and rural] as far as class partici-
> pation is concerned, you will find that students from town participate more. They talk
> and ask questions.
>
> These students are really dull. No matter how hard you try to motivate them they just
> remain lifeless in class. All they want is information from you.
>
> They are not confident. They do not believe in themselves. They do not believe that they
> are capable of knowing anything that does not come from the teacher or the textbook.

The teachers thought that interactive methods of teaching (such as those
associated with learner-centred pedagogy) were more suited to students in
urban areas (although there is no evidence to that effect), and that directive/
transmission teaching was appropriate for the students they were teaching:

> We try some of these new methods of teaching. Say you give them a textbook and a
> topic and ask them to sit in groups and discuss. At the end of the lesson you realize
> that they haven't done anything because they believe that the teacher should impart the
> knowledge to them.

What should simply be seen as 'differences' between urban and rural students
is turned into 'deficits' on the part of the latter. The deficit view becomes
the basis for comparing these groups of students and for constituting their
identities (as 'dull' or 'brilliant'). In the classroom these deficiencies translate
into information that helps structure events. One effect of the deficit view is
that it invariably calls for more control from the teacher, thus exacerbating the
already prevailing asymmetrical power relations in the classroom.

Given the perceived student deficiencies, it is not surprising that teachers
viewed their own responsibility in therapeutic terms: 'My duty is to mould
students into responsible citizens'; 'The teacher's role is to impart knowledge
to the students'; 'Because they do not participate in class activities, I am
compelled to spoon-feed them'. Just like the doctor, the teachers viewed
themselves as charged with the responsibility for restoring to health those
they were in charge of (the students). Students, on their part, appeared
to be willing patients. The descriptions of their own classroom roles and
responsibilities were remarkably consistent with their understanding of
learning as a process of receiving the teacher's knowledge: 'Listening to the
teacher, reading and asking questions where I do not understand, doing
my homework and handing it in on time.' 'We should co-operate with our
teachers and whenever they ask us questions we should always try to answer.'
'To give the teacher the feedback to show that I understand his teaching.'
'Doing the work assigned to us by the teacher.'

The teachers' responsibilities, on the other hand, were described as: 'Giving us work and marking it.' 'Making sure we do our school work'. 'Giving us notes.' 'Clearly explaining things to us.' 'Keeping order in class.' It is interesting to note the symmetry between the way the students described their teachers' and their own responsibilities, and vice versa. For both groups, the teachers' responsibilities are described in terms of making students do something, keeping order, and imparting knowledge. Students' responsibilities are described in terms of listening to the teacher, asking and answering questions, and acquiring knowledge. These are the relationships necessary for the transmission-reception model of learning.

A further consequence of the view of the teacher as therapist was the call for the imposition upon the schoolroom of the teacher's commanding presence' (Jones 1990:71). Teacher visibility, in the image of teaching as a therapeutic exercise, is paramount. And as discussed in the preceding chapter, in the lessons observed, this visibility was heightened by the oblong-shaped classroom architecture and the arrangement of desks in rows and columns, which ensured unobstructed movement for the teacher in the classroom. This ensured that students were under constant surveillance.

However, the surveillance did not always require the teacher's physical enforcement. It appeared that students themselves had internalized the need for surveillance. For example, students characterized teachers who 'teach while seated' and who 'speak slowly' as *majesa*. What has the teacher's teaching while seated, or speaking slowly, to do with whether or not the teacher is doing his or her job 'effectively'? I suggest that in a context in which the teacher's job is perceived in therapeutic terms, the teacher's visibility becomes crucial, and he or she ensures it through both voice and physical projection. If a teacher's visibility is lost (because he or she is seated or speaks slowly), classroom processes may be paralysed, thus deleteriously affecting teaching and learning. The teacher, therefore, has to ensure his or her visibility, both physically and vocally. However, it should be noted that this is not always the result of the teacher's orchestration; the teacher's 'physical' and 'vocal' presence is a demand from the students themselves. Teacher visibility becomes a control mechanism that sustains asymmetrical power relations in the classroom, leading to both the production and reproduction of teacher dominance.

Not only had the students internalized the need for surveillance, they had also internalized their own perceived deficit status, thus reinforcing the teacher's image as therapist. Such internalization ensured that the students took 'responsibility for behaving "appropriately" without the "look" of the teacher' (Gore 1994:116). This was achieved through students turning in 'upon themselves, creating reinforcing gazes among [themselves]' (Anderson and Grinberg 1998:336).

In the classroom this self-regulation is achieved through measures such as peer pressure. In the classes I observed, the students' awareness of their classmates had a profound effect on whether or not they participated in class activities. For example, it was common for students to laugh (in a ridiculing fashion) at those students who had made an attempt at answering the teacher's questions but gave incorrect answers or were struggling with expression in English – not that the laughing students would themselves have given any better answers or expressed themselves better. The laughing rather seemed to express the unpleasant sentiment that, 'Well, this serves you right. You think you are better than us'. Most students interviewed acknowledged that quite often they were inhibited from answering questions from the teacher for fear of being laughed at in case they gave a wrong answer or failed to express themselves well in English. In addition, students disliked fellow students who engaged the teacher in debates and arguments over subject content. Such students were seen as delaying progress and were often accused of posturing to win the teacher's favour, or even pretending to know more than the teacher. This was interpreted as unwarranted questioning of the teacher's authority. Given such an environment, many students withdrew into the safe cocoon of silence. The effect of this withdrawal is clear: the teacher is left to play the dominant role in classroom processes.

The analysis of teacher dominance I have been advancing suggests that the teacher is not entrusted with absolute power that is exercised willy-nilly over students. Rather, the teacher's encounter with students in the classroom engenders relations of power in which both the teacher and students are caught. As Foucault (1977:156) puts it, 'this machine [i.e. the classroom] is one in which everyone is caught, those who exercise power as well as those who are subjected to it'. In the process of this interaction, classroom practice is constructed. The constructed reality thus constitutes a 'shared field' or a mutually agreed 'definition of the situation' (Jones 1997:561). While this 'field' permits the participants' actions, at the same time it limits and regulates the diversity of possible and permissible actions.

Conclusion

Research on teaching in the African context has characterized classroom reality as teacher-centred or teacher-dominated, but deeply embedded in this discourse of teacher-centredness are two assumptions that the research never challenges: first, that it is the teacher who possesses power to influence classroom practices; and secondly, that students are powerless, passive spectators in the production of classroom reality. These assumptions are predicated on the conception of power as a commodity that can be exchanged, traded, transferred, and withheld. It is implausible (if not almost impossible), where such a view of power is held, to conceive of classroom reality as a co-construction, involving both the teacher and students.

However, once researchers adopt the view of power as a productive force (necessarily implying the capacity to act), they come to appreciate that students are active agents who influence their teachers' classroom practices – that far from being an imposition from above, the teacher's apparent dominance is a negotiated product resulting from teachers and students exercising power on one another. The resultant shared, taken-for-granted classroom reality termed 'teacher-centredness' is, therefore, a co-construction. Students are active agents in the construction of teacher-centredness and it is a 'world' whose boundaries they police very effectively. I have sought to show how their perceived deficit status, their expectations of teacher behaviour, and their 'playing possum' influenced teachers to assume the 'dominant' position in lessons. The students' internalization of the need for teacher visibility/surveillance and of their perceived deficit status produced and reproduced teacher dominance. Thus, the taken-for-granted view in classroom research that teacher dominance is an imposition by the teacher needs to be problematised. When classroom practice is viewed as a dialectical co-construction, then what has been termed students' passivity must be recognized as their exercising of power. This study, like that of Willis (1977) on the 'lads', has shown that students exercise their own power to move the lesson in the direction the teacher never intended.

Conceptualizing classroom reality as a co-construction has important implications for the pedagogical reforms currently being implemented in many African countries. In such reform endeavours, no cognizance is taken of the students. This is not only in line with the tacit assumption that students do not make any significant contribution to classroom practice, it is also in line with the linear relationship between teacher behaviour and student learning that technical rationality encourages by suggesting that student classroom behaviour will change as that of the teacher changes. However, this position becomes a fallacy once it is acknowledged that classroom reality (such as 'teacher-centredness') is as much a student construction as it is a teacher construction. It is a reality that validates and imbues the participants' actions with meaning.

5

Social Structure and Pedagogy

Introduction

In classroom research, it is often maintained that culture (i.e. the enveloping social structure) has an effect not only on what is taught in schools but also on how it is taught. For example, researchers have attributed classroom practices to the social structure in which such practices occur (e.g. Yoder and Mautle 1991; Harber 1994; Cleghorn et al. 1989; Fuller and Clarke 1996; Vavrus 2009). It is often stated as an article of faith that the 'oppressive' African culture contributes heavily to the substance and resilience of the teacher-centred pedagogy. Often lacking, however, is an articulation of how exactly the social structure finds its way into the classroom. For example, in the Botswana context, Prophet (1990:114) observes that:

> .... no research appears to have been carried out concerning the extent to which fundamental world-views of Setswana culture reinforce or contradict the views being put forward in schooling.

He goes on to make this pertinent observation:

> .... the quality of learning in the classroom here in Botswana may not be drastically improved by curriculum reform which simply alters the surface features of that which is on offer to the pupils.... The problem is more fundamental and is related to the issues of culture and language (p. 116).

It is clear that at the time of writing these words, Prophet may not have been aware of the anthropological work done by Alverson (1978) which demonstrates the relationship between Tswana child-rearing practices and didactic teaching practices. This oversight notwithstanding, Prophet's observations were apposite in that they demonstrated an awareness of the social/cultural groundedness of teaching and learning – a position that negates technical rationality and all that it stands for. What Prophet is calling for in the statements cited above is the linking of the macro (structural features) and the micro (classroom practice), in particular the following three aspects: the enveloping social structure, education as the transmission of culture, and pedagogical practices in the classroom.

In this chapter I examine aspects of the African social structure, child-rearing practices and pedagogical practice. Salient aspects of social structure are the structures of domination and subordination which govern interpersonal relations and practices in the African context. Child rearing in Africa generally emphasizes the domination and subordination of the child. During both overt and covert socialization, children internalize these structures as their subjective reality which in turn informs their habits of thought and positively orients them towards their society's authority structures. The habits of thought thus engendered are perfectly congruent with the prevailing traditional social structure and are, therefore, essential for the perpetuation and reproduction of the latter. Agents (e.g. teachers and students) who are products of more or less the same objective conditions will tend to share a commonsense world as well as harmonized and homogenized actions and practices. The mode of thought produced through the internalization of these objective conditions is what students and teachers carry to the school situation as their 'cultural baggage'. Teachers and students do not leave this baggage at the school gate. Being part of their 'unconscious' (Bourdieu 1971), they take it with them into the classroom where, through the mediation of pedagogical style, it influences their classroom practices and actions. Viewed in this way, teaching ceases to be a neutral activity that is dislocated from its broader social context (Flanagan 1992). Freire (1972) has argued that education is never a value-neutral activity; it either functions as an instrument for integrating the young into the logic of the present so that they conform to it, or it becomes the practice of freedom. Research on classroom processes in sub-Saharan Africa, as indicated in the previous chapters, clearly shows that education there serves to integrate students into the existing paternalistic social structure, a point emphasized by Harber (1994).

Taking the cosmology of the Tswana of southern Africa as an example, I demonstrate the relationship between the social structure and classroom practices. The reader is encouraged to relate my rendition to their own context as a way of establishing how their own culture interacts with education. I begin by a brief consideration of Bourdieu's thinking on education as a social institution and its role in the transmission of culture. Such explication is necessary if we are to appreciate how schools in the African context and elsewhere for that matter, produce and reproduce the social structure that in the first place shaped them. This will be followed by a consideration of how structures of domination and subordination found in many African contexts are engendered and how ultimately they become part of the consciousness of those inhabiting the structures. It is these structures that the education system reproduces and it is the pedagogical style that connects the school to the enveloping social structure.

Bourdieu on Education and Cultural Transmission

Sociologists (such as Berger and Pullberg 1966; Berger and Luckmann 1967) maintain that we are all born into social structures that predate us and that the whole process of 'becoming', by definition, implies the gradual internalization of the social structure in which one is born. It is only through internalization that one becomes a member of their society, that is, it is only when objective reality has been internalized that we may talk of one as possessing a 'habit of thought' or mode of thinking which is at the basis of their actions and behaviour. Objective structures differ from one society to another and even within the same society, leading to variations in cultural practices. Berger (1963:133) has observed that:

> Each society can be viewed in terms of its social structure and its socio-psychological mechanisms, and also in terms of the world view that serves as the common universe inhabited by its members. World views vary socially, from one society to another and within different segments of the same society. It is in this sense that one says that a Chinese "lives in a different world" from that of a Westerner.

Internalization of the social structure is a function given to the institutions of the family and education system in most societies. It is through the family that the child acquires its 'formative' identity. The school, in later years, shares this responsibility with the family when the child has to spend more than eight hours in each week day away from home, or in the case of secondary education, ten months away in a boarding school. Thus the power of these institutions to shape the identity of the child in many societies cannot be compared to any other institution. Bourdieu (1977:87) captures the mutuality of the family and school when he observes that the disposition 'acquired in the family underlies the structuring of school experiences (in particular the reception and assimilation of the specifically pedagogic message)....'

Through their socialisation function these institutions are heavily implicated in the production and reproduction of the enveloping social structure. For these institutions to carry out this function an 'affinity must exist between the cognitive style [what Bourdieu terms "habit of thought"] of the society and the pedagogical style employed in the schools' (Farquharson 1990: 4). That is, if schools are to effectively mould individuals into desired members of society the pedagogical style used in the schools must be instrumental to the social structure in which the school is located.

Although social structures predate us, they are social constructions in that they are constructed by humans and are essential for human existence (Berger and Luckmann 1967), which means that they have to be maintained and legitimated so as to ensure their continuity and reproduction. In their daily activities, human beings construct society, or more specifically, social structures. As Berger and Pullberg (1966:63) point out, 'Any specific social structure exists only insofar as human beings realize it as part of their world'. Social structures, therefore, have no reality without a human one. A dialectical perspective of social constructions contends that these, through time, tend to assume an independent, objective existence and appear to constrain human actions. That is, social reality becomes objectified and a constraint on action. Structures in this sense then can be defined as 'ideologically based social relationships expressed in an objectivised form' (Giroux 1980:241). For Giddens (1976) structures are series of reproduced practices. The task of sociological theorizing, according to Giddens, is to explain how structures are constituted through action and reciprocally, how action is constituted structurally. Berger and Pullberg (1966:57) put this task of sociological theorizing in a question form: 'How is it possible that subjectively intended meanings become objective facticities?' I do not intend answering this question here; it has been competently addressed by others (see Berger and Luckmann 1967). My interest is in understanding how, once constructed, social structures are maintained and legitimated. Education, being one of the legitimating processes of the social structure, has to function in ways instrumental to the existence of the latter.

Bourdieu argues that the content of the curriculum and the pedagogical style of an education system are determined by the cultural apparatus of which they are part. Farquharson (1990) makes the same point when he states that we can only understand the nature of pedagogical styles by reference to the particular society within which they find expression. In short, teaching methods have social and cultural origins; they are contextual. Bourdieu (1971) attributes the acquisition of a whole system of perception and thought which individuals use in making sense of their society to formal education. Thus, schooling implicitly defines and transmits a culturally-valued 'habit of thought' which Bourdieu (1971) defines as a 'set of basic, deeply interiorized master-patterns' (pp. 192-3) on the basis of which individuals subsequently acquire other patterns. Bourdieu describes culture as a common code that enables all individuals possessing that code to attach the same meaning to the same words and to the same type of behavior. Culture is a 'common set of previously assimilated master-patterns from which an infinite number of individual patterns directly applicable to specific situations are generated' (Bourdieu 1971:192). To emphasise the socialization role of the school, Bourdieu states that its function is:

> consciously (and also, in part, unconsciously) to transmit the unconscious or, to be more precise, to produce individuals equipped with the system of unconscious (or deeply buried) master-patterns that constitute their culture (Bourdieu 1971:194).

The cultural code has two basic elements: a master-pattern (which is closely related to the concept of 'background' as described in the previous chapter) and 'patterns of invention and improvisation' (which is related to the concept of 'foreground') (Bourdieu 1971:192). The relationship between these two elements is a dialectical one, meaning that culture is dynamic. The 'master-pattern' ensures stability and constancy of practices while the 'foreground' permits innovation and improvisation. That is, the existence of the background and foreground is what is responsible for cultural/historical change:

> History culminates in an ongoing and seamless series of moments, and is continuously carried forward in a process of production and reproduction in the practices of everyday life (Jenkins 1992:80)

Through exposure to the education system, the master-pattern becomes deeply internalized as the cognitive style or habit of thought (Farquharson 1990). The master-pattern organizes, for the individual, 'a marked-out area covered with compulsory turnings and one-way streets, avenues and blind alleys' (Bourdieu 1971:196), thus setting limits to what is thinkable and do-able. With limits set by the master-pattern on consciousness and actions, the individual's ability to innovate is likewise constrained. Radical change, because it tends to threaten the stability of the master-pattern, usually is not welcome. For example, innovations that seem to question the teacher's and students' taken-for-granted assumptions about teaching and learning are likely to face tissue rejection.

   If education is involved in the transmission and internalization of a society's habit of thought that is reflective of, and instrumental to the continued existence of the social structure, it is therefore also an agent of the legitimation of the existing social order and its relations of power. Bourdieu (1973:83) states that 'the education system fulfils a function of legitimation which is more necessary to the perpetuation of the social order'. Since it is the 'most effective means of perpetuating the existing social pattern' (Bourdieu 1974:32), education essentially has a conservative function. In this sense, schools are instrumental in maintaining the status quo. If schools are to mould individuals effectively into desired members of society, the pedagogical style used in them must be instrumental to the reproduction of the social structure in which the school is located. Thus, it would be expected that a society that emphasizes structures of domination and subordination of the child in its child-rearing practices would tend to employ a pedagogical style in the schools that is instrumental to the perpetuation of such structures. This position is summarized by Freire (1972:152) in the following words:

> ... a rigid and oppressive social structure necessarily influences the institutions of child-rearing and education within that structure. These institutions pattern their action after the style of the structure, and transmit the myths of the latter. Homes and schools (from nurseries to universities) exist not in abstract, but in time and space.

Bourdieu's explication of the education-society relationship is significant in two ways. First, it demonstrates that the relationship is a symbiotic one in that both education and society, through mediation by the pedagogical style, constitute one another. Secondly, it helps us appreciate the social/cultural embeddedness of pedagogical styles such as teacher-centred and learner-centred pedagogies. Social structures function as support systems for these pedagogies, and the same social structures only allow for the production and reproduction of those classroom practices that are pre-adapted to the same social structures. In other words, social structures set limits to pedagogical change. Thus, reasons for failure to shift teachers' and students' classroom practices from teacher-centredness to learner-centredness for example, should be sought not only from technical factors (such as lack of resources and time, large student-teacher ratios, and poorly trained teachers), but also from the surrounding social structures (Farquharson 1990).

How, then, can this framework help us understand not only the social/cultural genesis of the teacher-centred pedagogy in the African context, but also its resilience? This is the question we attempt to answer in the remaining sections of this chapter. I borrow heavily from Alverson's (1978) anthropological study of the Tswana of southern Africa to illustrate how the social structures of domination and subordination find their way into African classrooms. Alverson attributes these structures to Tswana cosmology which is not markedly different from what other scholars (e.g. Mbiti 1969) have said about African cosmology in general.

Tswana Cosmology as a Variant of African Cosmology

This section begins with a note of caution – what follows should not be read to mean that Tswana society is static and homogeneous; far from it. In addition to changes due to its own internal dynamics, Tswana society has changed as a result of increasing contact with other cultures. This has affected its internal structures. Africa's long colonial history ensured adoption/adaption of institutional structures and values of modern, structurally differentiated societies of the West. Thus Tswana values exist side-by-side with imported Western values. This has profoundly altered traditional structures such as child rearing. However, this should not be read to mean that the habit of thought engendered by earlier 'traditional' social structures has also been profoundly changed. There is no one-to-one correspondence between social structures and habits of thought. Indigenous values, practices or generally, ways of doing things are known to have resisted powerful forces of urbanization, education and industrialization, forces that have obliterated social structures in some instances. For example, 'revolutions' such as the Scientific Revolution of the seventeenth century which ushered in modern science, profoundly changed social structures but took centuries to shake habits of thought. Butterfield (1949) contends that although modern science overthrew the ancient world and the Middle Ages and replaced them by a new world view, this was just the beginning of a process which was to take hundreds of years, and is not complete even now. He explains this resilience of the 'old' world view in this way:

> Our [the West's] Graeco-Roman roots and Christian heritage were so profound – so central to our thinking – that it has required centuries of pulls and pressures, and almost a conflict of civilizations in our midst, to make clear that the centre had long ago shifted (Butterfield 1949:189)

Thus, the introduction of new structures to replace existing ones does not necessarily change profoundly the way people in a society think or do things. These established ways of doing things have evolved over hundreds of years and it may take as many years to change them. In the same vein, although colonialism and other forces of modernity have altered structural features of Tswana society, some have remained relatively stable, for example, structures of child domination and subordination. However, even these are being altered as a result of increased differentiation within Tswana society engendered by forces of urbanisation and formal education, leading in some segments of society to more democratic child-rearing practices. For example, we see increasing differentiation along social class lines, meaning that socialization practices will tend to differ from one social class to the other, leading to variations in habits of thought. This is so because – and this is a general rule of thumb – individuals occupying the same positions within the social world will tend to share a world view. In a differentiated society, therefore, people will tend to differ in their habits of thought according to their social class. As DiMaggio (1979:1464) puts it:

> To the extent that members of different social classes differ in the nature of their primary socialization…. each class has its own characteristics [habit of thought] with individual variations.

That said, we must always bear in mind that individual and class habits of thought are but structural variants of the collective habit of thought which acts as the 'canopy' of society, giving rise to a structure plausible to all individuals well-integrated into society. Thus, although contemporary Tswana society may be characterised by segmentation (in terms of rural-urban areas, social class, etc.) there are nevertheless 'overarching reality definitions' (Berger et al. 1974:21) which hold the whole society together and give its members a shared frame of reference. It is precisely this frame of reference which maintains institutional order. The kinship system is one such overarching structure in Tswana society, and is underpinned by the principles of lineage membership, sex and age. In the socialization of children, age and sex have always served as common denominators, not just among the Tswana, but among Bantu-speaking people in general. Age, however, cuts across all other positional factors such as gender, ethnicity, social class and so forth (for a superb discussion of socialization on the basis of gender in Tswana society, see Mafela 1993; Alverson 1978 and Schapera 1941). One cannot overemphasise the centrality of the principle of age in Tswana socialization. Without a clear conceptualization of this principle, particularly its intersection with the Tswana conception of time, it is doubtful if socialization practices of the Tswana can be understood. The intersection is critical in that it leads to social hierarchy based on age which in turn structures socialization practices.

The Tswana Conception of Age and Time: The determinate Intersection

At the centre of Alverson's rendition of Tswana cosmology is the factor of 'age'. Great emphasis in Tswana society is put on kinship as the basis on which political, judicial, economic and religious aspects of society are organised (Alverson 1978: 12). Embedded in the kinship concept are three important principles for recruitment to social roles. These are sex, age of the individual relative to that of another (senior versus junior), and lineage membership. Of the three, age is the most relevant to our study and shall later be considered in more detail. It will be demonstrated that the structures of domination and subordination in Tswana, and indeed in African society in general, emanate directly from the social importance accorded to age. Suffice it to say at this stage that age has been recognised by anthropologists such as Alverson and Schapera as one of the important ranking criteria in Tswana society. In this regard, Alverson observes that in Tswana society 'any senior of the same sex is one's superior and any junior of the same sex one's subordinate' (1978:13). Traditionally, ranking by age was elaborated in a system of age-sets or age-regiments. These are common amongst almost all Bantu-speaking people of southern Africa. Bray et al. (1986) also observe that age-sets are pervasive in Africa in general. Age-sets amongst the Tswana were based upon tribe-wide groupings of men and women who came to maturity at about the same time. They remained in their age-regiments throughout their lives. They remained deferential towards age-sets of their seniors and expected the same from junior age-sets. Already we can see that Tswana social hierarchy and interpersonal relations have always been regulated by a rigid, paternalistic structure, and this same authority structure pervaded traditional education which was, to say the least, training in conformity.

Age and ageing cannot be adequately conceptualised if their temporal dimension is ignored. It is essential to grasp the intersection of age and time and, how it, in the context of the Tswana, influences their child-rearing practices. This is because for the Tswana, ageing is not just the mere progression of the biological being through universal linear time.

Mbiti (1969:21) observes that the 'linear concept of time in Western thought, with an indefinite past, present and infinite future, is practically foreign to African thinking'. Traditionally, time is a two-dimensional phenomenon, with a long past, a present, and virtually no future. Taking off from this basic premise, Alverson (1978:170) also characterises Tswana time as two dimensional, comprising what he terms 'existing time' and 'cosmologic time'. The two conceptions of time are co-ordinated and are essential for our understanding of Tswana 'lived time', that is, age and ageing. Alverson describes 'cosmologic time' as progressive, atemporal and eternally present. The Tswana believe that the 'cosmos' had a beginning and that beginning continues throughout cosmologic time, hence it is always present. Existing time, on the other hand, has two aspects; world time and ancestral time, and it is a union of the two, with world time being finite. For the Tswana therefore, age and ageing cannot be conceived of as the progression through the linear and homogeneous time of the Western world. Age for the Tswana, Alverson (1978:170) argues, has its basis 'in a set of social and ancestral relationships'. Social order in this sense is in both the world of the living and of the dead, the latter being closest to the origins of society. Age is one's relation to this social order. Ageing, defined as a movement towards death, is simultaneously a movement towards the origins of society, a movement towards the beginning. In this sense, an individual's age is defined in terms of their nearness to the ancestors.

Inextricably linked to age is the accumulation of experience. The amount of experience one accumulates is directly dependent on one's age. Experience in this context is the depth of one's knowledge of the past, towards which the future is moving. As Alverson (1978) puts it:

> .... for the Tswana aging is a simultaneous movement in two directions from the centre: to a primordial past which is the goal of the future and to the end of one's future, which is defined in terms of experience accumulated while alive (p. 170).

In Tswana cosmology, both children (because of their recent arrival from the world of the ancestors) and the very old are spiritually closest to the ancestors, 'to the final order' which is also the beginning of their society. Now, this brings us to the significance of growth. Growth of the biological being from childhood has the adverse effect of cutting it off from its closeness to the ancestors. However, continued growth to old age increases the individual's closeness to the ancestors, that is, to the past which is also the beginning. It is precisely this understanding of 'growth' that structures the child-adult relationship among the Tswana. Although the child and the old share their closeness to the final order, the latter has an edge over the former; the child's closeness to the origins of society is only defined in terms of its recent 'arrival' from the world of ancestors, whereas the old man/woman is wise both because (s)he is growing closer to the ancestors, and because during his/her occupation of a position in the world, (s)he has accumulated knowledge through experience compared to the child. This puts the child in an inherently subordinate position vis-à-vis the adult. Practically, the child may never accumulate as much knowledge as the elders in the whole of its life. For this reason, the child must always learn from the elders. This must be so because for the Tswana 'knowledge' is 'remembering things past' (Alverson 1978:171), and compared to their elders, children have little to remember.

Tswana understanding of life is that it is not a 'race against time'. Living is an accumulation of time and engenders wisdom which is equated to knowledge. The more time one accumulates, that is, the longer one lives, the wiser a person is considered to be. Ageing, therefore, is synonymous with increased wisdom. For this reason, it is not surprising that the oldest in Tswana society are normally the most influential and command great respect. Their experience/knowledge is supposedly deep because it has been accumulated over a long period of time. On the contrary, children have a shorter past and, therefore, a shallower life experience compared to the elders because they have not accumulated as much time. As a direct result of this, the Tswana in general feel that there is very little of value that an elder can learn from his/her junior.

It is clear from the foregoing discussion that age and time intersect in determinate ways. The subordinate status of children means that the Tswana regard them as a 'deficit system', to use Esland's (1971:89) terminology. One must emphasise that this subordinate status of children in Tswana society is not only in relation to their elders, but is also in relation to knowledge. The child, therefore, has no capacity to constitute the world and must be initiated into it by 'knowledgeable' elders. Thus, Tswana society emphasises structures of domination and subordination of the child both to the elders and to knowledge. Children are exposed to these authority structures quite early in their lives. These structures of domination and subordination are internalised by children during primary socialisation as their subjective reality, giving rise to a form of consciousness we may term the 'dependent' mode of thinking. This mode of thinking is compatible with Tswana social structure and is essential for the latter's continuity, maintenance and reproduction. It is this mode of thinking that children take with them into classroom as their cultural baggage; it helps structure classroom social relations.

Tswana children are brought up in a way that respects age and its many prerogatives. Children are taught that obedience to and respect for the elders is very important. It is for this reason that Alverson (1978:68) has described Tswana child rearing as 'training in deference'. Child rearing in Tswana culture involves instruction in matters of 'propriety, morality and character'. The emphasis is on self control, respect for others, obedience to elders, courtesy and generosity. As Alverson (1978:68) observes of Tswana culture; '[m]uch of child training consists in imparting the etiquette that an older individual (doing the instruction) feels should govern how a junior person acts toward a senior person.'

Children are expected to learn and appreciate their responsibilities towards their seniors. The Tswana are known to be '... rigid and authoritarian disciplinarians who enjoy teaching legalistic dos and don'ts in manners of public decorum, etiquette and role obligations' (Alverson 1978:68). Children are taught from an early age values and attitudes related to collectivism (which is related to the extended family) and submission to authority. Even Western-educated prominent African personalities have expressed the social valuation of collectivism and ascriptive authority. Jomo Kenyatta, the late President of Kenya, expressed this view five decades ago: 'To the European, individuality is the ideal of life, to the Africans, the ideal is the right relations with, and behaviour to, other people' (Kenyatta 1961:122).

This is the sort of culture Tswana children are inducted into during primary socialisation. It constitutes their objective, taken-for-granted world. The socialisation practices engendered by such a world ensure its continuity and reproduction. As a way of legitimising this social world, a whole universe of ritual practices, discourses, sayings, stories, maxims and proverbs is employed to make sure that the child does not stray away from the socially-patterned form of behaviour. A well-socialised Tswana child, therefore, is expected to obey legitimate instructions and requests, to follow the *'canons of decorum and etiquette',* and to have learnt the duties and rights of one's station in life (Alverson 1978:69). All these customs and practices go a long way in teaching young children who they are and what their limited rights are before they enter the classroom (Kay 1975; Apple 1990). Before the child enters the first year of primary school, these values have been firmly impressed in the mind. The practices help the child establish a frame of reference by which to approach systems s/he will later encounter, and this includes the classroom as a system.

Tswana Child-rearing Practices and Formal Education: The link

An important offshoot of Tswana child-rearing practices is the rigid, domineering and one-sided child-adult relationship. Such a relationship, Freire (1972) argues, usually reflects the objective cultural conditions of the surrounding social structure which penetrate the home environment. He goes on to argue that the home atmosphere is carried over to the school 'where the students soon discover that (as in the home) in order to achieve some satisfaction they must adapt to the precepts which have been set from above' (Freire 1972:153). Students come to 'fear freedom', to 'learn not to think', thus reinforcing their cultural image of a deficit system or empty vessels. When these young people become professionals (e.g. teachers) they will tend to reproduce the rigid patterns in which they were educated. In this way, the dominant authority structure is legitimated and the culture of dependency on the part of the students augmented, with the resultant effect of reinforcing the teachers' social roles as authorities. The end result, once again, is the cultural reproduction of authoritarian teaching practices.

Alverson (1978) discerns a direct link between Tswana child-rearing practices and formal education in Botswana. He sees formal education in Botswana as a perfect analogue of Tswana patterns of child rearing. The learner learns by rote and is punished for errors, mistakes and general incompetence. Teachers clearly see themselves as figures of authority. Alverson (1978:69) observes that in Botswana:

> There is no conception, like that currently in vogue in the Anglo-Saxon world, of developing "the whole personality" by means of self-discovery . . . of rewarding exploratory or innovative behaviour even if it is absurd to the adults.

To be innovative and critical is actively discouraged by the rote learning approach. Spontaneity, creativity, self-reliance and autonomy are stifled. A good student must show docility, obedience and submissiveness towards his/ her teacher. It is significant to note how this resonates with educational thinking in nineteenth century Europe, although as we saw in Chapter Three, there such education was aimed at 'civilising' the 'depraved' working class children.

In a different study, Alverson (1977) claims to have heard American Peace Corp Volunteers (PCV) complaining about the authoritarian and domineering approach to teaching of their Tswana colleagues. A connected complaint was the PCVs' inability to get the students to 'think critically and independently'. Many of the PCVs, as Alverson (1978:69) puts it:

> ... go to Botswana imbued with a Summerhill-type world view in which their goal is to help the Tswana "find themselves" and discover the rich experience of creative self-expression.

However, these ambitions are shattered both by the Botswana education system and the response of most Tswana students who want clear instructions as to what is expected of them and clear standards by which they must perform (Alverson 1977). What the PCVs are expressing is indicative of a 'collision of consciousnesses'. Coming from a different socio-cultural setting where values different from those of the Tswana are cherished, they find it difficult to cope and innovate in their new setting. This may also mean that an attempt to promote a 'Summerhill-type world view' in Botswana schools may be resisted by teachers and students, for this would be incompatible with their habit of thought. In fact, a qualitative study by Prophet and Rowell (1993:207) indicated that teachers, students, parents and school administrators in Botswana public schools are generally happy with the qualities of these teacher-dominated classroom interactions and see no need for change. For example, the parents I interviewed in the course of this study indicated that 'showing traditional respect' towards their teachers was a prerequisite for the students' learning and success in their examinations. Showing respect meant a number of things to parents. It meant students not challenging the authority of the teacher (as discussed in Chapter Four), not criticizing their teachers, dutifully carrying out instructions from teachers, and having the 'correct' attitude towards their elders. Parents also expected the school to have a restraining effect on their children; they expected the school to play the same functions as the family. So, when they 'handed over' their children to the school they expected teachers to treat them the same way they themselves treated them at home. This tended to put a lot of pressure on the students to be submissive, at the same time empowering teachers to act as domineering figures.

Harmony in the teachers', students', parents' and administrators' perceptions of classroom practice may be explained by recourse to the fact that being products of the same objective conditions, the practices of the four groups of participants are immediately mutually intelligible and predictable. This leads to teachers' and students' homogenised pedagogical expectations of the other. They live in a well-established, taken-for-granted, commonsensical classroom 'world' in which both hold tacit assumptions about issues of curriculum, assessment and pedagogy. This common-sense world, coupled with years of classroom experience, makes both the teacher and students have very specific expectations of each other. For example, students expect teachers to be certain in their behaviour and subject knowledge. They expect them to maintain control, enforce rules and present the curriculum (Britzman 1986). Any deviation by the teachers from this traditional image is articulated by both students (as we saw in the preceding chapter) and administrators, and even also by other teachers.

The discussion above leaves no doubt that the pedagogical style (which most research has identified as teacher-centred) employed in the transmission of school knowledge in many African contexts is instrumental to the existing social structure in which the child is dominated and subordinated. It is in this relationship to adults and to knowledge that the child can become a fully integrated member of this society. The point has been made that teaching style mediates the classroom and the wider social structure, that is, it is through the pedagogical style that the social structure finds expression in the classroom setting (Farquharson 1990). As the school has to reproduce the social structure (with its emphasis on the domination and subordination of the child) it has to employ a style of pedagogy that best serves the process of 'filling' the children with knowledge. It is only fair to say that the transmission-reception pedagogical style in Botswana and elsewhere in Africa has now become institutionalised as an educational tradition, leaving very little room for alternative pedagogies such as learner-centredness. However, as King (1989) argues, once a pedagogical style has become embedded in a society it becomes resilient to changes in government, major curriculum reform or even changes in teacher training. In short, this pedagogy is now institutionalized; it constitutes a pedagogical paradigm and for this reason it is difficult to dislodge. The resistance of teachers, students and administrators to pedagogical change in Botswana and the sub-Saharan African region generally may, therefore, be explained by arguing that they are operating within 'normal science' (which is the banking- education pedagogical paradigm) and see no need for a 'paradigm shift' to the learner-centred pedagogical paradigm. Banking education constitutes their plausibility structure. Attempts to make this structure implausible by introducing an innovation which requires them to operate in a different paradigm can only result in the tissue rejection of that innovation by the participants. This observation buttresses the argument made in Chapter Three that paradigms have implications for pedagogical change.

Linkage of a pedagogical paradigm to the enveloping structure implicitly suggests that dislodging this pedagogical paradigm may require fundamental changes in the social structure itself, in particular, child-rearing practices. However, changing the latter, as has been argued above, is a very slow and difficult process. Because of its neglect of the socio-culturally embedded nature of pedagogy the technicist approach to pedagogical change cannot be expected to be effective in altering the classroom practices of both teachers and students.

Conclusion

This chapter has argued that Tswana child-rearing practices are structured in accordance with the structures of domination and subordination, leading to the production of a compatible habit of thought. It is this habit of thought which children and teachers internalize as their subjective reality and which they use to make sense of the world that surrounds them. It is this same habit of thought which they carry to the classroom situation as their cultural baggage and which in turn informs their classroom practice, classroom practical knowledge and their assumptions about pedagogy and curriculum. Effectively, this means that pedagogical assumptions are social in that they derive from the existing social structure and are therefore socio-culturally determined. It is in this sense that we talk of the socio-cultural context as a constraint on teachers' and students' classroom actions and as setting parameters for change. Schools as agents of reproduction of the social structure have to employ a pedagogical style instrumental to the continued existence of that structure. In the African context, banking education is the pedagogical paradigm that is compatible with the social structure. That is, the teacher-centred pedagogical style is simultaneously engendered by and instrumental to the continued existence of the social structure. A fundamentally different pedagogical style, such as learner-centredness, is most likely to face tissue rejection in this socio-cultural context. This rejection cannot just be explained away in terms of technical issues (e.g. the resource scarcity thesis discussed in Chapter One) associated with the delivery of the innovation. The problem is more fundamental since it is related to the issue of culture. For this reason then, when explanations are being sought for the rejection by teachers and students of pedagogical innovations, the socio-cultural context should not be neglected.

6

Post-independence Educational Planning and Classroom Practice

Introduction

Chapter Five posited that the objective conditions of the socio-cultural environment permit the production and reproduction of human practices. This means that in every context where reproduction is possible, there must be certain stable elements which allow both production and reproduction of stable practices to take place. If there were no such elements, reproduction would be extremely difficult. The same logic pertains to pedagogical styles as human practices. We can argue that the production and reproduction of teaching methods that are associated with the banking-education pedagogical paradigm in public schools in Botswana and Africa in general is sustained by certain stable elements in the socio-cultural ambiance. In the words of Bartlett (1991:24):

> Persistent actions require a set of stabilised elements or set of conditions which allow the actions themselves to be reproduced. The elements or conditions are defined as social structure...

What then are the stabilized elements or conditions that allow the persistence of teacher-centred methods in the African context? They include the dominant objectivist view of knowledge and the structures of domination and subordination. I would like to add to these the utilitarian view of schooling/education engendered by manpower planning, the education system's (centralized or decentralized) organizational structure and, lastly, curricula arrangements. The latter is discussed in detail in Chapter Eight. In this chapter,

I concentrate on the first two. These stabilized elements, being aspects of the socio-cultural context, inform teachers' and students' classroom practices. Because they are part of the immunological condition of the environment, they have implications for pedagogical change. Overlooking their potential as barriers to pedagogical innovation in favour of a technicist stance may lead to innovation rejection.

Human Resource Planning in the Post-1966 era

Britain's indifferent attitude towards native education was to have a profound effect on Botswana. At independence in 1966, Botswana found itself with a poorly developed educational infrastructure with which to support the country's expanding administrative services. The government's priority, therefore, became the expansion of educational provision in order to meet the country's human resource development needs. Vanqa (1989:28) clearly captures this dire situation:

> To read the story of education and its development in Botswana after 1966 is to read the story of manpower (sic) needs for an emerging country. When Botswana gained her independence from Britain, it became crucial for the country to have a viable programme to produce manpower (sic) to cater for the growing social, economic and administrative services.

This human resource development-oriented educational planning of post-independence Botswana had pedagogical consequences. The mode of planning may have assisted in perpetuating the pedagogical style which had a foundation laid by traditional and missionary education. The mode of planning led to the development of a *utilitarian perception* of education – the view that education/schooling is an important vehicle for social mobility. This view of education promotes the liberal myth that everyone has the chance to climb the social ladder through education, that is, by passing examinations. It is not an overstatement to say that in Botswana and indeed sub-Saharan Africa as a whole there is no conception of education other than the utilitarian one. It pervades most aspects of schooling. It is often reflected in school logos and mottos, which are imprinted on the badges of students' school uniforms as a constant reminder that through education they will ultimately be able to lead better lives. For example, take this motto from one of the schools studied: '*Thuto ke thobo ya Bokamoso*', translated as '*Education is a harvest for the future*'. This 'harvest' is none other than an economic one. The utilitarian view is shared by teachers, students and parents. Davies (1988:300), in an ethnographic study of two senior secondary schools in Botswana, reported this 'extraordinary congruence in the aims of teachers and students'. Whether this utilitarian view of education/schooling is realistic or misplaced is not the concern here. Instead, the concern is the effect of this conception of education on teachers' and students' understanding of teaching and learning.

Botswana's economic growth rate increased significantly after independence in 1966, from 7 percent per year at independence to 15 percent per year at the end of the 1960s (Colclough and McCarthy 1980:57). Between 1966 and 1974, two important mines – Orapa (diamonds) and Selibe-Phikwe (copper/nickel) – were opened, increasing both public and private sector employment. A desperate situation developed in which job opportunities were increasing but with very few qualified citizens to take them up. Securing a clerical job depended on one holding a certificate. There developed a quest for certificates, and consequently, for the education that provided this result.

In no way is it being suggested that this craving for certificates was an exclusively post-independence phenomenon. In fact, it is interesting to see how the colonial administration's policy of recruiting locals encouraged this yearning for certificates. At the time of colonial administration, Africans were denied the opportunity to occupy important positions in the administrative structures. This was often justified by arguing that they 'lacked the formal qualifications of European incumbents' (Gossett 1986:304). It was to be expected that many individual Batswana would begin to aim at obtaining equivalent qualifications. As Cooper (1982) observes, salaries depended directly on academic qualifications. In view of the recurring droughts and the limits on the numbers of migrant labourers going to South African mines, employment in the colonial administration became the only viable means of leading a better life. That education paid dividends was conspicuously clear to everyone. An African bureaucrat in the colonial administration was much better off than the peasant. Better income for the African bureaucrat (as compared to the peasant) was often justified by pointing to the importance of education as qualification. Sir Richard Ramage, who was appointed in 1961 to review the structures of the public services in Basutoland (present-day Lesotho), Bechuanaland (Botswana) and Swaziland, justified the big gap in earnings between the African bureaucrat and the peasant by arguing that the gap 'provides the inducement to the peasant to educate his children so as to qualify them in that respect for a higher standard of living than that of the parents' (1961:13-14).

Education/schooling (and a certificate) naturally came to be seen as the gateway to procuring a job, and as a result, a better life, not just for oneself, but for one's parents as well. The term 'qualification' became a catchword. Even securing a clerical job in the formal sector depended on one holding a required minimum qualification. Education became synonymous with certification. This situation prevails today and has led to an even greater quest for certificates, a syndrome Dore (1976) describes in his book, *The Diploma Disease*. Gossett (1986:307) describes the current situation in Botswana in the following words:

> In recruiting administrative personnel, Botswana makes extensive use of certificates. Direct entry to any but the lowest levels of the service has been tied to possession of a particular certificate…. few applicants or hiring officials seem to expect many without the proper certificate to achieve a higher rank. At least since independence, Botswana has viewed education as a way to provide individuals with the certificates, and hopefully the skills to fill various occupations in the public and private sector.

It is also one's level of education that determines the level of entry and progress in the labour market:

> And since there are few alternative patterns of mobility in Botswana access to the most senior and financially rewarding positions in the occupational structure became more and more dependent upon the certifying functions of schools and hence upon examination success. The certificate thus becomes the major filter, determining life chances and the more external the examination is the more the allocation appears objective and just" (Francis 1979:7).

The higher the demand for certificates, the more competitive and selective examinations become. Education, therefore, becomes a vehicle for social mobility. Francis (1979) has employed Turner's (1961) classificatory framework of modes of ascent, specifically 'sponsored' and 'contest' mobility, to explain the selective nature of education in Botswana. Sponsored mobility is a controlled selection process. As Francis (1979:8) puts it, 'Mobility is neither won nor seized but rather is a process of sponsored induction into the elite subsequent upon selection'. Contest mobility, on the other hand, implies that there is a competition open to all on an equal footing, with victory being gained by one's own efforts:

> The governing objective of contest mobility is to give elite status to those who earn it, while the goal of sponsored mobility is to make the best use of the talents in society by sorting each person into his proper niche (Turner 1961:123).

Francis concludes that the educational system in Botswana closely approximates Turner's model of sponsored mobility, the major selection criterion being success in school examinations. Human resource projections by the government determine the number of students entering post-secondary schooling each year. Only a minority of students who take the Senior Certificate examinations proceeds to tertiary level institutions. Human resource planning, therefore, has reinforced the sponsored mobility system. The former has also restricted educational opportunities but has at the same time greatly rewarded success (by way of high salaries). Such a system promotes the liberal myth that everyone has the chance of climbing the social ladder through education, that is, by passing examinations. The 'backwash' effects of such a view of education are clear. Teaching/learning become geared towards preparing students for the examinations. In the classroom, the tendency is for the teacher to emphasise factual information which can be communicated to the students in a didactic fashion.

Classroom research studies reviewed in Chapter One overwhelmingly reveal that teachers in sub-Saharan Africa see their job as one of mainly imparting and delivering school knowledge and keeping order in the classroom. Conversely, students see their own role as that of receiving the teachers' knowledge. Parents, on their part, see the role of students as one of listening to and carrying out the teachers' orders. These views, in addition to shaping classroom practice, produce certain pressures on the school, on teachers and on students. The school is under pressure from the state and the general public to produce good results; the teacher is under double pressure from parents and the school administration to produce good results; students are under pressure from parents to do well. These pressures give rise to implicit views on teaching and learning. If the role of the teacher is perceived as that of providing knowledge then his/her duty is to 'teach'. Where the role of the student is to receive knowledge, then her/his duty is to 'learn' by assimilating the knowledge provided by the teacher. The best teaching method in this context becomes one that is thought most likely to produce the best examinations results. If teachers see their primary task as that of helping students pass examinations, the tendency is to teach for the examination. If students in turn equate schooling with passing examinations, the tendency is to expect the teacher to 'spoon-feed' them to pass the examinations. Ultimately, the emphasis in teaching and learning is placed on facts and learning by rote, the sort of 'right-answerism' discussed in Chapter Three.

Jones (1989:27) argues that a 'positive view of school is coupled with particular ideas about how to go about acquiring the necessary credentials'. Interviews with students, teachers and parents revealed that these groups held a strong, utilitarian view of education/schooling and the view promoted and sustained a transmission-reception pedagogical style.

Teachers' Perspectives on Schooling/Education

Teachers understood schooling in terms such as: 'Schooling prepares our students for the future, for different vocations in society.' 'Schooling is meant to prepare students for certificates so that they can have a career to follow.' 'The whole aim of schooling is for one to have a brighter future, find a job and live better.' Because of this vocational view of schooling, all the teachers interviewed had one main future expectation of their students – for them to pass their Cambridge Overseas School Certificate (COSC) examinations and go on to further education which would then guarantee them well-paid jobs. The teachers' classroom activities, therefore, revolved around preparing their students for the COSC examinations. In the teachers' view, the schools possessed the curriculum knowledge which the students needed in order to pass their examinations. Their main duty as teachers was to ensure that their students acquired the curriculum knowledge. It is not surprising, therefore, that teachers described their own classroom roles and responsibilities in terms such as, 'My foremost responsibility is to impart knowledge and to manage the class, making sure there is order'. 'My role is to deliver the goods to the students. I have to make sure that I give them notes, and I have to test their understanding by assessing them.' 'The main role of the teacher is to teach students and also to get feedback from students through tests and assignments.' If the pattern of school work was centred on the teacher, with control being of prime concern to the teacher, then only paternalistic student-teacher relationships could be expected. Teachers made it clear in staff room gossip that they expected deference and subservience from students.

Conversely, students' roles were described as those of acquiring and assimilating knowledge. Furthermore, teaching was described in terms of giving out and imparting school knowledge. Learning, on the other hand, was described in terms of acquiring and assimilating knowledge. The pedagogic implications of this schism between teaching and learning are discussed below.

Students' Perspectives on Schooling/Education

Like their teachers, the students interviewed saw schooling/education in purely utilitarian terms. Their learning activities had a single goal: to enable them to pass their COSC examinations so as to obtain a certificate that would subsequently enable them to either go on to further education or join the (shrinking) labour market. 'I want to acquire knowledge so that I can be marketable in future.' 'I want to get the necessary grades that will allow me to pursue a course at the tertiary level of education.' 'I want to gain knowledge and a certificate. I want to attain credits in all subjects so that I may get a certificate.'

All the students interviewed stressed that they could only obtain the necessary credentials for furthering their education or getting a well-paid job by 'working hard'. Asked to elaborate on what they understood by working hard the students mentioned the following: 'Doing work assigned by the teacher.' 'Following teacher instructions.' 'Revising work done with the teacher.' 'Listening attentively to the teacher.' 'Reading extensively.' 'Asking and answering questions.' It was by being engaged in such activities that the students felt they were gaining the school knowledge that they needed to get the certificates. It was also clear from the students' statements that school knowledge more or less meant the same thing as the teacher's knowledge. Since it was the teacher who possessed school knowledge, these students saw their primary task as that of receiving the teacher's knowledge. This receiving of the teacher's knowledge constituted their understanding of doing school work: 'Doing school work means doing what the teacher says you must do and cooperating with teachers and other students in class activities.' 'It means being taught by the teacher in class, doing practicals and reading privately.' 'Reading and obtaining as much information from the teacher in the form of exercises and notes.' 'Studying by yourself and asking the teacher when you do not understand.' It was the students' understanding of *doing school work as receiving* the teacher's knowledge that helped them define their own as well as the teachers' roles and responsibilities in class. This was also a view shared by parents who also believed that students acquired school knowledge by listening and carrying out orders from the teacher and by studying hard.

The utilitarian view causes a significant schism between teaching and learning. As we have just seen from the empirical study, there is a tendency to view these as two distinct but inextricably related activities. They are often viewed as converse terms. One becomes meaningless without the other. This teach-learn converse places the teacher in a very powerful position and it also serves to demarcate role boundaries between the teacher and the students. The teacher 'teaches' and the student 'learns'. Paradoxically, this distinction also describes a relationship, and one that indicates the direction of the flow of information in the classroom: from the teacher to the learner. Such a relationship is in perfect harmony with the banking theory of education. Because in this theory, teaching and learning are mechanistic and deductive processes, it is inevitable that emphasis in the classroom would be placed on fact-learning and rote-learning. Interactive teaching/learning methods (such as group discussions and role play) which characterize a learner-centred pedagogy come to be viewed as dysfunctional in that they are not perceived as being directly related to the passing of examinations, and also that they deprive the learners of an opportunity to apply their rote-learning skills (Holliday 1991). This is a critical point because to these students, learning by rote is not necessarily perceived as a burden, but rather as an asset because it is directly related to their utilitarian view of schooling. Hence the observation by Prophet and Rowell (1993) that teachers, students and school administrators in Botswana are generally happy with the quality of teacher-dominated classroom interactions.

Also, it would be unreasonable to expect teachers to see anything wrong with emphasizing facts and rote learning. After all, this kind of learning worked well for them, hence their privileged position in society. If it worked for them then there is no reason why it should not work for the students as well. Moreover, to the majority of local teachers this is the only form of learning and teaching they know of. Research shows that teachers are conservative. Lortie (1975) argues that teachers have never left the classroom. As students, they internalized certain models of teacher behaviour so they tend to emulate those models in their teaching.

Implications of the Utilitarian view for Pedagogical Change

The views of education held by parents, teachers and students have implications for classroom practice, and ultimately, for pedagogic change. Innovations that seem to be working against those views may not be acceptable to classroom participants. I have made an attempt to demonstrate how the state's human resource development policy might have helped to promote a utilitarian view of education. The empirical study also revealed that students and their teachers saw education as a means to an end, this being in line with a utilitarian view of education. What the empirical study was not able to establish conclusively though, was that these conceptions (of teachers and students) were necessarily or directly shaped by government policy on human resources development. But because the policy encourages the utilitarian view of education, it is plausible to postulate that it might have helped shape teachers', students' and parents' perspectives on teaching and learning. These perspectives, as I have argued above, might have evolved as antithetical to the learner-centred pedagogy that is advocated in both *Education for Kagisano* (Social Harmony) (1977) and the *Revised National Policy on Education* (RNPE) (1994) but quite compatible with the demands of the banking education pedagogy. The latter demands the separation of the subject of the learning process from its object, that is, it encourages the teach-learn converse, thus a deductive approach to teaching/learning. Learner-centred pedagogy, on the other hand, demands the blurring of the subject-object, teach-learn dichotomies and encourages an inductive approach to learning. It demands that the teacher acts as a facilitator in the students' learning process and that the latter be active participants in their own learning. To expect teachers and students to shift from the banking-education pedagogical style to a learner-centred one is necessarily to expect them to make a paradigm shift. However, they may not be prepared to do this as it would have a destabilizing effect on their taken-for-granted classroom world, possibly leading to deskilling and cognitive dissonance. The shift might also be made difficult by the fact that these teachers and students might know very little or nothing at all about the inductive approach. Barjesteh and Holliday, as cited in Holliday (1991:346) argue that:

> Students who seem to have been brought up on the deductive approach . . . want superficial knowledge (to learn) for the examinations (through which) they want to move quickly and are unwilling to discuss and explore.

This emphasis upon examinations (hence on the deductive approach), as I have already stated, is inextricably tied to the utilitarian perception of education/schooling. It now becomes easy to understand why and how the utilitarian view of education may act as a buffer to pedagogic change. This means that for as long as this view of schooling prevails, it will continue promoting deductive approaches that are antithetical to the inductive, learner-centred approaches advocated in major education policy texts. The utilitarian view of education, therefore, constitutes a stabilized element in Africa which allows for the production and reproduction of teaching/learning methods closely associated with banking education. It gives meaning to the teachers' and students' day-to-day classroom practices. It exists as an objective condition which students, teachers and parents have internalized as part of their mode of thinking or consciousness, and it sets parameters within which they may innovate, while at the same time giving rise to spontaneous practices that are pre-adapted to it and taken for granted by teachers and students. In short, the utilitarian view of education is part and parcel of the immunological condition of the educational environment in Botswana, and in Africa generally. Pedagogical innovations such as those proposed in many countries in Africa have to comply with this condition or risk tissue rejection. This appears to have been the fate of the learner-centred pedagogy advocated by the two commissions on education in Botswana. The historical and empirical evidence indicates that the authoritarian pedagogical style that characterizes classroom practice in Botswana schools to such an extent evolved over a long period of time and is now part of the immunological condition of the education system. Pedagogic innovations that are not pre-adapted to this condition cannot be easily institutionalized. I have attempted to demonstrate that the values central to the learner-centred pedagogy are incompatible with the immunological condition of the Botswana education system. For this reason we may regard this pedagogy as foreign to Botswana, and it would be most appropriate to treat it as a transferred innovation.

That the transfer of educational innovations in general from developed to developing countries is problematic has been noted by many researchers with interest in innovation transfer. Hurst (1975) notes that the practice of importing innovations from the Western world began with the importation into colonial territories (such as Bechuanaland) of formal educational systems and institutions based on Western models. Little cognizance was taken of the fact that the social context from which the innovations originated could have been significantly different from their new host environment. Dalin (1978) rightly cautions us against the blind borrowing of Western-initiated innovations. He argues that many of the innovations that have been implemented throughout the Western world (e.g. student-active learning, inquiry-based learning and open education) reflect social and cultural changes in that environment, a point discussed in Chapter Three. Similar changes may not be occurring in less-developed countries (LDCs). For this reason, Dalin predicted (and experience has vindicated him) that many LDCs would experience difficulties in implementing these very same innovations since their success or failure would be influenced by factors beyond the reach of the educational system – factors such as cultural traditions, traditional authority structures and parental expectations. This was indeed a prophetic observation.

The argument advanced above should not be misconstrued to mean that the borrowing of innovations is wrong *per se*. It only serves to sensitise us to the fact that it becomes imperative to assess the feasibility of a transferred innovation *vis-à-vis* the changed cultural setting in order to minimize the chances of tissue rejection of the innovation. This is an area seriously under-researched in Africa which, ironically, is a big borrower of Western-initiated curricular and pedagogic innovations. This gap in the case of Botswana has been observed by Prophet (1990), who has called for research on the extent to which the worldview of Tswana culture reinforces or contradicts the views being promoted in schooling, an attempt I have made in Chapter Five. As part of their contribution to the general literature on the international transfer of innovations, Vulliamy and Carrier (1985:29) urge Third World educational planners to do away with the fallacious belief that '...educational planning can proceed in a sociological vacuum, that socio-cultural studies are of negligible importance compared to curriculum evaluation, in-service training and the inculcation of technical skills". This effectively is an attack on the technicist approach to issues of curriculum and pedagogy.

The Education System's Organisational Structure: A Support Structure

One other factor that has helped shape classroom practice in Botswana, as in many other countries, has been the highly centralised system of education which, as Fuller (1991) observes, was built from colonial forms of administration, relying on hierarchical social relations. Why did the Botswana government 'opt' for a centralised system of education at independence? Many different reasons may be given for this, but two stand out as more plausible. The first, which we have already discussed, is that the economic imperative to provide human resources to run the economy was overwhelming. It was thought that a centralised system in full government control would accomplish this mammoth task. The second reason was political. Education was widely seen as a tool that could be used for nation building through political integration. At independence, Botswana comprised disparate tribal groupings, with each group seeing itself as an 'independent' nation. There was, therefore, a need to build a nation-state with inhabitants whose loyalty was to the nation, not to their tribes. As Marope (1994:34) notes:

> Strong tribal patriotism still prevailed even after independence, with most Batswa- na perceiving themselves as belonging to their tribes and as owing tribute and loyalty to their chiefs.

In light of this situation, it was imperative to forge a national identity. A centralized national system was the favoured arrangement because it held the promise, real or illusory, of addressing regional disparities in educational opportunities that was self-evident at independence in 1966. Political integration was a priority for the Seretse administration:

> The primary aim of the Government of the new Republic of Botswana will be to take all steps necessary to create a strongly united nation, to overcome all pa- rochial, tribal or racial rivalries and make clear to the whole world our deter- mination to preserve the territorial integrity and sovereign independence of our country" (Republic of Botswana 1966 Foreword)

Inequity in education posed a serious threat to the realization of the political integration objective. The ideal arrangement for dealing with this potential threat, it was surmised, was a framework of a centralized national education system with a homogenized view of the child in which the curriculum, pedagogy and assessment were standardized (Pansiri 2007). This system would turn out to be highly centralized, with a standardized and uniform curriculum driven by the ideology of 'educational merit', defined as 'ability plus effort' (Marginson 1999:28). The ideology was aimed at breaking up the traditional, ascriptive, status-allocation mechanism prevalent in pre-independence 'fiefdoms', the ultimate objective being the weakening of tribal patriotism and bolstering of loyalty to the emerging nation-state. Furthermore, a centralized education system was expected to facilitate fair and equitable distribution of educational resources, thereby achieving the goal of equity. Such a centralized education system with a standardized curriculum and assessment regime leaves little room for celebrating diversity and the local. In fact, diversity was frowned upon since, in the eyes of the national polity, it stood in stark contrast to political integration. Centralised control of education was not in any way a consideration peculiar to Botswana, though. All over Africa post-colonial governments viewed education as an instrument for nation building, and to leave it to local authorities was a move few politicians would ever countenance.

However, the central or local control of education has implications for pedagogical practices. With regard to the effects of the national context of an education system, Broadfoot and Osborn (1988:265) observe that:

> ...the national context within which teachers work deeply influences their professional ideology, their perceptions of their professional responsibility, and the way they carry out their day to day work.

The hypothesis that the way education is organised in a country (centralised or decentralised) will affect the classroom practices of teachers and students has been explored in a growing number of studies adopting a comparative perspective (e.g. Broadfoot and Osborn 1988; Fuller 1991; Stevenson and Baker 1991).

Stevenson and Baker (1991) set out in their study to find out whether the institutional issues of fifteen educational systems constrained the classroom practices of mathematics teachers. Their general finding was that the level of state control of the curriculum impacted upon teachers' classroom instruction. Teachers in centralised educational systems were more likely to use more didactic and inflexible teaching methods, whereas those in decentralised systems had the 'discretion in how they handle classroom instruction and learning' (Stevenson and Baker 1991:2).

In their comparative study of how two contrasting national educational systems (the French system and the English and Welsh system) influenced teachers' conceptions of their work, Broadfoot and Osborn (1988) found that French primary schools teachers had a restricted view of their professional role, an axiomatic conception of teaching, and tended to put more stress on the product than on the process of learning. Teachers in England and Wales, on the other hand, had an extended view of their role, saw teaching as problematic and stressed the process of learning rather than its product. Broadfoot and Osborn attributed these differences in role conceptions to the different educational systems – the highly centralised French system tended to routinise teachers' work, hence their restricted and axiomatic conception of their role. The decentralised English and Welsh systems offered teachers autonomy, hence their extended and problematised conception of teaching. Their study was carried out within the context of an educational system (the English and Welsh system) that had become more centralised since the Conservative Party assumed power in 1979. Fuller (1991:68) also stresses that in many 'fragile' states, education ministries control curriculum content by offering a 'universal curriculum, standard materials, teachers' guides, and national examinations that enforce routinised forms of knowledge and facts'. Thus, the national context of an educational system is an important variable in educational change. This is because the context has a considerable 'impact on the way teachers see their task and the way they do their work (Broadfoot and Osborn 1988:267).

In the case of Botswana, researchers have found that the country's centralised educational system negatively affects classroom instruction. Davies (1988) identifies two aspects of 'central' control in Botswana that standardise and routinise official practice: international examinations and national syllabuses. Fuller et al. (1994:143) argue that, *'over time, these structural foundations may have encouraged a pedagogical emphasis on relaying factual information via simple didactic routines'.* Fuller (1991) contends that because the teachers' duties are predetermined by central authority, their role becomes routinised and mechanical. The result is a technicist approach to teaching, paralleling deskilling, (Davies 1988) and a pedagogical style reflecting the bureaucratic organisation of the school structure, knowledge and the educational system as a whole.

To illustrate the general point about the impact of organizational structures on teachers' and students' classroom, I present below the case of Mapoka Senior Secondary School (a pseudonym) which had an organisational structure that not only mirrored the general structure of the education system in the country but also typified the structures of public schools.

Organisational Features of Mapoka Senior Secondary School (MSSS)

The organisational structure of MSSS was typical of all other public senior secondary schools in the country. The headmaster was at the top (and accountable to the Director of Teaching Service Management in the Ministry of Education), followed by his deputy, then heads of department (senior teachers), and these were followed by 'ordinary' teachers. At the bottom of the pyramid were the students. In this hierarchical structure, power and authority decrease as one moves down the hierarchy. Students had no *formal* power. The school's administration was centralised in a single building although science teachers tended largely to confine themselves to their laboratories. As in Everhart's (1983) study, there was emphasis on student separateness at MSSS. The significance of this separateness lies in the fact that it emphasises the difference between teachers as adults and students as children, portraying the latter as immature, thus perpetuating the view of students as empty vessels. Officially, the staff room and staff houses were no-go areas for students. This tended to ensure that the relationship between the teachers and students was formal.

The notion of formality is important here. Waller (1965) associates formality with impersonality and social distance, as well as with relationships between juniors and superiors. Formality implies hierarchical relationships. Teachers at MSSS insisted on students addressing them by their title of 'Mr.' For students to call teachers by their first name was unimaginable. All the teachers interviewed at the school stated that they would 'go wild' if a student dared call them by their first name. This insistence on formality was a way of maintaining social distance between themselves and the students. Edwards and Furlong (1978:25) contend that when formality is repeatedly practiced it becomes 'part of the definition of the relationship'. However, by formalizing most social and learning aspects of classroom practice, teachers are able to remain in control of the situation. Unfortunately for classroom practice, formality sustains asymmetrical classroom relationships and an implicit authoritarian pedagogy.

All these official rules and regulations emphasise to students who they are in the school structure. Not only do they come to know that they are not teachers, they also come to know that they are *different* from teachers. Although student separateness is an ubiquitous phenomenon found in even the most progressive of schools, its effects on the other aspects of schooling tend to be more deleterious where it (student separateness) is sanctioned through official rules and regulations. One such effect is that it tends to widen the teach-learn schism. The more students see themselves as 'learners' the more dependent on the teacher they become. The more the teachers see themselves as different from students, the more authoritarian their teaching and relationship with students become. The final result is the cyclical reproduction of authoritarianism and the deepening of the myth of students as 'deficit systems'.

This was what appeared to be happening at MSSS. One would reasonably expect the same in schools that are similarly hierarchically structured. Such organisational conditions are not favourable for the introduction of a learner-centred pedagogy. As Rowell (1995) has stated, a learner-centred pedagogy is 'democratic in action' and sees the learner as capable of constituting the world. Democratic action may not be sustained where the structures themselves are undemocratic. A hierarchically organised educational system can only be expected to promote an authoritarian pedagogical style in schools. We saw in Chapter Three in the case of the private, independent secondary school that democratic action was reflected in and facilitated by the school's architectural design and organizational structure. This shows that even within a single educational system, teaching practices may vary among schools depending on their organizational structures and whether they are private or public schools. It is in this sense that I am arguing that the centralized, hierarchically organized education system of many sub-Saharan African education systems constitute a stabilized element which allows for the persistence of teacher-centred pedagogical styles.

Conclusion

This chapter has argued that the persistence of the teacher-centred pedagogical paradigm in Botswana or Africa in general is made possible by a set of conditions, among them the utilitarian view of schooling (which is engendered by the view that formal education bestows material benefits on those who are able to acquire it) and hierarchical organizational structures. The utilitarian view of education in turn structures teacher and student perspectives on what constitutes acceptable behaviour in the classroom. It also helps to define a host of other issues, such as understanding of 'teaching' and 'learning', 'doing school work as receiving teacher's knowledge', 'working hard' as the student's successful move into the teacher's world of meanings (Edwards and Furlong 1978) and so forth. These definitions demarcate very clearly the role boundaries. Persistence of these internalized definitions has a reproductive function. This is compounded further by the hierarchical social relations encouraged by hierarchical organizational structures characteristic of many schools in sub-Saharan Africa. All this acts as a support structure for teacher-centredness.

7

Missionary Education and Pedagogical Practice

Introduction

The main focus of the previous chapters was on the philosophical and social/ cultural contexts of the teacher-centred pedagogical paradigm. This chapter and the next adopt a more historical approach to the evolution of teacher-centredness in Botswana in particular and Africa in general. This chapter looks at how the colonial governments neglected education, leaving it to the missionaries. Their imported model of education was bureaucratic and premised on structures of domination and subordination, and it interacted productively with an authoritarian African cultural ambiance to engender and subsequently entrench a correspondingly bureaucratic and authoritarian pedagogical style. I focus on three aspects of the imported model, namely, its condescending conception of the child, the nature of religious knowledge and the embedded ideology of cultural supremacy.

In the case of the Tswana for example, these aspects combined with a correspondingly authoritarian traditional education, a deficit view of the child and the active involvement of traditional chiefs in educational matters to promote authoritarianism in the schools. The existence of this correspondence challenges directly the popular notion that mass Western education conflicted with traditional African society. Proponents (e.g. Namuddu 1991) of this 'incongruence thesis' have tended to focus on the *content* of education at the expense of its *form*. There is no doubt that the content of missionary/ colonial education differed with, and aimed to obliterate any trace of traditional knowledge systems. For this reason, it was to be expected that the content of missionary education would not only differ from, but would also challenge traditional notions of knowledge. However, the proponents of this thesis ignore the *form* of education, and its subtle, hidden messages that are embedded in the ways classrooms are socially organized. And yet it is the *form* of education that is more powerful than its content. In terms of form there was synergy between mass Western education and traditional African education. Thus, in some ways, the supposed chasm between the two forms of education is exaggerated.

Broadly, this and the next chapters assess the manner in which the historical development of education (taking Botswana as an example) might have helped shape classroom practices in schools. These chapters highlight the thread that binds together all the chapters of the book, namely that there is nothing value-neutral about pedagogical styles; the latter are products of the surrounding cultural, social and historical milieu. To this end, Giroux (1985) advises that:

> .... to understand the present.... educators must place all pedagogical contexts in a historical context in order to see clearly their genesis and development (Giroux 1985:xxiv).

This chapter traces the historical development of primary and secondary education in Botswana from the time of British rule to independence in 1966. I then extrapolate from these educational developments their likely effects on pedagogy in the schools. As already stated, the pedagogical style characteristic of Botswana schools and classroom organisation is a product of cultural, social, economic and historical forces, and it has evolved over a period of time. It is now firmly embedded in our educational institutions to such an extent that it is almost a tradition. It is part of the teachers' and students' institutional biographies and they implicitly implement it in their day-to-day classroom activities. If education is to effectively transmit the 'myths' of the social structure in which it is embedded, it has to employ a pedagogical style that is compatible with society's habit of thought.

Educational Development in Botswana under British administration

Botswana (then Bechuanaland) became a British Protectorate in 1885. However, the latter's commitment to the protection of the territory was not matched by a commitment to develop it. Why did Britain offer protection to a territory it had no commitment to develop? A number of explanations have been proffered. One such explanation is that the British thought that the territory was just a desert with no exploitable resources. This view is undeniably true as the statement of Lord Derby, Colonial Secretary from 1882 to 1885, indicates: 'Bechuanaland is of no value to us . . . for any Imperial purposes it is of no consequence to us whether Boers or Native Chiefs are in possession' (as quoted in Gossett 1986:143).

However, to argue that British adventures in Africa were solely motivated by economic considerations would be an oversimplification of a complex issue. Gossett (1986) has added humanitarian and strategic motives to the economic motive for colonisation. He argues that the extent to which Britain invested in any of its colonies (including investment in human resource development) was dependent on the motive for colonisation, and this would later determine the gravity of local manpower shortages at independence. For example, where the motive for colonisation was purely economic, that is, involving the exploitation of natural resources, one would expect that human resources would be developed insofar as they were needed to develop the natural resources. This would inadvertently have led to the emergence of an 'African bourgeoisie' which would have occupied some of the public sector and management positions at independence. And where the motive for colonisation was humanitarian, one would expect the colonial power to invest substantially in human resource development. Where the motive was for strategic purposes, one would expect very little investment both in human and natural resource development. These motives, however, are not mutually exclusive. In the case of Bechuanaland, it would appear on the surface that Britain offered protection to the territory on purely humanitarian grounds since Tswana chiefs and the missionaries had asked for it. However, a closer look would show that the protection was offered neither for economic nor for humanitarian reasons, but rather for strategic reasons.

To understand this, it is crucial to first understand that the territory was granted protection in 1885, just before the Berlin Conference was held, and about thirty years after the protection had been requested. It was at this conference (which was held at the height of the 'Scramble for Africa') that European powers systematically divided Africa among themselves. The British, therefore, were to use the Bechuanaland Protectorate as a bargaining chip at the conference. By proclaiming jurisdiction over Bechuanaland, Britain effectively halted further northward expansion of the Afrikaners and eastward movement of the Germans who were in present-day Namibia. Britain's 'road to the North' (from the Cape Colony) which passed through Bechuanaland was thus secured. This is but a small part of a complex story that serves to show that Britain's interests in Bechuanaland were more of a strategic nature than anything else.

Gossett's conceptual framework puts in doubt the popular view that Botswana's protection was secured by three Chiefs. What is clear is that the British had neither economic nor humanitarian interests in Botswana. Otherwise Botswana would have inherited a more robust economic and human resources infrastructure at independence, the same way Zimbabwe or Kenya did. Thus, the conceptual framework built around the three motives for colonisation helps us understand why different countries which were under the rule of the same colonial power had differential manpower needs at independence. Perhaps more important for the argument in this chapter is that Gossett's framework helps us appreciate why the development of education throughout the eighty years of British protection was left to the missions and local authorities (Colclough and McCarthy 1980), institutions that had limited capacity to produce the territory's human resources needs in the long term.

Primary Education

Primary education in the then Bechuanaland was started by missionaries in the 1840s. As would be expected, the concentration in these schools was on evangelical education. Its main purpose was to enable the students to read the Bible so that they would later on assist the missionaries in spreading the Gospel (Gossett 1986). Students also learnt the 3Rs ('reading, writing and arithmetic') and some vocational skills. By the turn of the century, the missions had established twenty primary schools in the territory, with an enrolment of one thousand pupils. There were three major missions: the London Missionary Society (LMS), the Lutheran and the Dutch Reformed Church. There was, therefore, some danger of these denominations becoming involved in disputes, with each trying to bring as much territory as it could into its sphere of influence, as happened, for example, in Nigeria (see Bassey 1999). In view of this danger, the LMS, which was the most widespread of all the missions in the territory, proposed in 1910 that committees which would supervise the work of the schools be established in each tribal area. This marked the first move towards some form of a system of local administration. The interest groups which were represented in these committees were the tribal authority, district administration and the missions themselves. These committees were replaced by Local Education Authorities in 1966.

By leaving the provision of education to tribal administration, the colonial administration was not expressing any reasoned belief in the efficacy and value of tribal administration. Rather it wanted to limit its own administrative responsibilities for financial reasons (Hodgson and Ballinger 1932:150), and above all, its presence in the territory was motivated more by the latter's strategic position than anything else and so there was no need to invest in the territory. Gossett (1986) also sees the decision by the colonial administration to leave education to tribal administration as an extension of indirect rule, since the Africans had only nominal independence to organise their own education. It only went as far as finance was concerned. Beyond that, for example, the realm of the curriculum, was the province of the Director of Education who was, so to speak, a surrogate of the colonial administration. Thus, although London was not directly involved in the provision of education in the territory, it nonetheless controlled and monitored what the schools provided.

In the 1950s, while primary school enrolment started to expand (see Table 6.1 below), problems still remained. Resources were inadequate to cope with this expansion. There was also an acute shortage of trained teachers. These problems plagued primary education beyond independence.

Table 6.1: Enrolment in the school system, 1946-1976

YEAR	PRIMARY SCHOOLS			SECONDARY SCHOOLS			
	STANDARD 1	STANDARD 7	TOTAL	FORM 1	FORM 3	FORM 5	TOTAL
1946	7,478	428	21,174	n.a.	n.a.	-	50
1959	5,812	383	16,293	n.a.	n.a	-	132
1955	6,793	448	20,475	129	35	4	242
1960	11,541	684	36,287	278	107	18	561
1964	17,633	3,985	62,839	429	222	39	1,036
1966	20,616	4,614	71,546	530	316	80	1,531
1968	17,825	5,021	78,963	885	465	161	2,299
1970	12,721	6,913	83,002	1,336	826	252	3,905
1972	13,506	9,749	81,662	1,854	1,230	386	5,538
1974	20,756	13,811	103,711	2,362	1,650	531	7,055
1976	23,833	13,602	125,588	2,861	2,206	861	9,558

Source: Colclough and McCarthy (1980:207)

Secondary Education

Attempts to provide secondary education were made before the second World War (for example, the Tati Training Institute) but these were not successful. Secondary education in the Bechuanaland Protectorate was, therefore, a post-war phenomenon. Swartland and Taylor (1988:143) state that:

> various attempts to start secondary school classes in the 1930s were resisted by the colonial government, which believed that students from Bechuanaland would be better educated at schools in South Africa and Southern Rhodesia.

Here also the colonial administration left the provision of education to the missionaries and the various tribal groupings. That secondary education was massively neglected during colonial rule is evident from the figures in Table 6.1. For example, in 1964, two years before independence, only 39 students sat for their matriculation examinations.

The first school to introduce junior classes was St. Joseph's College, a mission school, in 1944. It was followed by Moeng College (which was modeled on the English grammar school) in 1948 and was built on tribal initiative. Three more schools built on tribal initiative followed. At independence in 1966, there were nine secondary schools in the territory. Three were mission schools, four were built on tribal initiatives, one had been established with neither mission nor government assistance (Swaneng Hill School in Serowe, established by Patrick Van Rensburg), and the last one, Gaborone Secondary School in the capital, was conceived and built as a government school before independence and was opened in 1965. Studies leading to the Cambridge Overseas School Certificate (COSC) were not introduced until 1955. Even by 1964, only four of the eight secondary schools in the whole protectorate offered a five-year course leading to the COSC (Colclough and McCarthy 1980:209). Only two teacher training colleges (for primary school teachers) and a government training centre in Gaborone existed before independence.

It is clear from the above that although the protectorate was politically administered by the British government, the latter did very little to develop formal education. One reason was that it was considered cheaper to send students from the protectorate for post-primary education to South Africa or Southern Rhodesia than to build facilities within the territory. This resonated well with the colonial government's strategic motive for colonizing Botswana. It was this dependence on neighbouring countries that was to later dictate educational developments in the protectorate in the 1940s and 1950s. This was the time when decisive political developments were taking place both in

South Africa and Southern Rhodesia. The irony, as Parsons (1984:39) has observed, is that this policy of dependence was being pursued with rigour at a time when *those countries were beginning to squeeze out pupils from the Bechuanaland Protectorate*.

Pressure mounted in the 1940s to keep students from the protectorate out of South African and Southern Rhodesian schools and universities. At this time, demand for education in those countries was also high. More serious perhaps was South Africa's determination to introduce Bantu education which, *inter alia*, entailed restricting the admission of protectorate students.

It was these events, therefore, that were to mark a turning point in the provision of educational facilities in order to facilitate education from within the territory. Thus, the colonial administration's decision to increase primary education expenditure in the 1950s and early 1960s was more a response to political developments in the neighbouring countries than a genuine willingness to fund educational development in the territory. As Parsons (1984:40) puts it:

> political and educational divergence from South Africa in the 1950s was forced on the Bechuanaland Protectorate by South African initiative and British colonial response, rather than vice-versa.

Thus, Botswana's educational landscape up to independence in 1966 was shaped more by historical developments in the sub-region than by deliberate policy from the colonial administration.

This brief overview has brought to the surface two salient points. The first is that the colonial administration largely left educational provision to the missionaries and tribal groupings in Bechuanaland and that these had a limited capacity to develop education. The second point (which was a consequence of the first) is that at independence, Botswana had serious shortages of trained and trainable manpower to run the burgeoning government administrative machinery.

Missionary Education and Classroom Practice

What were the pedagogical consequences of leaving the provision of education to the missionaries and tribal authorities? To answer this question we must first understand the nature of the schooling model that was imported from Britain and imposed on the peoples of Botswana and Africa in general. It is important in this endeavour to isolate the assumptions and values which appeared to inform the model. One of the premises of this study is that this model was imported into Botswana by the missionaries who introduced Western formal education in most colonial territories. While missionary education contributed in no small measure to the development of the authoritarianism that research has found to characterize the classroom climate in Botswana, it can also be argued that this model interacted in productive ways with contemporary Tswana values and practices to entrench the authoritarianism.

Namuddu (1991) observes that the evolution of mass education in Western Europe was a response to certain important philosophical, cultural, social and economic imperatives. The same imperatives did not exist for the African population when mass education was introduced with the advent of colonialism. Mass schooling as it is known today came into being towards the end of the nineteenth century. Its organisational structure was bureaucratic, reflecting the then predominant mode of manufacturing and commerce in Britain. This organisational structure was essential for the production of a work force which would occupy subordinate positions in factories and offices. Because the education was for subordination and submission, it was authoritarian in practice. Emphasis in the schools, as Ottaway (1962) states, was on inculcating into pupils attitudes related to 'hard work, strict discipline, subordination to their betters, and Christian humility' (p.64). This strict rigidity of the school programme has since remained a salient aspect of schooling, as Shipman (1971:54-55) observes:

> Punctuality, quiet orderly work in groups, response to orders, bells and timetables, respect for authority, even tolerance for monotony, boredom, punishment, lack of reward and regular attendance at place of work are the habits to be learned at school.

To carry out this function effectively, schools had to be organised along bureaucratic- authoritarian lines. This model of schooling has ever since remained prototypical of schooling programmes in Africa. Attempts to reform it have come to no avail (Serpell 1983). In the case of present-day Botswana, the schooling model is bureaucratic and centralized, with the state in total control of the curriculum. However, a bureaucratic-authoritarian schooling model relying on hierarchical social relations (Fuller 1991) can only be expected to engender a similarly authoritarian pedagogical style in the schools. The authoritarian nature of the pedagogical style which characterized nineteenth-century mass education in Britain was further compounded by two other factors: the then prevailing conception of childhood, and the conception of knowledge as objective, scientific and factual.

As discussed in Chapter Three, nineteenth century Europe, particularly its Christian theology, conceived of the child as innately depraved (Rusk 1954), and education was a way of morally straightening children. The child was viewed as an incomplete and immature 'young adult' who was in perpetual need of some guidance, and it was precisely this conception that Rousseau decried in Emile. This conception of childhood led to the development of an 'image of education as a condescending process in which the teacher has an obligation to control and direct the student along a predetermined path' (Serpell 1993:91-92). This condescension assured the maintenance of asymmetrical relationships between the teacher and the student, resulting in a unidirectional flow of information in the classroom. Thus, the asymmetrical power relations mandated the teacher to authoritatively direct all classroom activities and to correct any 'deviations by the student from the prescribed form of behavior' (Serpell 1993).

The view of knowledge prevalent in the nineteenth century (and perhaps even to this day) further compounded the asymmetrical teacher-student relationships. Knowledge was viewed as scientific, objective and as a certainty. This epistemology was a product of the Enlightenment era of the eighteenth century. The general belief was that:

> To every genuine question there were many false answers, and only one true one; once discovered it was final — It remained for ever true (Berlin 1956:16).

There was a general consensus that:

> all problems were soluble by the discovery of objective answers which once found — and why should they not be? — would be clear to all to see and valid eternally (Berlin 1954:28).

As argued in Chapter Three, this objectivist, rationalist epistemology had implications for pedagogical practice in schools. If knowledge was perceived as objective and independent of the learner, emphasis had to be on the transmission of these immutable and incontestable facts from the knower to the novitiate, the knower being the teacher, and the novitiate being the student.

In summary, therefore, the nineteenth- and twentieth-century schooling model was bureaucratic and authoritarian in style, based on a deficit-system conception of the child and on the objectivist, rationalist epistemology. Such then was the nature of the educational model that was exported, not only to Botswana, but also to many other African countries by missionaries in the nineteenth and twentieth centuries. What remains now is to demonstrate that Botswana provides a specific example of the general point that the social context influences classroom practice.

As stated above, formal Western education was first introduced in Botswana (then Bechuanaland) by missionaries in the late 1840s. The whole institution was foreign. Therefore, the curriculum, teaching methods, assessment procedures, and its aims were alien to local communities. As would be expected, teaching in missionary schools concentrated on evangelical education. Its main aim was to enable students to read the Bible so that later they could assist the missionaries in the propagation of the Gospel. So important was this aim that the Bible was translated into the various languages of Bechuanaland. The schools emphasised reading, writing and the Scriptures, and the pedagogic principle was essentially the monitor system (Parsons 1984:25). This pedagogical principle involved training the older students by the direct method so that they could later drill the younger ones in small groups. It was a strategy David Livingstone (the first missionary to establish a formal school in Botswana in 1844) called the use of native agency in education. It must be noted that the pedagogic principle of the monitor system was imported directly from Britain. There, it had been developed at the beginning of the nineteenth century by an Anglican clergyman, Andrew Bell, and a school teacher, Joseph Lancaster. They saw it as most appropriate method for mass education since *masters* (teachers) had to deal with large groups of students. The lesson was broken down into its simplest elements by the master for the monitors (usually older boys) to teach in a mechanical fashion to small groups of children. Though cheap, such instruction did not take into consideration the unique needs of individual children.

The nature of religious knowledge itself made it naturally amenable to the direct method – religious knowledge was viewed as objective, factual and unchanging. This is as true today as it was in the nineteenth century. In such epistemological circumstances, it is difficult to think of any other pedagogical style that would have suited the teaching and learning of religious facts more than the transmission-reception pedagogical style. This authoritarian pedagogical style is what perhaps best characterizes schooling in Africa, as research indicates. As an educational tradition, the style is very resistant to change since it is now part of the 'unconscious' of teachers, students and the general community; it is now history sedimented at the base of society. A technicist approach alone is unlikely to ever be able to change it. As Dewey (1952) (cited in Skilbeck 1970:42) states:

> To change long-established habits in the individual is a slow, difficult and far more complicated process. To change long-established institutions – which are social habits organised in the structure of the common life – is a much slower, more difficult and

far more complicated process. The drive of established institutions is to assimilate and distort the new into conformity with them.

However, the contribution of missionary education in the development of the banking-education pedagogical style in Botswana should not be over-emphasised. Indeed, it would be wrong to assume that missionary education, with its attendant bureaucratic-authoritarian educational model, was solely responsible for the evolution of this style of pedagogy in the country. In fact, it is only fair to argue that its authoritarian nature notwithstanding, the model found a conducive environment to flourish in local communities. After all, as noted in Chapter Five, traditional education was just as authoritarian. Tswana social hierarchy and interpersonal relations have always been regulated by a rigid, paternalistic structure, and the same authority structure pervaded traditional education, which to say the least, was training in conformity.

The influence of the wider social structure on educational practice has always been very much evident in Tswana society. In pre-colonial Tswana chiefdoms education was both formal and informal. Informal training was life-long since it was embedded in day-to-day socialization. Formal education, however, was more elaborate and involved initiation rituals for both boys and girls. The rituals 'were the ideological reference point for Tswana daily activity' (Mafela 1993:39) and they formed the fabric of society. Specifically, through these rituals, traditional education served to maintain the sharp hierarchical distinction between children and elders. This shows that traditional education shared some aspects with the imported Western model of education, such as the deficit-view of the child. This symmetry of views about the child helped to institute a pedagogical style in which the relationship between the student and the teacher was clearly authoritarian. This symmetry is often overlooked by those who tend to over-emphasise the conflict that existed between mass Western education and traditional society. So powerful is the influence of the latter that some have suggested that modern, formal primary education in Botswana, for example, 'should be understood, at least in part, as carrying on something of the traditional role of the extended family in the teaching, socializing and disciplining of young children' (Yoder and Mautle 1991:12). The rote learning that traditional culture fosters discourages the development of attributes such as spontaneity, self-reliance, creativity and learner autonomy. A good student must display docility, obedience and submissiveness towards her/his teachers. As argued in Chapter Five, these role patterns are inculcated by child-rearing practices, formal education and other established organizations in society. However, these are antithetical to a learner-centred pedagogy.

Also interesting is the form the administration of education took in colonial Botswana. Throughout the eighty years of British administration, the development of education was largely left to missionaries and local authorities. This, however, was not an expression (by the colonial administration) of any reasoned belief in the efficacy and value of native control of education. This could never be, given the condescending attitude of the missionaries/colonialists towards the local people and Britain's strategic motive for its presence in the territory. Britain simply wanted to limit its own administrative responsibilities. Furthermore, leaving the administration of education to local control was an extension of the strategy of indirect rule. This strategy, however, ensured that tribal chiefs were actively involved in educational matters, to the extent that conflict between them and the missionaries over education was common. Nevertheless, local control was nominal, going only as far as finance. Beyond that into, for example, the realm of the curriculum was the exclusive province of the Director of Education who was a representative of the colonial administration.

Although nominal, local control of education had more than just a symbolic meaning. It linked education closely with tribal organization. In particular, the active involvement of tribal chiefs in educational matters ensured the influence of conservative indigenous forces in education. As a result, traditional authority tended to be perpetuated at the expense of progressive educational ideas. Indeed, innovations to make colonial education more progressive were attempted. In 1931, for example, a more locally-oriented syllabus was received for adoption. It urged teachers to use 'activity, creativeness, song, story and dramatization as vehicles for instruction' (Parsons 1984). However, the innovation appears never to have really taken off. The adoption of these methods of instruction would have constituted a paradigm shift in classroom practice in colonial Botswana. Undoubtedly, the lack of suitably trained teachers and shortages of teaching materials contributed to the failure to institute these new methods. More fundamental perhaps may have been the fact that the proposed pedagogic innovations, which would have required students to exercise some degree of initiative, were out of step with the objective social conditions where conformity, not initiative, was the expectation from both missionaries and traditional society. Thus, local control of education, because it involved the infusion of traditional structures and values into a Western institution (i.e. formal education), might have inadvertently acted as a barrier to innovativeness, thus perpetuating authoritarianism in educational practice.

The Ideology of Cultural Supremacy

However, to say that missionary educational practices in Bechuanaland were informed by a bureaucratic-authoritarian model, complemented by the authoritarian nature of the traditional Tswana social structure, does not seem to capture the total picture. Riveted to this model was the missionaries' own condescending attitude towards the local people and their cultures. The source of this condescension is not very difficult to establish; it was inherent in the very aim of the missionaries – the aim of 'saving native souls'. No wonder they described Africans in crude terms such as 'heathens' and 'primitives' who had to be transformed. These sentiments were clearly shared by John Mackenzie, a London Missionary Society (LMS) missionary working amongst the Bangwato of Botswana's Central District. Mackenzie believed that, 'The heathen was to be converted in his (sic) beliefs and customs, industry was to be encouraged, education fostered, a new society created and western civilization established' (Dachs 1975, cited in Mgadla 1986:82). Native refusal to embrace the missionaries' worldview was often met with hostility. For example, Chief Sekgoma of the Bangwato was described as a 'savage', 'heathen', 'fiend' and 'barbarian' because he had refused to be converted and did not personally approve of missionary education.

These sentiments must be understood within the wider framework of the missionaries' attitude towards Africans. Generally, the missionaries saw nothing of worth in Africans and their culture:

> They regarded the people as immoral, lazy, and drunken, steeped in superstition and witchcraft, and doomed to spiritual damnation. There could be no question of grafting the Christian message on to the traditional culture. That whole culture was rotten, in their view, and had to be replaced, root and branch (Snelson 1974:11, cited in Serpel 1993:92).

As a consequence of such convictions, Tswana 'indigenous culture became submerged and many Batswana were encouraged to believe that their own cultural inheritance was inferior to that imported by the British' (Republic of Botswana 1977:11). This was clearly reflected in the curriculum content; it was biased against the local culture, in favour of European (particularly the British) culture. For example, even by the turn of the century, English rhymes, recitations, and the Oxford English Readers continued to dominate the curriculum (Mgadla 1986). Local history was not taught in the schools, and the reasoning was very simple – the natives had no history that was worth teaching. Teaching them their own history, therefore, would send the wrong message – that they had a history. Instead, students were taught about Britain and its national figures. Thus missionary education, to say the least, was alienating and depersonalizing. It had to be so if the missionaries were to attain their objective of profoundly transforming the 'heathens' into fully-fledged persons. This shows that the missionaries' educational practice was inherently cloaked in an ethnocentric assumption of cultural supremacy. Batswana, by and large, internalized their supposed cultural inferiority as part of their subjective reality and this in turn guided their relationship with their European 'superiors'. The relationship was, as would be expected, inherently asymmetrical. Missionaries had nothing to learn from the 'rotten' Tswana culture, and by extension, Batswana had nothing to contribute towards their own civilizing process. Whatever exchange of ideas took place, one can only surmise that it necessarily involved a 'unidirectional transfer of information, skills, understanding and civilization' (Serpel 1993:95) from the European to the African. It is, therefore, plausible to conclude that the missionaries' assumption of Western cultural superiority in Bechuanaland implicitly justified a condescending pedagogical style in schools. This style of pedagogy functioned as an instrument of social control. Thus, missionary education was necessarily a domesticating education. Only an equally domesticating pedagogical style could be expected to accomplish this objective.

It is, nevertheless, critical to reiterate the point made in Chapter Three that this use of education as an agent of social control characterized mass education in nineteenth century Britain. Such education was meant for the working class, which was 'generally regarded as having no system of values' (Prophet and Hodson 1988:134). The task of education, therefore, was to inculcate Christian moral values into working-class children. This is the same task that was assigned to missionary education in colonial Africa (although here the task was broader since it involved the total uprooting of a people's culture). It is for this reason that Curtin (1965:427) asserts that the curriculum and teaching methods that Christian missionaries introduced in Africa were designed for the working class in Europe and were naturally of a condescending nature.

Conclusion

Using a socio-historical approach, this chapter sought to trace the historical evolution of teacher-centred pedagogy to the imported bureaucratic-authoritarian model of education of nineteenth-century Britain and the missionary/colonialist belief in the supremacy of Western culture. The imported model had three problematic qualities; first, it was bureaucratic and authoritarian; secondly, it was based on a deficit-system conception of the child; and thirdly, it was based on the objectivist, rationalist view of knowledge. Interestingly, it found in Africa a cultural ambiance that was equally authoritarian, based on structures of child domination and subordination and an 'empty vessel' conception of the child. These qualities taken together authenticated a bureaucratic, authoritarian pedagogical style which has since remained prototypical of teaching in Africa. The missionary/colonialist belief in their cultural supremacy promoted asymmetrical power relationships between themselves and the colonized. Looking down upon the latter's culture, the former promoted a unidirectional flow of information in interactional situations. In the classroom (as one such situation), the ideology of cultural supremacy implicitly justified a condescending pedagogical style. However, the arguments advanced here are not meant to dismiss as inconsequential the technical issues associated with the innovation delivery system (such as lack of resources, poorly trained teachers and high teacher-student ratios). Indeed, these interact with aspects of the social context in complex ways to determine the fate of innovations. Rather, the chapter merely challenges the weight that they are often accorded when accounting for failure by teachers and students to adopt and/or implement pedagogic innovations. In short, the chapter sought to demonstrate the social embeddedness of pedagogy.

8

Curriculum as Context of Teaching and Learning

Introduction

This penultimate chapter considers the powerful influence the curriculum exerts on teachers' and students' classroom practices. More often than not, the curriculum is presented as an innocuous arrangement of subject-matter to be presented to the learners by the teachers and for the learner to assimilate in an unproblematic manner. However, the curriculum is both an enabling and a constraining structure. This position is reminiscent of Gidden's (1976) 'structuration postulate' which posits that 'the course of social history results from mutually constituting agent choices and structural dispositions' (Scholte 2000:91). As already stated, actors (such as teachers and students) do not act in a sociological vacuum. Their actions are simultaneously enabled and constrained by the context within which they operate. If structures (e.g. the curriculum) and acting agents (e.g. teachers and students) are mutually constitutive then it is necessary to:

> situate the individual [teacher and/or student] in a social context [the curriculum], to be able to say something about that context in terms of its internal structure and dynamics, of the opportunities it makes available and the constraints it imposes, and at the same time grasp that essential individuality and uniqueness of man (sic) that evades any total categorization (Sharp and Green 1975:17).

Thus, the actions of individuals cannot be understood when abstracted from their context. Structuration theory is, therefore, useful in exploring the ability/inability of teachers and students to innovate. How then can the theory help us analyse the ways in which the curriculum constrains pedagogical innovations? Put differently, how does the curriculum, as structure, contribute to the regularity of teacher-centred teaching practices and their intractability in sub-Saharan Africa?

I attempt to answer this question by analysing curriculum development in the past two decades in Botswana, where the constructivist, learner-centred pedagogy has been declared the official pedagogy in schools. Ironically, emphasis on the pedagogy is intensifying at a time when the school curriculum is increasingly becoming behaviourist in orientation. Bearing in mind the fundamental differences between constructivism and behaviourism (see Chapter Three), this conflation of behaviourism and constructivism is contradictory: how are the two expected to co-exist? The tension between the two is further exacerbated by the recent emergence of the League Table – the ranking of schools by performance in terminal examinations. It is, therefore, important to look at these developments more closely with a view to establishing their implications for pedagogical reform.

To develop some useful insight into the Botswana curriculum, it is important to locate the curriculum in a global context. This is a context characterized by a discourse of economic competitiveness, a discourse that calls for reform of education and training to align them more closely with the labour and skills demands of the 'new' economy. While Botswana, just like most sub-Saharan African countries, has always had a national, prescriptive curriculum that heavily limits teachers' and students' room to act, the curriculum reforms of the 1990s further attenuated that space. Specifically, the emergence of the "Objectives-based Curriculum" has constrained the little autonomy the teacher had. The result was a further tightening of state control of teachers' work. In other words, we have witnessed since the 1990s hyper-entrenchment of state surveillance of teachers in Botswana. This development was to be aided by the rise of accountability measures in the country occasioned by public sector reforms which were encapsulated in the discourse of productivity. Accountability in the education sector comes in the form of ranking of schools by performance in public school examinations results. School principals today are asked by their employer, the Ministry of Education and Skills Development (ME&SD), to account for the position of their schools in the League Table. The media have taken keen interest in the rankings and the general public gets the opportunity to discuss the examinations results on both public and private radio stations. In short, the performance of schools has become a public spectacle. This combination of surveillance and spectacle (Vinson and Ross 2003) has fundamentally altered teacher-student relationships by making them even more hierarchical and impersonal, leading to further entrenchment of banking education.

Contexts of Reform

The past two decades have witnessed an unprecedented global attempt to attune education to the demands of the 'new' economy. This has impacted on education in major ways, including leading to fundamental curricular reforms. One strand of this reform agenda is the production of a new kind of learner, worker or citizen. As noted in Chapter Two, the education system is expected to develop in learners attributes such as creativity, versatility, innovativeness, critical thinking, problem-solving skills, and a positive disposition towards teamwork – attributes deemed essential in today's changed work environment. Promotion of these attributes is not new in education, though. The Progressive Education Movement of the 1960s and 1970s purported to promote these qualities in learners. As Silcock (1996:200) states, 'Progressivists have always promised to deliver the independence of thought and action which life in modem societies demands'. However, Progressive Education retreated in the 1980s in the face of attacks from 'new right organisations and governments for supposedly reinforcing and failing to overcome the "underachievement" of many children in schools resulting in falling standards' (Usher and Edwards 1994:197). Interest in the attributes stated above was rekindled in the 1990s, this time reoriented to meet the demands of the 'flexible economy' (Rassool 1993). Their desirability is now couched in the discourse of international economic competitiveness. It is alleged that new patterns of economic production and organisation, leading to a changed workplace, have emerged and require a new kind of worker – what we identified in Chapter Two as Castells' (1997) 'self-programmable' worker. The call in the new patterns of production is for a multi-skilled, adaptable, and flexible workforce. Education has a major role to play in the production of this 'new' kind of worker. It is precisely (though not solely) for this reason that education is being reformed in many countries across the globe. Since the driving force is the urge to have a competitive edge in the global market, the move is towards what King and McGrath (2002:78) term 'a curriculum for competitiveness'.

Botswana was not to be left behind in this education reform stampede. In 1994, it unveiled the Revised National Policy on Education (RNPE) which, in many ways, was a response to the economic production and industrial restructuring taking place globally.

The Global Context of the RNPE

The evolution of the RNPE was in a context of global restructuring of education spurred by globalisation. Globalisation has been defined as:

> ...the intensification of worldwide social relations that link distant localities in such a way that local happenings are shaped by events occurring many miles away, and vice-versa. This is a dialectical process because such local happenings may move in an obverse direction from the very distanciated relations that shape them. Local transformation is as much a part of globalization as lateral extension of social connections across time and space (Giddens 1990:64).

By emphasising the interplay of the global and local, Giddens' definition of globalisation eschews a deterministic relationship between the global and local in which the former is portrayed as determining processes in the latter. Although it is intensifying 'policy migration' (Edwards et al. 1999) or 'policy borrowing' (Tikly 2001), leading to a 'convergence in policy and practice throughout [the world]' (Priestley 2002:122), globalisation does not impose the globally circulating discourses on those countries' 'borrowing' policy. That is, the relationship between the global and local is a dialectical one (Christie 1997; Arnove and Torres 1999). Internationally circulating policy discourses, Hartley (2003:82) observes, are 'mediated by the cultural and political conditions which prevail [in any given context]'.

Thus, although it is important to draw upon global influences in trying to understand educational policy directions in Botswana or anywhere else, it is essential to recognise that the ultimate shape policy assumes is also a function of local circumstances and concerns. It is this mediation of the global by the local that gives globalisation its contradictory and paradoxical character, this in turn leading to gaps, contradictions and paradoxes in policies that emerge as a response to it. Formulation of the RNPE, as an education policy determined to produce a new learner, was not immune from these gaps, tensions, contradictions and paradoxes. These contradictions and paradoxes have implications for the success of pedagogical reforms.

The Local Context of the RNPE

The RNPE was published against the backdrop of harsh, global economic conditions that saw Botswana's revenues decline owing to a depressed world diamond market. This resulted in an upsurge in the unemployment rate, especially among the youth. For example, in the early 1990s youth unemployment stood at 41 percent of the 15-24 age group, compared to the total unemployment rate of 21 percent reported for the labour force as a whole in 1993/94 (Leith 2005). In the face of this reality, concerns were raised about the relevance of the education being provided. The government instituted the Kedikilwe Commission (named after its chairman) in 1992, with a mandate to, among other things, 'identify problems and strategies for [the education system's] further development in the context of Botswana's changing and complex economy' (Republic of Botswana 1993:v). The Commission submitted its report, the *Report of the National Commission on Education* (RNCE), in 1993. The government's reaction to the Commission's recommendations came in April 1994 in the form of Government White Paper No. 2, the *Revised National Policy on Education* (RNPE). The text, together with other policy documents, reflects major discourses associated with globalisation, such as 'economic competitiveness', 'lifelong learning', and 'world of work'.

The thrust of this policy text was the alignment of education to labour requirements of the economy. This discourse of the economy-education nexus was emphasized in the RNPE and associated texts: 'The level and type of education that is offered is partly responsible for the speed with which industrialization can proceed' (Republic of Botswana 1993:8). The education system was to 'offer individuals a life-long opportunity to develop themselves and to make their country competitive internationally' (Republic of Botswana 1993:4). To prepare the workforce for higher productivity, education was urged to provide a 'high level of technical and scientific skills' (Republic of Botswana, 1993:8). To justify this policy direction, the Commission invoked the much-touted economic success of the Asian Tigers (Taiwan, Singapore, Hong Kong and South Korea), attributing their success to heavy investments in education and workforce training.

Given its concern for the economy-education dislocation, it is not surprising that the RNPE attributed growing youth unemployment in the country to the perceived dislocation. The Botswana Democratic Party (BDP) government insisted that the economy was in good shape. It was the education system that was failing to produce people with the requisite skills to take up available opportunities in the local labour market:

> In the past decade rapid economic growth and the resulting changes in the structure of the economy have resulted in shortages of skilled personnel. However, the education system was not structured to respond to the demand (Republic of Botswana 1994:3).

This pronouncement needs to be treated with some skepticism. Given that Botswana was badly affected by the global economic crisis of the late 1980s and early 1990s, it smacks of disingenuousness to argue that the country's economy was in good shape. However, to pronounce otherwise would have been potentially suicidal on the part of the government, given that the 1994 general elections were just around the corner. It seems that the party ingeniously appropriated or 'bought into' the circulating global education discourse (of the economy-education dislocation) to deflect attention from the state of the economy as the source of youth unemployment. The perceived global economy-education dislocation offered a less controversial explanation for youth unemployment, an explanation that struck a chord with the electorate – the education system was not responsive to the new demands of a changing economy; it needed reforming.

What in fact were those 'new' demands and how was the economy changing? How was education to respond to these changes and new demands? The *Report of the National Commission on Education* (RNCE) of 1993 observes that:

> Manufacturing techniques are changing and there is a general movement away from low skill, mass production assembly techniques towards higher degrees of automation and flexible specialization which require higher levels of skills (Republic of Botswana 1993:8).

Clearly a claim is being made here that Botswana's economy is to some extent post-Fordist and globalised, a claim that is more an aspiration than a reality. It has been suggested by some commentators (e.g. Kraak 1995; Chisholm 1997; King and McGrath 2002) that the adoption of post-Fordist work processes has been limited in South Africa (perhaps the only sub-Saharan economy integrated into the world economy). It would, therefore, be absurd to talk of flexible specialization in Botswana, with its pre-industrial economy. It, therefore, makes better sense to view the RNPE's emphasis on high skills as reflecting present and future economic aspirations, to somehow leapfrog the industrial stage. Furthermore, since the 1990s Botswana has aggressively pursued neo-liberal economic policies such as privatisation, cost recovery, deregulation and liberalisation. These are deemed essential if the country is to move away from the periphery and be better integrated into the global economy. Botswana is involved in the 'scramble' for foreign direct investment (FDI), and so it has to do everything necessary to position itself as an attractive destination for global capital. Among the demands of global capital are an open 'market' economy and a skilled workforce which displays attributes associated with a post-Fordist dispensation. Thus, the RNPE's emphasis on attributes associated with post-Fordism, in spite of the fact that Botswana's economy is not post-Fordist, should be understood in terms of the country's desire to be competitive, especially in attracting foreign investment. As Stewart (1996) observes, education in the era of globalization is pivotal in enhancing productivity and attracting foreign capital.

There are other ways policy texts reflect general post-Fordist thinking. Pedagogically, the RNPE explicitly espoused a learner-centred pedagogy based on social constructivism. As argued in Chapters Two and Three, social constructivism implies democratic social relations. In some sense, therefore, constructivism resonates with post-Fordism in that the flattened hierarchies that characterise post-Fordist production processes also require democratic work relations. In the context of the RNPE, it is believed that through activity-oriented teaching and learning methods such as 'project-work, fieldwork, group discussions, pair-work, class presentations…' (Republic of Botswana 1999:iii), learners would develop the capacity to think autonomously and work collaboratively with others. In fact, the homology between the RNPE's preferred skills and those deemed essential in a post-Fordist setup is striking. Just like the latter, the RNPE identified the following attributes as central to a reformed education in Botswana: critical thinking skills, individual initiative, interpersonal skills and problem-solving ability. It is also telling that the Botswana Confederation of Commerce, Industry and Manpower (BOCCIM) recommended these attributes to the Kedikilwe Commission. Learner-centred pedagogy was identified as the 'vehicle' by which these workplace-related attributes would be inculcated in the learners. Given learner-centred pedagogy's resonance with post-Fordist production processes, it is not surprising that the RNPE declared it the official pedagogy in schools.

A 'New' Role for Education?

In the light of these global and local economic developments, the RNPE envisaged a new role for education – the fashioning of a new kind of learner and, by extension, a new kind of worker and citizen. Changing classroom practices, therefore, was at the core of the RNPE initiative. And the RNCE had no illusions about the radical nature of the initiative since it would 'require a transformation in the curriculum, school organization, teaching approaches, teacher training' (Republic of Botswana 1993:40). Riddell (1996) also echoes the need for a radical reorientation of education when he argues that developing the capacities of the self-programmable learner/worker will demand more than just additional schooling and revision of the formal school. It will require a new form of schooling, one with a new ethos and new demands on the teacher.

Following publication of the RNPE, task forces for the various subjects were established to carry out syllabus reviews. The task forces were broad based, comprising academics, teachers, ministry officials in charge of curriculum development and non-governmental organisations (NGOs). Guided by the Curriculum Blueprints for the three cycles of general education (primary, junior secondary and senior secondary) they were to develop 'skill-based syllabi' for all subjects. It was through these syllabi that Botswana's industrial and other human resource needs were, hopefully, to be met. Although there was vagueness regarding what qualified as a 'skill', essential employability skills – as identified by the Botswana Confederation of Commerce, Industry and Manpower (BOCCIM) – guided the review of syllabi. These generic/transferable skills included critical thinking skills, individual initiative, interpersonal skills and problem-solving ability (Republic of Botswana 1993). Task forces were expected to subordinate knowledge/content to these skills. Content was not to be covered just for its own sake. It was to act as a medium through which the learner acquired these skills. Thus content that could not demonstrate potential to promote a particular set of skills related to the world of work was not to be included in the syllabus. The pitfalls of this approach are very clear: how were the task forces to determine what constituted a skill in any particular context? How were task forces to identify content that was vocational in nature? How were they to balance vocational elements (where they could be identified) with academic ones? These practical constraints were worsened by the lack of clear practical guidelines on how the task forces were to carry out the reviews.

The case of the task force for geography (a subject offered in the senior secondary cycle of the general education programme) can illustrate the syllabus review process. It has been indicated elsewhere that the development of the Botswana General Certificate of Secondary Education (BGCSE) geography syllabus was a deductive process based on the behaviourist objectives model of curriculum development (Tabulawa 2002). The task force was presented with the senior secondary Curriculum Blueprint, which stipulated the goals and aims of the senior secondary education programme. The task force then generated general aims of the subject (geography), aligning the aims with those of the senior secondary programme, as laid down in the Curriculum Blueprint. Then specific topics (content) were suggested. Every suggested topic was discussed, focusing mainly on identifying the vocational skills the topic would most likely promote. Once agreement had been reached on its appropriateness, then general objectives pertaining to the topic were generated. These defined in general terms what the student should be able to do after completing a topic. Specific objectives were then generated from the general objectives. These were specific skills that the learner should be able to demonstrate as a result of having undergone instruction, and were to be stated in *assessable, observable and measurable behavioural terms* (Tabulawa 2002). Figure 8.1 illustrates the general arrangement of topics in the Botswana General Certificate of Secondary Education (BGCSE) geography syllabus.

Topic	General Objective	Specific Objective
Weather	Understand and appreciate the elements of weather	• Distinguish between weather and climate. • Demonstrate the ability to measure, record and analyse weather statistics of temperature, rainfall, humidity, air pressure, cloud cover, sunshine, wind speed and wind direction. • Describe factors influencing weather. • Analyse synoptic charts and interpret weather photographs. • Explain the atmospheric process that leads to difference in air pressure. • Identify global wind patterns. • Describe and explain the formation of relief, frontal and convection rainfall with reference to Botswana • Define the concepts of El Niño and La Niña. • Describe and explain the effects of El Niño and La Niña to human activity in Southern Africa.

Figure 8.1: Extract from the Botswana General Certificate of Secondary Education Geography Teaching Syllabus (Republic of Botswana 2000).

This syllabus displays four features reminiscent of the behavioural objectives movement: (a) knowledge is atomised; (b) skills are understood as narrow technical competencies; (c) content is tightly specified; and (d) outcomes are pre-specified/pre-determined as well as cast in measurable behavioural terms. Taken together, these features describe the technical/rational model of teaching discussed in Chapter One. Globally, we are witnessing a resurgence of technical rationality re-packaged as competency-based/outcome-based education which is supported by a rugged form of behaviourism. The latter is undoubtedly the philosophical underpinning of the current school curriculum in Botswana. This is problematic in a number of ways, one of which is the way it conflates constructivism with behaviourism. What are the pedagogical implications of this conflation?

One problematic conclusion emerges, namely that a learner-centred education was to be delivered through a behaviourist curriculum. As already stated, the RNPE settled for the constructivist learner-centred pedagogy as the official pedagogy in schools, and by extension, as the pedagogy that was to deliver the self-programmable learner. I argued in Chapter Three that both learner-centred and teacher-centred pedagogies are value-laden and embed epistemological assumptions that are diametrically opposed to each other. Constructivism and behaviourism are worldviews that engender in human subjects actions or practices that are not necessarily compatible. While the constructivist learner-centred pedagogy stresses process, dialogue, cooperative learning and the constructedness/situatedness of knowledge, behaviourism on the other hand stresses product and an atomised view of knowledge (Weber 2002). Clearly, behaviourism and constructivism are at odds with each other. But how is conflation of such apparently contradictory constructs possible? There may be many reasons. First among them is that policy makers in Botswana are often not adept at critically analysing concepts (such as learner-centredness and behaviourism), and isolating the values that inform each one of the concepts. If they were skilled in that, they probably would have realised that there is tension between the two concepts. Secondly, as argued in Chapter Two, it is seldom the case that learner-centredness is attractive to policy makers for its educational value. Learner-centredness has social, economic and political appeal. Ordinarily, this is more attractive to policy makers than any avowed educational value of the pedagogy. As a matter of fact, the RNPE and associated policy texts do not advance any robust arguments for the cognitive/educational efficacy of the pedagogy whereas social and political arguments for the pedagogy abound in the texts. Thus casting the value of learner-centredness in educational terms in the RNPE was more of a symbolic gesture than anything else. Its real import lay in its value as a legitimating device or justification for linking general education to the world of work. In such circumstances, one does not expect much attention to be paid to (epistemological) assumptions underpinning concepts such as constructivist learner-centredness and behaviourism. Conflating them, therefore, is hardly viewed as problematic. However, at a conceptual level, conflating them sends 'mixed messages' to teachers and can be expected only to lead to pedagogical confusion. The behaviourist curriculum currently obtaining in Botswana undercuts the preferred constructivist learner-centred pedagogy. While it would be disingenuous to suggest a deterministic relationship between behaviourism and didactic teaching, it should, nonetheless, be observed that prospects for such a relationship to develop are enhanced by a tightly framed assessment regime such as the one Botswana has. To look at these issues in more detail, I return to the four features of the Botswana curriculum that are reminiscent of the behavioural objectives movement. These features turn the curriculum into a very potent tool of teacher control/surveillance. Surveillance combined with accountability imperatives attenuate teacher and student autonomy, thereby reducing teaching and learning to technical activities in which teachers' preoccupation is to dispense knowledge for the students to assimilate uncritically.

Surveillance Through Atomization and Tight Specification of Content

Use of behavioural objectives in curriculum design has been criticised for fragmenting 'learning into narrowly conceived categories of behaviour' (Tennant 1988:117) and for leading to an atomised, 'tightly constrained curriculum with closely, specified content' (Naish 1996:73). The holistic and contextual nature of knowledge is lost. A closer look at Figure 8.1 shows that an attempt is made to break topic content into small, discrete units. This decontextualisation of knowledge is accentuated by the fact that the teacher receives the curriculum sealed with the Teacher's Guide to assist them to implement it. The highly specified content (as illustrated in Figure 8.1) leaves absolutely no room for the teacher to determine what to teach. The teacher's role is reduced to that of a technician who dispenses pre-packaged chunks of knowledge without any ethical consideration of what they are doing. In short, the curriculum is teacher-proof. What gets lost as a result is the social nature of learning and skill acquisition, the very attributes learner-centredness is meant to promote. This situation, in Purpel and Shapiro's (1995:109) words, 'robs [teachers] of the opportunity to think creatively about how they teach or what it is that should be taught…'

However, as Knight et al. (1998) observe, to promote and develop creativity, independence, innovativeness and critical thinking, some degree of student and teacher autonomy is a prerequisite. The autonomy is further constricted by an assessment system that is strictly related to the highly specified behavioural objectives. In effect, in the examinations students may not be assessed on an objective that is not reflected in the syllabus. The tendency, therefore, is for teachers to focus almost exclusively on those objectives reflected in the syllabus. Because the syllabus content is atomized, and teachers focus exclusively on those 'atoms', students do not acquire a holistic appreciation of a topic; only content pertaining to those specific objectives of the topic is covered. What of that content which is not covered by the objectives but which is essential for a holistic appreciation of the topic? That tends to be lost. As a result, it is highly probable that students only gain disjointed, partial and fragmented chunks of knowledge that, even when put together, do not cohere into a topic.

In previous curriculum arrangements, syllabi simply listed the topics to be covered without breaking them down into their constituent elements, that is, without specifying objectives. Because the teacher did not know what aspect of the topic would possibly be set for the examination, the tendency was to be as comprehensive in the coverage of the topic as possible. The benefit to the student was more holistic coverage and probably also better understanding of a topic. In other words, even though the content in the previous syllabus was also prescribed, there was still room for the teacher to cover it as extensively as he/she wanted. That room is considerably reduced in the current behaviourist/rationalist curriculum. Thus, the highly prescriptive curriculum that emanated from the RNPE represented a further tightening of the framing and classification of the curriculum, leading in turn to intensified teacher surveillance and control (Bates 1999).

Pre-specified Outcomes and Classroom Practices

Hyland (1994:54) observes that: 'If behavioural objectives... are constructed in highly specific terms or are pursued to the exclusion of all else, they can easily become educationally counter-productive and vulnerable to all the weaknesses of behaviourism...' For example, emphasis on measurable behavioural objectives ensures effective marginalisation of the more humanistic concerns of education in favour of the instrumental. Figure 8.1 above displays this quality; it is clear that it is only the cognitive aspect that is accommodated. 'Fuzzy' achievements such as teamwork, independence and autonomy, creativity, critical thinking and innovativeness which are part of the affective, are effectively excluded. Performance outcomes are therefore valued over process, leading to a 'monocultural view based on the satisfaction of narrow performance criteria [directed] towards fixed and predetermined ends' (Hyland 1994:54). The result may be a 'limited model of teacher-student interaction' (Bull 1985:79). In short, the behaviourist approach to curriculum development embeds a model of teaching and learning that is mechanistic and reductionist. Thus the model undercuts the constructivist learner-centred pedagogy that is meant to deliver the self-programmable worker of the future. While the rhetoric of the RNPE is generally post-Fordist, the curriculum development approach is top-down, hierarchical and therefore inherently concerned with regulation, surveillance and control, all these being qualities of Fordist production processes.

Although teachers are encouraged to go beyond the syllabus objectives, there is no incentive to do so, given the spectre of too many objectives to cover in a year. In conversation, teachers confessed that the emphasis on measurable performance outcomes encourages them to 'teach to the objective'. Treated in this manner, knowledge assumes an objective existence, far removed from student experience. This has implications for classroom pedagogical practices: teachers 'spoon-feed' students with the information they need to pass examinations. 'Delivery' of information to meek and passive students becomes the teacher's preoccupation. The social nature of learning is lost, as Gewirtz 1997:230) observes:

> [There is] a decline in the sociability of teaching [and] pressure on teachers to adopt more traditional pedagogies, with a focus on output rather than process and on particular groups of higher-attaining students.

In this scenario, prospects for the development of generic skills such as interpersonal, communication and teamwork skills are considerably diminished.

While the case has been made above for the deleterious effects (on the possible production of the self-programmable learner) of features (such as atomisation of knowledge and skills, pre-specification of content and the focus on performance outcomes) characterising the RNPE, it is important to point out that the features do not in themselves compel certain classroom practices. Their effect on classroom practices is contextual. For this reason it is necessary to explain why these features play out in the Botswana context in ways that are similar to or different from the way they play out in other education systems. A comparative perspective would be helpful here. For example, the use of behaviourist objectives in both New Zealand's Competence Based Education and Training (CBET) approach to unit standard and the United Kingdom's (UK) General National Vocational Qualifications (GNVQs) had different and contrasting effects on teaching and learning. In the case of New Zealand's unit standards, the use of behaviourist objectives led to didactic teaching, while in the case of the GNVQs (even though competence-based just like the unit standards in New Zealand) evaluations of the programme (see Bates 1999, and Knight et al. 1998 for example) confirmed a relatively easy co-existence of learner-centred pedagogy and a competence-based assessment.

The reason for the deterministic relationship between behaviourist objectives and didactic teaching in the case of unit standards had to do with the fact that standards were tied to content, leading to tightly framed assessments. The GNVQs, on the contrary, explicitly tried to separate pedagogy from curriculum and assessment leaving room for a high degree of procedural autonomy. The case of Botswana is akin to that of the unit standards in New Zealand. As already observed, curriculum in Botswana is centrally orchestrated and is prescriptive to the point of being teacher-proof. When this aspect of the Botswana curriculum is dovetailed to a tightly framed assessment regime in which tests and examinations precisely reflect the myriad of specific objectives, it is not difficult to see how behaviourist outcomes are likely to contrast with learner-centred pedagogy. Thus, whether or not the use of the behaviourist model compels certain classroom practices will depend on how tightly or loosely outcomes are tied to content, this in turn leading to tightly or loosely framed assessments.

The Rise of Accountability

If the objectives-based curriculum and the attendant tightly-framed assessment regime have constricted teachers' autonomy, that is, if the two have augmented the surveillance of the teachers' work, then the emergence of the League Table ranking of schools by performance in public schools examinations results has turned school performance into a public spectacle, the latter defined as the watching of the few (teachers, students, classrooms, schools, etc.) by the many (the entire news-interested public) (Vinson and Ross 2003). Teachers' work-as-spectacle has not directly emanated from the RNPE. Instead, it emanates from the state-inspired public sector reforms that started in the late 1990s. This background is necessary if we are to appreciate the effect of the accountability movement on the education sector.

The global economic crisis of the 1980s affected Botswana badly. Due to a slump in the demand for diamonds in the major markets such as Japan and the United States of America, Botswana, as an economy dependent on diamonds, experienced an unprecedented decline in foreign revenue earnings, and was forced to stockpile diamond production. This adversely impacted the government's ability to deliver on development. For example, in National Development Plan (NDP) 8 (1997/1998-2002/2003) the government forecast gloomy economic prospects and called for austerity measures across the entire public sector. As a result, issues of economy, efficiency and effectiveness came to the fore. This then called for improved *productivity*, defined as 'getting more output from more or less given resources' (Tomlinson 1994:170), on the part of the civil service. This led to a flurry of initiatives, most of which were imported from Malaysia and Singapore, aimed at boosting productivity, such as Work Improvement Teams (WITS), Performance Management System

(PMS) and its derivative, Performance-Based Reward System (PBRS) and Balanced Score Card. All these initiatives aimed at improving the productivity of workers. PBRS, for example, demanded that institutions and employees set themselves targets (couched in behaviourist terms) which they had to achieve within specified periods of time. There were to be rewards and sanctions for good performance and poor performance respectively.

Teaching as a public enterprise was not spared these accountability measures. No sooner had the government started rolling out its productivity drive than were schools expected to draw up plans indicating how they would improve terminal examinations results, in particular the Primary School Leaving Examinations (PLSE), Junior Secondary Certificate Examinations and the Botswana General Certificate of Secondary Education Examinations (BGCSEE). The results of these examinations became the sole indicators of a school's effectiveness. The emergence of the League Table means that the school's position on the Table matters more than anything else. The deleterious effects of league tables in other contexts have been noted (e.g. Jansen 2005; Gorard et al. 2002; Winter 2000; Goldstein 2003). Publication of examination results 'names and shames' those schools regarded as under-performing. In Botswana principals of 'under-performing' schools are written personal letters requesting them to account for their school's under-performance and state why they believe they should not be retired as a result. The effects of all this are not difficult to discern; some include (a) attempts by schools to 'game the system' (Leyva 2009:372) by employing strategies (some legal and some not) to improve examinations scores (e.g. poaching 'good' students from other schools); and (b) increased levels of stress on principals, teachers and students. This occurs as education officers put pressure on principals, who put pressure on teachers, who in turn pressurize students. Hierarchical relations become a defining feature of the system. However, as discussed in the preceding chapter, hierarchical relations reinforce central control which in turn standardizes and routinises official practice, including pedagogical practice.

Other counter-productive effects of accountability are:

(a) The tendency by teachers to 'teach to the specific objective'. This is least surprising given the close link between specific objectives as they appear in syllabi and assessment. With the ends justifying the means, teachers adopt didactic and authoritarian teaching and learning practices (see, for example, Prophet 1995 and Tabulawa 1997), the very practices that are antithetical to the production of a self-programmable, self-regulating learner. Thus, although at the level of policy rhetoric the RNPE promises a radical transformation of classroom pedagogical practices, in reality it may just serve to perpetuate extant didactic pedagogical practices associated with banking education;

(b) Increased competition among students. Learner-centred pedagogy stands for cooperative learning. Such learning, however, is seriously attenuated when out-performing others is more important than working together with them to achieve a common goal. A student at Botswana General Certificate Examinations level (the qualifying examinations for tertiary education) needs necessarily to out-perform others in order (i) to get admission into the most highly-prized programmes at tertiary institutions and (ii) to qualify for government sponsorship to study at the tertiary education level. In such situations, self-interest takes precedence over collective interest. Thus ironically, emphasis on accountability promotes rugged individualism;

(c) Increased competition between schools. It is difficult to imagine neighbouring schools engaging in genuine and authentic cooperation with one another in the interests of the students when each wants to lead the league table. It would seem that school-school cooperation is gradually being replaced by school-school competition.

Conclusion

In summary, it would seem that both the curriculum and the rise of accountability may be averse to a constructivist, learner-centred pedagogy. The behaviourist, skills-based curriculum that resulted from the attempt to attune education to the world of work and the strongly framed assessment regime have attenuated further whatever little existed of teacher autonomy and is encouraging both teachers and students to adopt pedagogical practices aligned to banking education. The objectives-based curriculum development model has attracted criticism, one of which is that it embeds a model of teaching and learning that is mechanistic, reductionist, technical and transmissive (Apple with Junk 1993) and that it neglects the 'examination of inaccessible and unobservable mental events' (Tennant 1988:107) such as critical thinking, creativity, independence of thought, innovativeness and flexibility, the very attributes of the self-programmable learner. 'Teaching to the objective' is rapidly becoming the norm. This is being exacerbated by the rise of accountability measures such as the performance-based reward system (reminiscent of the nineteenth century 'pay-by-results' system) and the publication of league tables of examination results. It would appear, therefore, that the evolving curriculum ambiance in Botswana has the potential to act as a powerful obstacle to pedagogical innovation.

9

Conclusion

Beyond Colonising Pedagogy

It is now time to bring together the central arguments of the book and to comment on the implications for teaching and learning of the socio-cultural approach to pedagogy. In the preceding chapters I have explored the effects of the ideology of technical rationality on pedagogy and how this rationality partially explains the failure to institutionalize learner-centred pedagogy in sub-Sahara African contexts. I have observed that the origins of this ideology can be traced back to the application of the scientific method, particularly the Newtonian, mechanistic cause-and-effect paradigm, to the study of teaching. Science prides itself for its supposedly objective, value-neutral methods of studying objective reality. It is the aim of science to 'discover' the laws that govern the operations of the universe. Scientific methods were adopted in a number of human sciences in the nineteenth and twentieth centuries. For example, cause and effect was used to discover the laws that governed the operation of human societies, leading to the emergence of the field of sociology. In the field of human thinking, cause and effect laid the foundations for the discipline of psychology and led to the most enduring version of psychology generally referred to as 'behaviourism'. Teaching was not to be left behind in this stampede for scientific status. At the beginning of the second half of the twentieth century, efforts to establish the 'scientific basis of the art of teaching' began, the result of which was the process-product paradigm of research on teaching. Teacher effectiveness research was born. At the beginning of the twenty-first century, we witnessed a resurgence of this form of research, but only after a short lull. The effects of positivistic approaches to teaching can be summarized as follows:

- They have led to the neglect of pedagogy, that is, if pedagogy is taken to mean more than just the techniques of teaching (see Alexander 2008). The equation of pedagogy with the 'observable acts of teaching' reduces the former to a technical undertaking. Teaching in this sense becomes an act of establishing the ends of the activity and selecting the most effective means of realizing those ends. This reduces teaching to an exercise in instrumental problem solving. What is lost in this instrumentalisation is a sense of teaching as an ethical and moral activity, in that during teaching, teachers make decisions that are informed by their context (e.g. what they understand to be the nature of knowledge, their views on teaching and learning, etc.).

- The neglect of context in teaching has led to the preponderance of standardized solutions to problems of teaching and learning. One such solution is the ubiquitous recommendation that learner-centred pedagogy can address problems of 'quality' in education anywhere, any time. It is supposedly a one-size-fits-all pedagogical style which works well irrespective of context. This view of pedagogy becomes problematic once we acknowledge pedagogy as shaped and informed by contexts, be they political, cultural or economic.

- In teacher-education programmes, the influence of technical rationality manifests itself in terms of emphasis on students' mastery of techniques of teaching. In other words, emphasis in these programmes is on the 'how', but rarely on the 'why' of teaching. Such an emphasis on technique tends to produce technicians, not professionals capable of reflecting on their teaching. Attention to the 'why' question can assist prospective teachers to appreciate better the complexity and problematic nature of teaching.

- Where teaching is abstracted from its context, a simplistic view of the process of pedagogical reform reigns – reform failure is rationalized in terms of insufficient resources, high student-teacher ratios, and defective teacher-education programmes resulting in poorly trained teachers. The remedy is to pour more resources into the 'deficient' system with the hope that things will change. Yet, pedagogical change in the direction of learner-centredness is still as elusive as ever.

What should be done then, in order to mitigate these deleterious effects of the technicist approach to pedagogical reform? This book's general suggestion is that if a socio-cultural approach to pedagogy were adopted, the chances of successful pedagogical reform in sub-Sahara

Africa would be enhanced. This should not be read as an endorsement of learner-centred pedagogy. In fact, a socio-cultural approach to pedagogy invariably questions the desirability of a universal 'one-true', 'one-size-fits-all' approach to teaching, which is exactly as learner-centredness is presented. This 'one-true approach' to teaching can only serve to entrench the marginalization of pedagogies based on alternative epistemologies. And this is precisely the purpose served by prescribing learner-centred pedagogy as a universal panacea. To the extent that it is a worldview, constructivist learner-centred pedagogy, according to Bowers (2005) is 'the Trojan horse of Western imperialism' since it is an imposition of a Western worldview on other cultures.

In this book, this argument has fully been developed in Chapter Two. If different contexts call for different ways of approaching teaching, then it does not make much sense to prescribe a single approach to teaching and learning for all contexts. In any case, such prescription would amount to a relapse into technical rationality, the object of critique in this book. A socio-cultural approach should be the basis for developing culturally responsive indigenous pedagogies. These may or may not turn out to be pedagogies akin to constructivist learner-centred ones. Guthrie (2011) discusses what he calls 'the Progressive Education fallacy in developing countries', arguing, just like Bowers (2005), that constructivist learner-centred pedagogy is hegemonic and therefore inappropriate for developing countries. Concluding his defense of 'formalistic teaching', Guthrie calls for its accommodation (not its vilification) in Third World contexts. After all, equating learner-centred pedagogy with 'quality' education is as dubious as equating inquiry teaching with development of inquiry skills. Formalistic teaching, properly used, Guthrie (2011) argues, is as effective as any form of teaching in promoting inquiry, critical thinking, problem solving, and other 'soft' skills that are often unduly associated with constructivist teaching. As we continue searching for more effective pedagogies we ought to keep in mind the following words by Edith Ackermann:

['I']here is nothing wrong in showing kids the right ways of doing things, in helping them unfold their natural gifts, or in letting them discover things by themselves. Yet, both *inneism* and *behaviorism* (the believe (sic) in either "fixity" or extreme malleability of mind) can become a formula for disaster when worldviews are at odds, value systems clash, or when some "unpopular views" stubbornly persist within a community. That's when we need to ask ourselves, in all simplicity, "who are we to tell the children of others what they should learn, and how? Who are we to know what's better for others, what's to be bettered? Such questions become particularly relevant in cultures that are not homogenous – in multi-cultural groups where different value systems have to learn to co-exist' (http://learning.media.mit.edu/content/publications/EA.Piaget%20_%20Paper.pdf)

In other words, where there is diversity (of epistemologies, for example), as is the case in our world, one-size-fits-all approaches to anything are not feasible. This is a direct questioning of the hegemony of technical rationality and of the presentation of constructivist learner-centred pedagogy as universal pedagogy.

Bibliography

Akyeampong, K., Pryor, J. and Ampiah, J.G., 2006, 'A vision of successful schooling: Ghanaian teachers' understandings of learning, teaching and assessment', *Comparative Education*, 42 (2), 155-176.

Alexander, R., 2008, 'Education for All, the Quality Imperative and the Problem of Pedagogy', *Create Pathways to Access: Research Monograph No. 20*, Institute of Education, University of London.

Altinyelken, H.K., 2010, 'Pedagogical renewal in sub-Saharan Africa: the case of Uganda', *Comparative Education*, 46 (2), 151-171.

Alverson, H., 1977 'Peace Corps Volunteers in rural Botswana', *Human Organization*, 36 (3), 274-281.

Alverson, H., 1978, *Mind in the Heart of Darkness: Value and Self-Identity among the Tswana of Southern Africa*, New Haven: Yale University Press.

Althusser, L., 1971, 'Ideology and the ideological state apparatuses', in Althusser, L., *Lenin and Philosophy and Other Essays*, London: New Left Books.

Amin, A. (ed.), 1994, *Post-Fordism: A reader*, Oxford: Blackwell.

Anderson, G.L. and Grinberg, J., 1998, 'Educational administration as a disciplinary practice: appropriating Foucault's view of power, discourse, and method', *Educational Administration Quarterly*, 34 (3), 329-353.

Anthony, W., 1979, 'Progressive learning theories: the evidence', in Bernbaum, G. (ed.), *Schooling in Decline*, London: Macmillan.

Anyon, J., 1980, 'Social class and the hidden curriculum at work', *Journal of Education*, 16 (1), 67-92.

Anyon, J., 1994, 'The retreat of Marxism and socialist feminism: postmodernism and post-structural theories in education', *Curriculum Inquiry*, 24 (2), 115-133.

Apple, M.W., 1990, *Ideology and Curriculum*, New York and London: Routledge.

Arnove, R., 1980, 'Comparative education and world systems analysis', *Comparative Education Review*, 24 (1), 48-62.

Arnove, R.F. and Torres, C.A. (eds), 1999, *Comparative Education: The Dialectic of the Global and the Local*, Oxford: Rowman and Littlefield.

Aronowitz, S. and Giroux, H.A., 1985, *Education Under Siege: The Conservative, Liberal, and Radical Debate Over Schooling*, South Hadley: Bergin & Garvey.

Arthur, J., 1998, 'Institutional practices and the cultural construction of primary school teaching in Botswana', *Comparative Education*, 34 (3), 313-326.

Baker, B., 1998, 'Child-centred teaching, redemption, and educational identities: a history of the present', *Educational Theory*, 48 (2), 155-174.

Ball, S. J., 1993, Education policy, power relations and teachers' work', *British Journal of Educational Studies*, XXXXI (2), 106-121.

Bantock, G.H., 1981, *The Parochialism of the Present: Contemporary Issues in Education*, London: Routledge & Kegan Paul.

Baptiste, I., 2001, 'Educating lone wolves: pedagogical implications of human capital theory', *Adult Education Quarterly*, 51 (3), 184-201.

Barrett, A., Chawla-Duggan, R., Lowe, J., Nikel, J. and Ukpo, E., 2006, 'The concept of quality in education: review of the 'international' literature on the concept of quality in education', found at http://www.edqual.org/edqual/publications/workingpaperquality02.pdf

Barrett, A., 2007, 'Beyond the polarization of pedagogy: models of classroom practice in Tanzania primary schools', *Comparative Education*, 43 (2), 273-294.

Bartlett, L., 1991, 'The dialectic between theory and method in critical interpretive research', *British Educational Research Journal*, 17 (1), 19-33.

Bartlett, V.L. and Cox, B., 1982, *Learning to Teach Geography*, Brisbane: John Wiley & Sons.

Bartolome, L.I., 1994, 'Beyond the Methods Fetish: Toward a Humanising Pedagogy', *Harvard Educational Review*, 64 (2), 173-194.

Bassey, M.O., 1999, *Western Education and Political Domination in Africa: A Study in Critical and Dialogical Pedagogy*, London: Bergin & Garvey.

Bates, I., 1999, 'The competence and outcomes movement: The landscape of research', in Flude, M. and Sieminski, S. (eds.), *Education, Training and the Future of Work: Developments in Vocational Educational and Training*, London and New York: Routledge, 98-123.

Beane, J., 1997, *Curriculum Integration: Designing the Core of Democratic Education*, New York: Teachers College Press.

Belenky, M.F., Clinchy, B.M., Goldberger, N.R. and Tarule, J.M., 1986, *Women's Ways of Knowing: The Development of Self, Voice, and Mind*, New York: Basic Books.

Bennett, N., 1976, *Teaching Styles and Pupil Progress*, London: Open Books.

Berger, P., 1963, *Invitation to Sociology: A Humanistic Perspective*, London: Penguin Books.

Berger, P.L., Berger, B. and Kellner, H., 1974, *The Homeless Mind*, Harmondsworth: Penguin.

Berger, P.L. and Kellner, H., 1965, 'Arnold Gehlen and the theory of institutions', *Social Research*, 32 (1), 110-115.

Berger, P.L. and Luckmann, T., 1967, *The Social Construction of Reality: A Treatise in the Sociology of Knowledge*, London: Penguin.

Berger, P.L. and Pullberg, S., 1966, 'Reification and the sociological critique of consciousness', *New Left Review*, 35 , 56-71.

Berlin, I., 1956, 'Introduction', in Berlin, I. (ed.), *The Age of Enlightenment*, New York: Mentor.

Boolstrom, R., 1998, '"Safe spaces": reflections on an educational metaphor', *Journal of Curriculum Studies*, 30 (4), 397-408.

Boron, A., 1995, State, *Capitalism, and Democracy in Latin America*, Boulder: Lynne Rienner Publishers.

Bourdieu:1971, 'Systems of education and systems of thought', in Young, M.F.D. (ed.), *Knowledge and Control: New Directions for the Sociology of Education*, London: Collier & Macmillan, 189-207

Bourdieu, P., 1973, 'Cultural Reproduction and Social Reproduction', in Brown, R. (ed.), *Knowledge, Education and Social Change*, London: Tavistock, 71-99.

Bourdieu, P., 1974, 'The School as a conservative force: scholastic and cultural inequalities', (translated by J.C. Whitehead), in Eggleston, J. (ed.), *Contemporary Research in the Sociology of Education*, London: Methuen, 32-46.

Bourdieu, P., 1977, *Outline of a Theory of Practice*, Cambridge: Cambridge University Press.

Bowen, J., 2003, *A History of Western Education (Vol. 111) The Modern West: Europe and the New World*, London and New York: Routledge.

Bowers, C.A., 2005, *The False Promises of Constructivist Theories of Learning: A Global and Ecological Critique*, New York: Peter Lang.

Bray, M. 1984, 'International influences on African educational development', *International Journal of Educational Development*, 4 (2), 129-136.

Bray, M., Clarke, P., and Stephens, D., 1986, *Education and Society in Africa*, London: Edward Arnold.

Britzman, D.P., 1986, 'Cultural Myths in the Making of a Teacher: Biography and Social Structure in Education', *Harvard Educational Review*, 56 (4), 442-456.

Broadfoot:and Osborn, M. with Gilly, M. and Paillet, A., 1988, 'What professional responsibility means to teachers: National contexts and classroom constants', *British Journal of Sociology of Education*, 9 No. 3: 265-287.

Brodie, K., Lelliott, A. and Davis, H., 2002, 'Forms and substance in learner-centred teaching: teachers' take-up from an in-service programme in South Africa', *Teaching and Teacher Education*, 18 (5), 541-559.

Brown:and Lauder, H., (1992) 'Education, economy, and society: An introduction to a new agenda', in Brown:and Launder, H. (eds.), *Education for Economic Survival: From Fordism to post-Fordism?*, London: Routledge, 1-44.

Bull, H., 1985, 'The use of behavioural objectives', *Journal of Further and Higher Education*, 9 (1) 74-80.

Burnell, P., 1991, 'Introduction to Britain's overseas aid: between idealism and self-interest', in Bose, A. and Burnell:(eds.), *Britain's Overseas Aid Since 1979*, Manchester and New York: Manchester University Press.

Butin, D.W., 2001, 'If this is resistance I would hate to see domination: retrieving Foucault's notion of resistance within educational research', *Educational Studies*, 32 (2), 157-176.

Butterfield, H., 1949, *The Origins of Modern Science*, London: Bell.

Carnoy, M. 1974, *Education as Cultural Imperialism*, New York: David McKay.

Carr, W. 1991, 'Education for democracy? A philosophical analysis of the National Curriculum', *Journal of Philosophy of Education*, 25 (2), pp. 183 -191.

Carter, J., 1997, 'Post-Fordism and the theorization of educational change: What's in a name?', *British Journal of Sociology of Education* 18 (I), 45-61.

Castells, M., 1997, *End of Millennium, Vol. 3 of The Information Age: Economy, Society and Culture,* Oxford: Blackwell.

Chambers, C.M., 1992, '(Other) ways of speaking: lessons from the Dene of Northern Canada', Paper presented at the 26th annual conference of the Teachers of English to Speakers of Other Languages, Vancouver, BC, Canada, University of Lethbridge, Lethbridge, Alberta, Canada.

Chisholm, L., 1997, 'The restructuring of South African education and training in comparative context', in Kallaway, P., Kross, G., Fataar, A. and Donn, G. (eds), *Education after Apartheid: South African Education in Transition*, Cape Town: University of Cape Town Press, 50-67.

Chisholm, L. and Leyendecker, R., 2008, 'Curriculum reform in post-1990s sub-Saharan Africa', *International Journal of Educational Development*, 28 (3), 195-205.

Christie, P., 1997, 'Globalisation and the curriculum: Proposals for the integration of education and training in South Africa', in Kallaway, P., Kross, G., Fataar, A. and Donn, G. (eds.), *Education after Apartheid: South African Education in Transition*, Cape Town: University of Cape Town Press, 111-126.

Clayton, T., 1998, 'Beyond mystification: reconnecting world-system theory for comparative education', *Comparative Education Review*, 42 (4), 479-496.

Clegg, S.C., 1999, 'Globalizing the intelligent organization: Learning organizations, smart workers, (not so) clever countries and the sociological imagination'. *Management Learning,* 30 (3), 259-280.

Cleghorn, A., Merritt, M. and Abagi, J., 1989, 'Language policy and science instruction in Kenyan primary schools', *Comparative Education Review, 33* (1), 21-39.

Cloete, N. and Bunting, I. 2000, *Higher Education Transformation: Assessing Performance in South Africa,* Pretoria: Chet.

Colclough, C. and McCarthy, S., 1980, *The Political Economy of Botswana: A Study of Growth and Distribution*, Oxford: Oxford University Press.

Connell, W.F., 1987, 'Teaching methods, History of', in Dunkin, M. (ed.), *The International Encyclopedia of Teaching and Teacher Education*, Oxford: Pergamon Press, 201-214.

Cooper, D.M., 1982, 'An Interpretation of the Emergent Urban Class Structure in Botswana: A case study of Selebe-Phikwe miners', (Unpublished PhD Thesis), University of Birmingham.

Cousins, M. and Hussain, A., 1984, *Michel Foucault*, London: Macmillan.

Craft, A., 2003 'The limits to "creativity" in education: Dilemmas for the educator', *British Journal of Educational Studies* 51 (2), 113-127.

Crawford, G. 1995, 'Promoting Democracy, Human Rights and Good Governance Through Development Aid: a comparative study of the policies of four northern donors', Working Papers on Democratization, Centre for Democratization Studies, University of Leeds.

Croft, A., 2002, 'Singing under a tree: does oral culture help lower primary teachers be learner-centred?', *International Journal of Educational Development*, 22 (3/4), 321-337.

Cross, M., Mungadi, R. and Rouhani, S., 2002, 'From policy to practice: Curriculum reform in South African education', *Comparative Education* 38 (2), 171-187.

Crossley, M. 1984, 'Strategies for curriculum change and the question of international transfer', *Journal of Curriculum Studies*, 16 (1), 75-88.

Crossley, M and Jarvis, P., 2001, 'Context matters', *Comparative Education*, 37 (4), 405-408.

Cuban, L. and Tyack, D., 1995, *Tinkering Towards Utopia: A Century of Public School Reform*, Boston: Harvard University Press.

Curtin, D., 1965, *The Image of Africa: British Ideas and Action*, 1780-1850, London: Macmillan.

Dalin, P., 1978, *Limits to Educational Change*, London: Macmillan.

Darnell, R., 1979, 'Reflections on Cree interactional etiquette: educational implications', Sociolinguistic Working Paper Number 57, Southwest Educational Development Laboratory, Austin, Texas.

Davies, L., 1988, 'Contradictions of Control: Lessons from exploring teachers' work in Botswana', *International Journal of Educational Development*. 8 (4), 293-303.

de Clercq, F., 1997, 'Effective policies and the reform process: an evaluation of South Africa's new development and education macro policies', in Kallaway, P., Kross, G., Fataar, A. and Donn, G. (eds), *Education After Apartheid: South African Education in Transition*, Cape Town: University of Cape Town Press, 143-168.

Delamont, S., 1976, *Interaction in the Classroom*, London: Methuen.

Denscombe, M., 1982, 'The "Hidden Pedagogy" and its implications for teacher training', *British Journal of Sociology of Education*, 3 (3), 249-265.

Department for International Development (DfID), 1997, *International Co-operation on Education. DfID Education Division Approach Paper* (Draft), produced for the 13th Commonwealth Conference of Education Ministers, 28 July-1 August.

DiMaggio, P., 1979, 'Review Essay: On Pierre Bourdieu', *American Journal of Sociology* 84 (6), 1460-1474.

Donmoyer, R. 2006, 'Take my paradigm ... please! The legacy of Kuhn's construct in educational research', *International Journal of Qualitative Studies in Education*, 19 (1), 11-34.

Dore, R., 1976, *The Diploma Disease*, London: Allen & Unwin.

Doyle, W., 1983, 'Academic work', *Review of Educational Research*, 53 (2), 159-199.

Doyle, W., 1992, 'Curriculum and pedagogy', in P. W. Jackson (ed.), *Handbook of Research on Curriculum*, New York: Macmillan, 486-516.

Dreyfus, H.L. and Rabinow, P., 1982, *Michel Foucault: Beyond Structuralism and Hermeneutics*, Brighton: Harvester.

Dryzek, J.S., 1996, *Democracy in Capitalist Times: ideals, limits and struggles*, New York: Oxford University Press.

Dupre, B., 2007, 50 *Philosophy Ideas you Really Need to Know*, London: Quercus.

Edwards, A.D. and Furlong, V.J., 1978, *The Language of Teaching: Meaning in Classroom Interaction*, London: Heinemann.

Elbaz, F., 1983, *Teacher Thinking: A Study of Practical Knowledge*, London: Croom Helm.

Edwards, R., Nicoll, K. and Tait, A., 1999, 'Migrating metaphors: The globalization of flexibility in   policy', *Journal of Education Policy*, 14 (6), 619-630.

Elliot, J., 1993, 'The assault on rationalism and the emergence of the social market perspectives', in: Elliot, J. (ed.), *Reconstructing Teacher Education: Teacher Development*, London: The Falmer Press.

Elliot, J., 1994, 'The teacher's role in curriculum development: an unresolved issue in English attempts at curriculum reform', *Curriculum Studies: A Journal of Educational Discussion and Debate*, 2 (1), 43-69.

Esland, G.M., 1971, 'Teaching and Learning as the Organization of Knowledge', in Young, M.F.D. (ed.), *Knowledge and Control: New Directions for the Sociology of Education*, London: Collier-Macmillan, 70-115.

Evans, M.W. and Knox, D.M. 1991, 'The Primary Education Improvement Project', in Evans, M.W. and Yoder, J.H. (eds.), *Patterns of Reform in Primary Education: The Case of Botswana*, Gaborone: Macmillan.

Everhart, R., 1983, *Reading, Writing and Resistance*, New York: Routledge and Kegan Paul.

Farquharson, E.A., 1990, '*Culture and Pedagogy: A Socio-historical Analysis of "Primary education in Scotland"*' (1965) (Unpublished PhD Thesis), University of Dundee.

Farrell, J.P. 2002, 'The Aga Khan Foundation experience compared with emerging alternatives to formal schooling', in Anderson, S.E. (ed.), *School Improvement Through Teacher Development: Case Studies of the Aga Khan Foundation Projects in East Africa*, Lisse: Swets and Zeitlinger Publishers.

Flanagan, W., 1992, 'Pedagogical Discourse, Teacher Education Programmes and Social Transformation in South Africa', *International Journal of Educational Development*. 12 (1), 27-35.

Foucault, M., 1977, *Discipline and Punish: The Birth of the Prison*, trans. A. Sheridan, New York: Pantheon.

Foucault, M., 1980, 'Power/Knowledge: Selected Interviews and other Writings, 1972-1977', Colin Gordon (ed.), trans. C. Gordon, L. Marshall, J. Mepham and K. Soper, New York: Pantheon Books.

Foucault, M., 1982, 'Afterword: the subject and power', in H.L. Dreyfus and P. Rabinow (eds.), *Michel Foucault: Beyond Structuralism and Hermeneutics*, Brighton: Harvester, 208-226.

Francis, M., 1979, 'Public Examinations and Educational Advance in Botswana', *Pula: Botswana Journal of African Studies*. 1 (2), 1-20.

Freire, P., 1972, *Pedagogy of the Oppressed*, London: Writers & Readers Publishing Cooperative.

Freire, P., 1985, *The Politics of Education: Culture, Power, and Liberation*, trans. D. Macedo, South Hadley: Bergin & Garvey.

Friedman, M., 1962, *Capitalism and Freedom*, Chicago: The University of Chicago Press.

Fullan, M.G. with Stiegelbauer, S., 1991, *The New Meaning of Educational Change*, 2nd ed., New York: Teachers College Press.

Fuller, B., 1991, *Growing-up Modern: The Western State Builds Third World Schools*, New York: Routledge.

Fuller, B. and Snyder, Jr., C.W., 1991, 'Vocal teachers, silent pupils? Life in Botswana classrooms', *Comparative Education Review*, 35 (2), 274-294.

Fuller, B., Snyder, Jr., C.W., Chapman, D. and Hua, H., 1994, 'Explaining variations in teaching practices: effects of state policy, teacher background, and curricula in southern Africa', *Teaching and Teacher Education*, 10 (2), 141-156.

Fuller, B. and Clarke, P., 1996, 'Raising school effects while ignoring culture? Local conditions and the influence of classroom tools, rules and pedagogy', *Review of Educational Research*, 94 (1), 119-157.

Gage, N.L., 1978, *The Scientific Base for the Art of Teaching*, New York: Teachers College Press.

Gage, N.L. 1989, 'The paradigm wars and their aftermath: A "historical" sketch of research on teaching since 1989', *Teachers College Record*, 91 (2), 135-150.

Gamble, A. and Walton, P., 1976, *Capitalism in Crisis: Inflation and the State*, London and Basingstoke: Macmillan.

Gaolathe, B., 2007, *Budget Speech 2007*, Gaborone: Government Printers.

Gee, J.P., Hull, G., and Lankshear, C., 1996, *The New Work Order: Behind the Language of the New Capitalism*, St Leonards: Allen and Unwin.

Gewirtz, S., 1997, 'Post-Welfarism and the Reconstruction of Teachers' Work in the UK', *Journal of Education Policy*, 12, 217-231.

Giddens, A., 1976, *New Rules of Sociological Method*, New York: Basic Books.

Giddens, A., 1990, *The consequences of modernity*, Stanford: Stanford University Press.

Gilbert, N., Burrows, R. and Pollert, A., 1992 (eds.), *Fordism and Flexibility Divisions and Change*, London: Macmillan.

Ginsburg, M.B., Kamat, S., Raghu, R. and Weaver, J., 1992, 'Educators/politics', *Comparative Education Review*, 36 (4), 417-445.

Giroux, H.A., 1980, 'Beyond the correspondence theory: notes on the dynamics of educational reproduction and transformation', *Curriculum Inquiry*, 10 (3), 225-247.

Giroux, H.A., 1985, 'Introduction', in Freire, P., The Politics of Education, New York: Bergin and Garvey.

Giroux, H.A. and McLaren, P., 1986, 'Teacher education and the politics of engagement: the case for democratic schooling', *Harvard Educational Review*, 56 (3), 213-238.

Goldberger, N.R., 1996, 'Cultural imperatives and diversity in ways of knowing', in Goldberger, N.R., Tarule, J.M., Clinchy, B.M. and Belenky, M.F. (eds), *Knowledge, Difference and Power: Essays Inspired by Women's Ways of Knowing*, New York: Basic Books, 335-371.

Goldstein, H., 2003, 'Education for All: the globalization of learning targets', *Research Intelligence*, 82, 18-22.

Gorard, S., Rees, G. and Selwyn, N., 2002, 'The conveyer belt effect: a re-assessment of the impact of national targets for lifelong learning, *Oxford Review of Education*, 28 (1), 75-89.

Gore, J.M., 1994, 'Enticing challenges: an introduction to Foucault and educational discourses', in Martusewicz, R.A. and Reynolds, W.M. (eds), *Inside/Out: Contemporary Critical Perspectives in Education*, New York: St. Martin's, 109-120.

Gossett, C.W., 1986, 'The Civil Service in Botswana: Personnel Policies in Comparative Perspective', (Unpublished PhD Thesis) Stanford University.

Gottlieb, E. 2000, 'Are we post-modern yet? Historical and theoretical explorations in comparative education', in Moon, B., Ben-Peretz, M. and Brown, S. (eds), *Routledge International Companion to Education*, London and New York: Routledge.

Gutek, G.L., 2005, *Historical and Philosophical Foundations of Education: A Biographical Introduction*. Upper Saddle: Pearson/Merrill/Prentice Hall.

Guthrie, G., 1980, 'Stages of educational development? Beeby revisited', *International Review of Education*, XXVI, 411-449.

Guthrie, G., 1990, 'To the defense of traditional teaching in lesser-developed countries', in Rust, V.D. and Daun: (eds), *Teachers and Teaching in the Developing World*, New York and London: Garland Publishing.

Guthrie, G., 2011, 'The Progressive Education Fallacy in Developing Countries: In Favour of Formalism', Dordrecht: Springer.

Harber, C., 1997, *Education, Democracy and Political Development in Africa*, Brighton: Sussex Academic Press.

Hartley, D., 2003, 'New economy, new pedagogy?', *Oxford Review of Education* 29 (1), 81-94.

Hayter, T., 1971, *Aid as Imperialism*, Harmondsworth: Penguin Books.

Henry, A., 1996, 'Five black women teachers critique child-centered pedagogy: possibilities and limitations of oppositional standpoints', *Curriculum Inquiry*, 26 (4), 363-384.

Hickox, M. and Moore, R., 1992 'Education and post-Fordism: A new correspondence?', in Brown:and Lauder, H. (eds.), *Education for Economic Survival: From Fordism to post-Fordism?*, London and New York: Routledge, 95-116.

Hodgson, M.L. and Bellinger, W.G., 1932, *Britain in Southern Africa (no. 2): Bechuanaland Protectorate*, London: London Press.

Hoffman, J., 1988, *State, Power and Democracy: Contentious Concepts in Practical Political Theory*, Brighton: Wheatsheaf.

Holliday, A.R., 1991, 'Dealing with Tissue Rejection in EFL projects: the role of an ethnographic Means Analysis', (Unpublished PhD Thesis), University of Lancaster.

Holt, J., 1964, *How Children Fail*, Harmondsworth: Penguin.

Holt-Jensen, A., 1980, *Geography: Its History and Concepts – A Student's Guide*, London: Harper and Row.

Hopkin, A., 1996, *Teaching and Learning in a Developmental Context: A Preliminary Assessment*, Paper presented at the 16th Annual International Seminar for Teacher Education, Porto Alegre, Brazil, April 17-23.

Horgan, G., Moss, M.M., Kesupile, A.S., Maphorisa, J. and Haseley, L., 1991, 'Toward a child-centred classroom', in Evans, M.M. and Yoder, J.H. (eds.), *Patterns of Reform in Primary Education: The Case of Botswana*, Gaborone: Macmillan.

Hoyle, E., 1969, 'How does the curriculum change? (2) Systems and strategies', *Journal of Curriculum Studies*, 1 (3).

Hoyle, E., 1970, 'Planning organizational change in education', *Research in Education*, May, 1-22.

Hoyle, E. and Bell, R., 1972, *Problems of Curriculum Innovation 1*, London: The Open University Press.

Hoyle, E., 1988, 'Micropolitics of educational organisations', in Westoby, A. (ed.), *Culture and Power in Educational Organizations*, Milton Keynes: Open University Press, 255-269.

Hurst, P., 1975, 'The criteria for the selective stage of the transfer of educational innovation', *Comparative Education*, 11 (1), 63-71.

Hurtado, A., 1996, 'Strategic suspensions: feminists of color theorize the production of Knowledge', in Goldberger, N.R., Tarule, J.M., Clinchy, B.M. and Belenky, M.F. (eds), *Knowledge, Difference, and Power: Essays Inspired by Women's Ways of Knowing*, New York: Basic Books, 372-392.

Hyland, T., 1994, *Competence, Education and NVQs: Dissenting Perspectives*, London: Cassell.

Jansen, J.D., 2002, 'Political symbolism as policy craft: Explaining non-reform in South African education after apartheid', *Journal of Education Policy* 17 (2), 199-215.

Jansen, J.D., 2005, 'Targeting education: the politics of performance and the prospects of 'Education for All', *International Journal of Educational Development*, 25 (4), 368-380.

Jenkins, R., 1992, *Pierre Bourdieu*, London: Routledge.

Jessop, T. and Penny, A., 1998, 'A study of teacher voice and vision in the narratives of rural South African and Gambian primary school teachers', *International Journal of Educational Development*, 18 (5), 393-403.

Johnson, D., Garrett, R. and Crossley, M., 2003, 'Global connectedness and local diversity: Forging "new" literacies at the point of confluence' in Sutherland, R., Claxton, G. and Pollard, A. (eds), *Learning and Teaching: Where World Views Meet*, Stoke-on-Trent: Trentham Books, 19-34.

Jones, D., 1990, 'The genealogy of the urban schoolteacher', in Ball, S.J. (ed.), *Foucault and Education: Disciplines and Knowledge*, London: Routledge, 57-77.

Jones, L., 1997, 'Talking about "everyday" issues in the formal classroom setting: a framework for understanding the dynamics of interaction', *Journal of Curriculum Studies*, 29 (5), 559-567.

Jones, A., 1989, 'The Cultural Production of Classroom Practice', *British Journal of Sociology of Education*, 10 (1), 19-31.

Kay, S., 1975, 'Curriculum Innovations and Traditional Culture: A Case History of Kenya', *Comparative Education*, 11 (3), 183-191.

Kelly, A.V., 1986, *Knowledge and Curriculum Planning*, London: Harper & Row.

Kenyatta, J. 1961, *Facing Mt. Kenya: The Tribal Life of the Gikuyu*, London: Mercury Books.

Kincheloe, J., 1997, 'Introduction', in Goodson, I.F., *The Changing Curriculum: Studies in Social Construction*, New York: Peter Lang, ix-xl.

King, K. 1989, 'Primary schooling and development knowledge in Africa', *Studies in Science Education*, 17, 29-56.

King, K., 1991, *Aid and Education in the Developing World: the Role of the Donor Agencies in Educational Analysis*, Essex: Longman.

King, K. and McGrath, S., 2002, *Globalisation, Enterprise and Knowledge: Education, Training and Development in Africa*, Oxford: Symposium Books.

Knight, P., Helsby, G. and Saunders, M., 1998, 'Independence and prescription in learning: Researching the paradox of Advanced GNVQs', *British Journal of Educational Studies*, 46 (1), 54-67.

Komba, W., 1998, 'Changes in liberal and non-liberal political and educational thought', *Journal of Philosophy of Education*, 32 (2), 195-206.

Kraak, A., 1995, 'Radical posturing, the challenge of policy-making and the RDP: A response to Wilderson', *Perspectives in Education*, 16 (1), 183-190.

Kuhn, T., 1962, 1970, *The Structure of Scientific Revolutions*, Chicago: University of Chicago Press.

Leith, J.C., 2005, *Why Botswana Prospered*, Montreal and Kingston: McGill-Queen's University Press.

Leyva, R. 2009, 'No Child Left Behind: A Neo-liberal repackaging of Social Darwinism', *Journal of Critical Education Policy Studies*, 7 (1), 364-381. Accessed 20th August 2011at http://www.jceps.com/?pageID=article&article=156

Lincoln, Y. and Guba, E., 1985, *Naturalistic Inquiry*, Beverley Hills: Sage.

Lipset, S.M., 1959, 'Some social requisites of democracy: economic development and political legitimacy', *American Political Science Review*, 53 (1), 69-105.

Lortie, D.C., 1975, *School Teacher: A Sociological Study*, Chicago: University of Chicago Press.

Macpherson, C.B., 1973, 'Elegant tombstones: a note on Friedman's freedom', in *Democratic Theory: Essays in Retrieval*, Oxford: Oxford University Press.

Mafela, L., 1993, 'Competing Gender Ideologies in Education in Bechuanaland Protectorate, c1840-c. 1945', (Unpublished PhD Thesis) Northwestern University.

Magdoff, H., 1982, 'Imperialism: a historical survey', in Alavi, H. and Shanin, T. (eds), *Introduction to the Sociology of 'Developing' Countries*, London: Macmillan.

Maher, F.A. and Tetreault, M.K.T., 1994, *The Feminist Classroom*, New York: Basic Books.

Marginson, S., 1999, 'After globalization: emerging politics of education', *Journal of Education Policy*, 14 (1), 19-31.

Marope, P.T.M., 1994, 'Expansion of national systems of education: the case of Botswana', in D'Oyley, V., Blunt, A. and Barnhardt, R. (eds.), *Education and Development: Lessons from the Third World*, Calgary: Detselig Enterprises Ltd, 21-45.

Marope, P.T.M. with Amey, A.A.K., 1995, *BEC [Basic Education Consolidation] Project Impact and Basic Education Teacher Effectiveness Study*, Gaborone: BEC Project/AED [Academy for Educational Development] and Department of Teacher Training and Development, Ministry of Education.

Maruatona, T., 1994, 'Hegemony and the curriculum process: A critique of curriculum development and implementation in Botswana' *Mosenodi: Journal of the Botswana Educational Research Association*, 2 (2), 15-32.

Mac an Ghaill, M., 1992, 'Student Perspectives on Curriculum Innovation and Change in an English Secondary School: an empirical study', *British Educational Research Journal*, 18 (3), 221-234.

Masterman, M., 1970, 'The Nature of a Paradigm', in Lakatos, I. and Musgrove, A. (eds.), *Criticism and the Growth of Knowledge*, Cambridge: Cambridge University Press, 59-90.

Mbiti, J., 1969, *African Religions and Philosophy*, London: Heinemann.

McEneaney, E.H., 2002, 'Power and knowledge produced by educationists', [Review of Popkewitz, T.S (ed.), *Educational Knowledge: Changing the Relationships Between the State, Civil Society, and the Educational Community*], *Journal of Curriculum Studies*, 34 (I), 103-115.

McGrath, S., 1997, 'Education and training in transition: Analysing the NQF', in Kallaway, P., Kross, G., Fataar, A. and Donn, G. (eds.), *Education after Apartheid: South African Education in Transition*, Cape Town: University of Cape Town Press, 169-182.

McGrath, S., 2008, 'Editorial: developing teachers and teaching', *International Journal of Educational Development*, 28 (1), 1-3.

McNiff, J., 1988, *Action research: Principles and Practices*, London: Macmillan Education.

Meyer-Bisch:(ed.), 1995, *Culture of Democracy: A Challenge for Schools*, Paris: UNESCO.

Organisation for Economic Co-operation and Development (OECD), 1987, *Structural Adjustment and Economic Performance*, Paris: OECD.

Ministry of Education and Culture (Namibia), 1993, *Toward Education for All*, Windhoek.

Mgadla, P.T., 1986, 'Missionary and colonial education among the Bangwato: 1862-1948', Unpublished PhD thesis, Boston University, Boston, MA.

Mtika:and Gates:2010, 'Developing learner-centred education among secondary trainee teachers in Malawi: the dilemma of appropriation and application, *International Journal of Educational Development*, 30, 396-404.

Muller, J., 2000, *Reclaiming Knowledge: Social theory, curriculum and education policy*, London and New York: RoutledgeFalmer.

Naish, M., 1996, 'The geography curriculum: A martyr to epistemology?', in Gerber, R. and Lidstone, J. (eds), *Development and Directions in Geographical Education*, C1evedon: Channel View Publications, 63-76.

Nakabugo, M.G. and Sieborger, R. 2001, 'Curriculum reform and teaching in South Africa: making a "paradigm shift"'? *International Journal of Educational Development*, 21 (1), 53-60.

Namuddu, K., 1991, 'Strengthening analytical and research capacity in education: lessons from national experience', in Gmelin, W. and King, K. (eds), *Strengthening Analytical Research Capacities in Education*, Bonn: German Foundation for International Development, 51-62.

Nash, R., 1976, 'Pupils' expectations of their teachers', in Stubbs, M. and Delamont, S. (eds.), *Explorations in Classroom Observation*, London: Wiley, 83-98.

Nola, R., 1997, 'Constructivism in science and science education: A philosophical critique', *Science and Education* 6 (1-2), 55-83.

Nykiel-Herbert, B., 2004, 'Mis-constructing knowledge: the case of learner-centred pedagogy in South Africa', *Prospects*, XXXIV (3), 249-265.

Orner, M., 1992, 'Interrupting the calls for student voice in 'liberatory' education: a feminist poststructural perspective', in Luke, C. and Gore, J. (eds), *Feminisms and Critical Pedagogy*, New York: Routledge, 74-89.

O-saki, K. K. and Agu, A.O., 2002, 'A study of classroom interaction in primary schools in the United Republic of Tanzania', *Prospects*, XXXII (1), 103-116.

O'Sullivan, M., 2004, 'The reconceptualisation of learner-centred approaches: a Namibian case study', *International Journal of Educational Development*, 24 (6), 585-602.

Ottaway, A.K.C., 1962, *Education and Society*, (2nd Edition), London: Routledge & Kegan Paul.

Overseas Development Administration (ODA), 1994, *Aid to Education in 1993 and Beyond*, London: ODA.

Pansiri, N.O., 2008, 'Improving commitment to basic education for the minorities in Botswana: a challenge for policy and practice', *International Journal of Educational Development*, 28 (4), 446-459.

Papert, S., 1980, *Mindstorms: Children, Computers, and Powerful Ideas*, New York: Basic Books.

Parsons, Q.N., 1984, 'Education and development in precolonial and colonial Botswana to 1965', in Crowder, M. (ed.), Education for Development in Botswana, Gaborone: Macmillan, 21-45.

Pearson, A.T. 1989, *The Teacher: Theory and Practice in Teacher Education*, New York: Routledge

Peet, R., 1991, *Global Capitalism: Theories of Societal Development*, London and New York: Routledge.

Peters, R.S., 1965, 'Education as initiation', in Archambault, R.D. (ed.), *Philosophical Analysis and Education*, London: Routledge.

Pignatelli, F., 1993, 'What can I do?: Foucault on freedom and the question of teacher agency', *Educational Theory*, 43 (4), 411-432.

Pogrow, S., 1996, 'Reforming the Wannabe Reformers: Why educational reforms almost always end up making things worse', *Phi Delta Kappan*, 77(10), 656-663.

Pontefract, C. and Hardman, F. 2005, 'The discourse of classroom interaction in Kenyan primary schools', *Comparative Education*, 41 (1), 87-106.

Priestly, M., 2002, 'Global discourses and national reconstruction: The impact of globalization on curriculum policy', *The Curriculum Journal*, 13 (1), 121-138.

Prophet, R.B., 1990, 'Experience, Language, Knowledge and Curriculum', in Snyder, C.W., and Ramatsui, P.T. (eds), *Curriculum in the Classroom*, Gaborone: Macmillan, 109-119.

Prophet, R., 1995, 'Views from the Botswana junior secondary classroom: Case study of a curriculum intervention', *International Journal of Educational Development*, 15 (2), 127-140.

Prophet, R.B. and Hodson, D. 1988, 'The science of common things: a study in social control', *History of Education*, 17 (2), 131-147.

Prophet, R. and Rowell, P., 1990, 'The curriculum observed', in Snyder, C.W. and Ramatsui, P.T. (eds), *Curriculum in the classroom*, Gaborone: Macmillan, I-56.

Prophet, R.B. and Rowell, P.M., 1993, 'Coping and control: science teaching strategies in Botswana, *International Journal of Qualitative Studies in Education*, 6 (3), 197-209.

Psacharopoulos, G., 1981, 'Returns to education: an updated international comparison', *Comparative Education*, 17 (3), 321-341.

Punch, M., 1977, *Progressive Retreat: A Sociological Study of Darlington Hall School,* 1926-1957, Cambridge: Cambridge University Press.

Purpel, D.E. and S. Shapiro, 1995, *Beyond Liberation and Excellence: Reconstructing the Public Discourse on Education,* Westport: Bergin and Garvey.

Ramage, Sir Richard, 1961, *Report on the Structures of the Public Services in Basotoland, Bechuanaland and Swaziland,* University of Botswana Library, Gaborone.

Rassool, N., 1993, 'Post-Fordism? Technology and new forms of control: The case of technology in the curriculum', *British Journal of Sociology of Education,* 14 (3), 227-244.

Republic of Botswana, 1977, *Education for Kagisano (Social Harmony): Report of the National Commission on Education,* Gaborone: Government Printers.

Republic of Botswana, 1993, *Report of the National Commission on Education,* Gaborone: Government Printers.

Republic of Botswana, 1994, *Revised National Policy on Education* (RNPE), Gaborone: Government Printers.

Republic of Botswana, 1999, *Botswana General Certificate of Secondary Education: The Geography Assessment Syllabus,* Gaborone: Educational Research and Testing Division, Ministry of Education.

Republic of Botswana, 2000, *Botswana General Certificate of Secondary Education: The Geography Teaching Syllabus,* Gaborone: Educational Research and Testing Division, Ministry of Education.

Reyes, M. de Luz, 1992, 'Challenging venerable assumptions: literacy instruction for linguistically different students', *Harvard Educational Review,* 62, 427-446.

Richardson, Y., Tidwell, D. and Lloyd, C. 1991, 'The relationship between teachers' beliefs and practices in reading comprehension instruction', *American Educational Research Association Journal,* 28 (3), 559-586.

Richardson, V., 1994, 'Conducting research on practice', *Educational Researcher,* 23 (5), 5-10.

Riddell, A.R., 1996, 'Globalisation: Emasculating or opportunity for educational planning?' *World Development,* 24 (8), 1357-1372.

Riseborough, G.F., 1985, 'Pupils, teachers' careers and schooling: an empirical study', in Ball, S.J. and Goodson, I.F. (eds.), *Teachers' Lives and Careers,* London: Falmer, 202-265.

Robins, K. and Webster, F. 1999, *Times of the Technoculture: From the Information Society to the Virtual Life,* London and New York: Routledge.

Rostow, W.W., 1960, *Stages of Economic Growth,* London: Cambridge University Press.

Rowell, P., 1995, 'Perspectives on pedagogy in teacher education: The case of Namibia', *International Journal of Educational Development,* 15 (1), 3-13.

Royal Norwegian Ministry of Foreign Affairs, 1993, *Support for Democratic Development,* Oslo: Ministry of Foreign Affairs.

Rueschemeyer, D., Stephens, E.H. and Stephens, J.D., 1992, *Capitalist Democracy and Development,* Cambridge: Polity Press.

Ruggie, J.G., 1982, 'International regimes, transactions, and change: embedded liberalism in the postwar economic order', *International Organization*, 36 (2), 379-415.

Rusk, R.R., 1954, *The Doctrines of Great Educators*, London: Macmillan.

Samoff, J., 1993, 'The reconstruction of schooling in Africa', *Comparative Education Review*, 37 (2), 186-222.

Sarason, S.B., 1990, *The Predictable Failure of Educational Reform: Can We Change Course Before It's Too Late?* Jossey-San Francisco: Bass Publishers.

Schapera, I. 1941, *Married Life in an African Tribe*, London: Faber & Faber.

Schlechty, P.C. and Atwood, H.E., 1977, 'The student-teacher relationship', *Theory into Practice*, 16 (4), 285-289.

Scholte, J.A., 2000, *Globalisation: A Critical Introduction*, Basingstoke: Palgrave.

Schon, D., 1983, *The Reflective Practitioner: How Professionals Think in Action*, New York: Basic Books.

Schon, D., 1987, *Educating the Reflective Practitioner*, San Francisco: Jossey-Bass.

Scruton, R., 1982, *A Dictionary of Political Thought*, London: Macmillan Press.

Semali, L., 2001, 'Review of Reagan, T. and Mahwah, N., 2000, *Non-Western Educational Traditions: Alternative Approaches to Educational Thought and Practice*, New Jersey: Lawrence Erlbaum Associates,. *Comparative Education Review*, 45 (4), 643-646.

Semali, L.M., 2000, *Literacy in Multimedia America: Integrating Media Education Across the Curriculum*, New York: Falmer Press.

Senge, P.M., 1991, *The Fifth Discipline: The Art and Practice of the Learning Organisation*, New York: Doubleday.

Serbessa, D.D., 2006, 'Tension between traditional and modern teaching-learning approaches in Ethiopian primary schools', *Journal of International Cooperation in Education*, 9 (1), 123-40.

Serpell, R., 1993, *The Significance of Schooling*, Cambridge: Cambridge University Press.

Sharp, R. and Green, A., 1975, *Education and Social Control: A Study in Progressive Primary Education*, London: Routledge and Kegan Paul.

Sharpes, D.K., 1988, *Curriculum Traditions and Practices*, London: Routledge.

Sharpes, D.K., 2002, *Advanced Educational Foundations for Teachers: The History, Philosophy, and Culture of Schooling*, New York: RoutledgeFalmer.

Shipman, M., 1971, *Education and Modernisation*, London: Faber & Faber.

Shukla, S., 1994, 'Democracy and education: reflections from the Third World in the late twentieth century', in Kumar, K. (ed.), *Democracy and Education in India*, London: Sangam Book Limited.

Shulman, L.S., 1986, 'Paradigms and research programs in the study of teaching: A contemporary perspective', in M.C. Wittrock (ed.), *Handbook of Research on Teaching* (3rd ed.), New York: Macmillan, 3-36.

Silcock, P., 1996, 'Three principles for a new progressivism', *Oxford Review of Education* 22 (2), 199-215.

Skilbeck, M. (ed.), 1970, *John Dewey*, London: Macmillan.

Smyth, W.J., 1984, 'Toward a "critical consciousness" in the instructional supervision of experienced teachers', *Curriculum Inquiry*, 14 (4), 425-436.

Smyth, J., 1986, 'An alternative and critical perspective for clinical supervision', in Sirotnik, K. and Oakes, J. (eds.), *Critical Perspective on Organisation and Improvement of Schooling*, Geelong: Deakin University Press.

Smyth, W.J., 1991, *Teachers as Collaborative Learners*, Milton Keynes: Open University Press.

St. Pierre, E.A., 2000, 'Poststructural feminism in education: an overview', *International Journal of Qualitative Studies in Education*, 13 (5), 477-515.

Stambach, A. 1994, '"Here in Africa, we teach; students listen": lessons about culture from Tanzania', *Journal of Curriculum and Supervision*, 9 (4), 368-385.

Stenhouse, L., 1980, 'Reflections', in Stenhouse, L. (ed.), *Curriculum Research and Development in Action*, London: Heinemann, 245-262.

Stern:and Shavelson, R., 1983, 'Reading, teachers' judgments, plans, and decision making', *Reading Teacher*, 37 (3), 280-286.

Stevenson, D.L. and Baker, D.P., 1991, 'State Control of the Curriculum and Classroom Instruction', *Sociology of Education* 64 (1), 1-10.

Stewart, F., 1996, '"Globalisation" and education', *International Journal of Educational Development*, 16 (4), 327-333.

Stocpol, T., 1977, 'Wallerstein's World Capitalist System: a theoretical and historical critique', *American Journal of Sociology*, 82 (5), 1075-1102.

Stokke, O.S., 1995, 'Aid and political conditionality: core issues and state of the art', in Stokke, O.S. (ed.), *Aid and Political Conditionality*, London: Frank Cass.

Swartland, J.R. and Taylor, D.C., 1988, 'Community Financing of Schools in Botswana', in Bray, M. (ed.), *Community Financing of Education*, Oxford: Pergamon Press, 139-153.

Tabulawa, R., 1995, 'A socio-cultural analysis of geography classroom practice in Botswana senior secondary schools', Unpublished PhD Thesis, University of Birmingham (UK)

Tabulawa, R., 1997, 'Pedagogical classroom practice and the social context: the case of Botswana', *International Journal of Educational Development*, Vol. 17 (2), pp. 189-204.

Tabulawa, R., 1998a, 'Pedagogical styles as paradigms: Towards an analytical framework for understanding classroom practice in Botswana', *Mosenodi: Journal of the Botswana Educational Research Association*, 6, No. 1: 3-15.

Tabulawa, R., 1998b, 'Teachers' perspectives on classroom practices in Botswana: implications for pedagogical change', *International Journal of Qualitative Studies in Education*, Vol. 11 (2), pp. 249-268.

Tabulawa, R., 2002, 'Geography in the Botswana secondary curriculum: A study in curriculum renewal and contraction, *International Research in Geographical and Environmental Education*, 11 (2), 102-118.

Tabulawa, R., 2003, 'International aid agencies, learner-centred pedagogy, and political democratization: a critique', *Comparative Education*, Vol. 39 (1), pp. 7-26.

Tabulawa, R., 2004, 'Geography students as constructors of classroom knowledge and practice: a case study from Botswana', *Journal of Curriculum Studies*, Vol. 36 (1), pp. 53-73.

Tabulawa, R., 2009, 'Education reform in Botswana: reflections on policy contradictions and paradoxes', *Comparative Education*, 45 (1), pp. 87-107.

Tabulawa, R., 2011, 'The rise and attenuation of the basic education programme (BEP) in Botswana: a global-local dialectic approach, *International Journal of Educational Development*, Vol. 31 (5), pp. 433-442.

Tennant, M., 1988, *Psychology and Adult Learning*, London: Routledge.

Terhart, E., 2003, 'Constructivism and teaching: A new paradigm in general didactics?', *Journal of Curriculum Studies*, 35 (1), 25-44.

Tikly, L., 2001, 'Globalisation and education in the postcolonial world: Towards a conceptual Framework', *Comparative Education*, 37 (2), 151-171.

Tikly, L., Lowe, J., Crossley, M., Dachi, H., Garrett, R. and Mukabaranga, B., 2003, *Globalisation and Skills for Development in Rwanda and Tanzania*, London: DFID.

Tisdell., E.J., 1998, 'Poststructural feminist pedagogies: the possibilities and limitations of feminist emancipatory adult learning theory and practice', *Adult Education Quarterly*, 48 (3), 139-156.

Tom, A.R., 1980, 'The reform of teacher education through research: a futile quest?', *Teachers College Record*, 82 (1), 15-29.

Tomlinson, J., 1984, 'The politics of economic measurement: the rise of the "productivity Problem" in the 1940s, in Hopwood, A.G. and Miller (eds), *Accounting as Social and Institutional Practice*, Cambridge: Cambridge University Press, 168-189.

Thompson, K.B., 1972, *Education and Philosophy*, Oxford: Blackwell.

Thomson, G.H., 1947, *A Modern Philosophy of Education*, London: George Allen & Unwin.

Turner, R.H., 1961, 'Modes of Social Ascent through Education: Sponsored and Contest Mobility', in Halsey, A.H., Floud, J., and Anderson, C.A. (eds), in *Education, Economy and Society: A Reader of the Sociology of Education*, London: The Free Press, 121-139.

United States Agency for International Development, 1986, *Primary Education Improvement Project*. Project Number 633-0222. Final Report (unpublished).

Tuthill, D. and Ashton, P., 1983, 'Improving educational research through the development of educational paradigms', *Educational Researcher*, 12 (10), 6-14.

Usher, R. and R. Edwards, 1994, *Post-modernism and Education*, London and New York: Routledge.

Vanqa, T., 1989, 'Issues in the Development of the Education System in Botswana (1966-1986)', *Pula: Botswana Journal of African Studies*, 6 (2) 28- 37.

Vavrus, F., 2009, 'The cultural politics of constructivist pedagogies: teacher education reform in the United Republic of Tanzania', *International Journal of Educational Development*, 29, 303-311.

Vinson, K.D. and Ross, E.W., 2003, *Image and Education: Teaching in the Face of the New Disciplinarity*, New York: Peter Lang.

Vulliamy, G. and Carrier, J., 1985, 'Sorcery and SSCEP: the cultural context of an educational innovation', *British Journal of Sociology of Education*, 6 (1), 17-33.

Walford, G., 1994, *Choice and Equity in Education*, London: Cassell.

Waller, W., 1965, *The Sociology of Teaching*, New York: Wiley, (first published in 1932).

Wallerstein, I. 1984, *The Politics of the World-Economy: The States, the Movements, and the Civilizations,* Cambridge: Cambridge University Press.

Weber, E., 2002, 'Shifting to the right: The evolution of equity in the South African government's development and education policies, 1990-1999', *Comparative Education Review*, 46 (3), 261-290.

Wildy, H. and Wallace, J., 1995, 'Understanding teaching or teaching for understanding: Alternative frameworks for science classrooms', *Journal of Research in Science Teaching,* 32(2), 143-156.

William, S.R., 1999, 'Mathematics (Grades 7-12)', in McCormick, R. and Paechter, C. (eds) *Learning and Knowledge*, Milton Keynes: P.C.P in association with The Open University.

Willis, P.E., 1977, *Learning to Labour: How Working Class Kids Get Working Class Jobs*, Aldershot: Saxon House.

Windschitl, M., 2002, 'Framing constructivism in practice as the negotiation of dilemmas: an analysis of the conceptual, pedagogical, cultural and political challenges facing teachers, *Review of Educational Research*, 72 (2), 131-175.

Winter, C., 2000, 'The state steers by remote control: standardizing teacher education', *International Studies in Sociology of Education*, 10 (2), 153-175.

Woodhall, M., 1985, 'Human capital', in Husen, T. and Postlethwaite, T.N. (eds), *The International Encyclopedia of Education: Research and Studies,* Vol. 4. Oxford: Pergamon Press.

World Bank, 1999, *Education Sector Strategy*, Washington DC: World Bank.

Yoder, J.H. and Mautle, G., 1991, 'The context of reform', in Evans, M. and Yoder, J. (eds), *Patterns of Reform in Primary Education: The Case of Botswana*, Gaborone: Macmillan.

Young, M., 1996, 'A curriculum for the twenty-first century? Towards a new basis for overcoming academic/vocational divisions', in Ahier, J., Cosin, B. and Hale, M. (eds), *Diversity and Change: Education, Policy and Selection*, London and New York: RoutledgeFalmer.

Zemiles, H., 1987, 'Progressive Education: On the Limits of Evaluation and the Development of Empowerment', *Teachers College Record*, 89 (2), 201-217.

www.ingramcontent.com/pod-product-compliance
Lightning Source LLC
Chambersburg PA
CBHW022316280326
41932CB00010B/1123